KHRUSHCHEV AND THE COMMUNIST WORLD

KHRUSHCHEV
and the
Communist
World

**Edited by
R. F. Miller
and F. Féhér**

CROOM HELM
London & Sydney

BARNES & NOBLE BOOKS
Totowa, New Jersey

© 1984 R.F. Miller and F. Féhér
Croom Helm Ltd, Provident House, Burrell Row,
Beckenham, Kent BR3 1AT

Croom Helm Australia Pty Ltd, 28 Kembla St.,
Fyshwick, ACT 2609, Australia

British Library Cataloguing in Publication Data

Khrushchev and the communist world.
1. Khruschchev, N 2. Soviet Union — Politics
and government — 1953- — Congresses
I. Miller, R.F. II. Feher, F.
947.085'0924   DK275.KS

ISBN 0-7099-1789-9

First published in the USA 1984 by
Barnes & Noble Books
81 Adams Drive,
Totowa, New Jersey 07512

Library of Congress Cataloging in Publication Data
Main entry under title:

Khrushchev and the Communist world.

Includes index.
1. Soviet Union — Politics and government — 1953-
— Addresses, essays, lectures. 2. Soviet Union —
Economic conditions — 1955-1965 — Addresses, essays,
lectures. 3. Khrushchev, Nikita Sergeevich, 1894-1971 —
Addresses, essays, lectures. 4. Europe, Eastern —
Politics and government — 1945- — Addresses, essays,
lectures. I. Miller, Robert F., 1932-
II. Féhér, Ferenc, 1933-
DK274.K518   1984   947.085'2   83-22287
ISBN 0-389-20445-5

Printed and bound in Great Britain

CONTENTS

Preface

When the idea of a symposium on 'Khrushchevism: Its Characteristics and Effects' was suggested as the program for the Socialist Countries Section of the 1981 Meeting of the Australasian Political Studies Association in Canberra not much thought was given to eventual publication of the proceedings. The success and coherence of the symposium and the quality of the papers and the discussion they provoked prompted the editors to look more seriously at the possibilities of publication. To that end they decided to commission several additional papers to round out the coverage of the theme. Most of these papers are included in the present volume.

The road to publication was longer than we had anticipated, partly because of resistance in some quarters to the notion that there was, or could be, anything called 'Khrushchevism'. As the reader will see, although the editors are convinced that 'Khrushchevism' is a viable concept, there is some dispute on this question even among the contributors. Nevertheless, we believe that the discussion of the pros and cons is in itself a valuable exercise for understanding the impact of Khrushchev on the communist world, and beyond.

The editorial preparation of the manuscript was actually a rather pleasant task. Many people contributed to making it so. The list is far too long to mention in its entirety, but we should like to express our appreciation to a few persons whose assistance was especially helpful. Drs Graeme Gill and Fred Teiwes of Sydney University provided valuable comments on the papers at the original symposium. Professor Bill Brugger of Flinders University and Dr T.H. Rigby of the ANU did likewise and also made useful suggestions for publication. In the painstaking work of preparing the manuscript we cannot say enough by way of gratitude for the backup support of Mrs Kath Bourke, the departmental secretary of the Department of Political Science, Research School of Social Sciences, the ANU, and especially to Mrs Gail Hewitt, of the same department, for her conscientious attention to detail and her mastery of the word processor in producing an attractive 'photo-ready' copy for publication. We should also like to acknowledge the both long-term and last-minute assistance of Messrs Russell McCaskie and Gregory Topchian, departmental Research Assistants. Finally, we wish to thank Dr Steve Fortescue and Ms Olga Prokopovich for assisting in the translation of Dr A.M. Nekrich's chapter from the Russian original and Mrs Marta Langridge for translating Dr Z. Mlynář's chapter from the Czech original. Ultimate responsibility lies with Bob Miller, however.

For errors of fact or judgement which remain in spite of this impressive team effort we, naturally, accept full responsibility.

Canberra   August 1983
Melbourne

Introduction

Robert F. Miller

Paradoxically, the further the Khrushchev era recedes into the past and the shorter it comes to appear in relation to the Stalin era which preceded it and the Brezhnev era which followed, the more interesting and unique it seems as a chapter in Soviet social and political history and the evolution of the erstwhile 'monolith' of international communism. Inevitably, comparisons are drawn between political and social life under Khrushchev and that under Stalin and Brezhnev. Some, who see in the Brezhnev and Andropov regimes a reversion to Stalinism or 'neo-Stalinism' tend either to regard the intervening Khrushchev years as an inconsequential interlude - a temporary, if welcome, aberration - or to emphasise the Stalinist features of Nikita Sergeevich Khrushchev's rule itself.(1) Such interpretations view the Khrushchev period as a mere transitory phase in Soviet and Bloc history.

Other observers, by contrast, including several of the authors in this volume, regard it as an important transitional stage: a period when the legacy of the Stalinist past was partially repudiated and the possibilities of reform within the USSR and the countries of the 'socialist camp' were explored. The lessons derived from this exploration by Bloc leaders and Khrushchev's successors unhappily led them to conclude that the scope for such reform was extremely limited. Many of Khrushchev's reform and reorganisational measures were indeed rescinded or emasculated. Nevertheless, an important residue of the period has remained. Above all, the notion was firmly implanted during his tenure that the naked terror of Stalinist rule and direct, centralised command over other socialist states were no longer necessary or even feasible. Some Western and émigré observers have argued that the mailed fist of Moscow has merely been covered by a velvet glove.(2) The events of 13 December 1981 in Poland suggest just how threadbare that glove really is. Even so, in comparison with Stalinism, the suppression of the Hungarian rebellion of 1956, and the invasion of Czechoslovakia in 1968, it is still arguable that some progress has been made. Thanks largely to Nikita Sergeevich's transitional efforts, Soviet leaders have been compelled to devise more sophisticated techniques of domination and adopt a more patient and tolerant attitude toward domestic and foreign diversity, although the aforementioned events in Poland and Czechoslovakia eloquently demonstrate that the limits of their sophistication and tolerance are very narrow.

For the present Soviet leaders the memory of Khrushchev's rule is a painful one, a record of the frenetic dismantling of a brutal, but curiously functional, control apparatus. It remains for them a chronicle of negative examples of techniques and structures which they have sought to avoid like the proverbial plague in trying to maintain the mechanisms and processes they deem necessary to confront the often unwelcome changes of an increasingly complex world. Under Andropov this assessment may be beginning to change, at least at the margin.

During the decade of Khrushchev's ascendance numerous works appeared in the West analyzing the complexities of Soviet politics and the important social and economic changes under his leadership.(3) However, in the Brezhnev period there was a tendency for Western authors to ignore the Khrushchev era, or, worse, to accept more or less without comment the deprecatory judgments upon it of his successors. It was commonly dismissed as an era of 'harebrained schemes' and 'hasty decisions', of no intrinsic value for understanding Soviet political evolution. Khrushchev's very real achievements and the changes in the tone and content of Soviet policies effected by him have been all too readily forgotten.(4) Notable exceptions to this pattern are the book on Khrushchev's 'years in power' by the Medvedev brothers(5), a more recent book by Roy Medvedev(6) and articles by Jeremy Azrael(7) and George Breslauer(8), which attempt to set the record straight to some extent and give Nikita Sergeevich his due.

The Medvedevs eloquently describe the great promise and inspiration of Khrushchev's early years in power, when some of the most gruesome aspects of Stalinist terror were officially exposed, and hopes were raised for more enlightened social and economic policies in the future. As committed Marxists the Medvedevs bitterly condemn Khrushchev for letting the democratic side down by the inconsistency of his liberalisation efforts, for his ideological primitivism, and for his increasingly arbitrary and erratic policy-making style.

It is worth noting that in his biography of Khrushchev written six years later (in 1982) Roy Medvedev is considerably more positive in his assessment of the former leader's achievements and less critical of his personal and political failings. Nowhere is the re-evaluation clearer than in the following eloquent statement near the end of the book:

Historians and politicians have appreciated more fully the importance of that radical change in the policy of the Communist Party of the Soviet Union, of the USSR herself and of the entire Communist movement that is linked with his name. For all his faults, Khrushchev was the only man in Stalin's circle who was capable of initiating and implementing that change. Under his influence nearly 20 million people were rehabilitated in the Soviet Union - many of them posthumously, alas. The fact alone outweighs all his shortcomings in the scales of history.(9)

In his 1975 article Jeremy Azrael emphasises the bona fides of Khrushchev's left Marxist-Leninist orientation. He traces the ideological lineage of Khrushchev's policies in a number of areas, arguing against the conventional view that arbitrariness and mere idiosyncrasy were the essential wellspring of his modus operandi. To illustrate Khrushchev's ideological leftism Azrael focuses on his commitments to specific social desiderata, such as enhanced popular involvement in state affairs, a more egalitarian and collectivist income distribution policy, and his fostering of a more positive attitude toward productive labour through polytechnic educational reforms and other devices for the creation of 'New Soviet Man'. Khrushchev's doggedness in pursuing these and other goals ultimately proved politically fatal for him and for the goals as well. The post-Khrushchevian regression to a more comfortable pattern of bureaucratic structures and routines may not be entirely irreversible, but, in Azrael's view, the chances for a resurgence of left ideological activism in the forseeable future are exceedingly remote.

Also writing in the mid-seventies, George Breslauer, likewise, found it necessary to 'rehabilitate' Khrushchev on certain points commonly distorted by Western - and Eastern - critics. In rebuttal of Jerry Hough's quantitative arguments concerning the expansion of popular participation under Brezhnev, as compared with the Khrushchev era, Breslauer rightly emphasises major qualitative aspects of participation under the latter. He characterises Khrushchev as a genuine 'populist' who introduced an atmosphere of trust toward the citizenry - especially the peasant masses - which had been notoriously lacking under Stalin and which has again been attenuated and distorted under Khrushchev's successors.

Breslauer acknowledges the ambivalence and ambiguities of many of Khrushchev's reform attempts: for example, his commitment to local initiative and criticism alongside his repudiation of political pluralism and his stifling of intellectual dissent. But he credits Khrushchev with raising the crucial issues of the Stalinist system and attempting to establish a more durable basis of legitimacy by forging a new nexus between rulers and ruled and curbing the bureaucratic arbitrariness of the former. Many, but not all, of these initiatives proved to be anathema to Khrushchev's successors and were directly scrapped or allowed to wither away by inattention. In this sense Breslauer denies that Khrushchev was merely a transitional leader, but rather someone who sought unsuccessfully to change the direction of Soviet politics.

These useful insights by the Medvedevs, Azrael, and Breslauer are expanded upon and added to from a range of different perspectives in the essays assembled in this volume. The original impetus for the symposium at which they were first presented was supplied by one of the editors, Ferenc Feher, who suggested that the 'Socialist Countries' section of the 1981 Meeting of the Australasian Political Studies Association devote its attention to 'Khrushchevism' as a distinct political and social phenomenon in the evolution of communist systems. The presentation and discussions of the papers at the APSA Conference at the Australian National University (ANU) in Canberra in August proved to be exceptionally fruitful, and the editors decided to commission several additional papers to round out the coverage of the main theme with an eye to subsequent publication.

The issue of the essential character of the Khrushchev era — whether it was merely a transitory phase or a definite stage in Soviet history — and the related, but obviously separate issue of whether 'Khrushchevism' can be identified as a specific political phenomenon are only tentatively settled in the essays here assembled. To be sure, these are largely definitional questions. Nevertheless, they are not without important substantive implications. If the Khrushchev era was only a transitory phase, and if Khrushchevism was only the unique, idiosyncratic manifestation of a particular Soviet leader's style of authoritarian rule, then Soviet politicians and historians (and the Western scholars who accept their premises) are right in treating the period as a mere, almost insignificant, aberration in the process of maturation of the post-Stalin Soviet system. If, on the other hand, it was a definite stage, marking a conscious effort to break with the past, with a range of specific normative criteria for how a socialist society and community of states ought to be organised and ought to function, then the period does have important intrinsic value as an object of study. Indeed, if ideology is not entirely dead in the communist world as a world view and source of policy inspiration, some aspects of the Khrushchev era - of 'Khrushchevism', if you will - may prove to be a recurrent phenomenon in the politics of that world, albeit in a highly altered form. Indeed, there are already a few signs that Andropov intends to revive at least some of the stylistic, if not the structural features of

Khrushchev's rule - talking with workers on the shop floor and demonstrably firing incompetent administrators.

Obviously, the contributors to this volume take the view that the period was indeed of more than transitory significance. Those among them who lived during the Khrushchev years in the Soviet Union or the countries in its orbit as citizens, like Drs Nekrich, Feher and Mlynar, as Western exchange graduate students, like the present writer, or as diplomats, like Dr Rigby, will recall the charged atmosphere of excitement and unexpected change. It was a period of the reappearance of returnees from the GULAG Archipelago, of exhibitions of previously forbidden works of art, of the publication of Solzhenitsyn's <u>A Day in the Life of Ivan Denisovich</u>, of relatively close and unimpeded contacts and friendships between Soviet citizens and foreigners, of the official repudiation of Stalinist arbitrariness and terror and the condemnation of some, at least, of their perpetrators. In China it was the period of the 'Hundred Flowers'. And throughout the Socialist Camp it was a time of readjustment and reconstruction of relationships - or at least the trappings of relationships - of subordination to authority. In short, it was a period of testing, when the limits of permissible deviance from the rigid Stalinist control system were being explored and assessed by both rulers and ruled.

Unfortunately, all too many of these often bold initiatives and decisions were found to be inconsistent with the party leaders' sense of political security, discipline, and Marxist-Leninist rectitude. That this reassessment partially occurred while Khrushchev was still in the saddle must inevitably add a deep layer of tarnish to the 'Golden-Age' image of his reign wistfully portrayed by some writers. Nonetheless, compared with what preceded them and what has followed, there can be little doubt that the Khrushchev years marked a significant turn for the better in Soviet life. And most of the enduring improvements of life in at least the Soviet-influenced part of the communist world since Khrushchev's fall must be credited to his efforts to effect a decisive break with the Stalinist past. It is almost inconceivable that Soviet and East European life would be as relatively bearable as it is today (even, or perhaps especially, in Poland) if Khrushchev's opponents, or the current crop of Soviet leaders had directly assumed Stalin's mantle.

But as obvious as it is that the contributors to this volume generally share the above assessment of the significance of Khrushchev's rule, it is equally obvious that they differ substantially on the nature, the basic tendencies, and the impact of his tenure. This is not merely a

consequence of differences in topical themes. On the question
of 'Khrushchevism', for example, while two of the authors
(Féher and Miller) perceive at least some elements of a more
generalisable type of communist leadership in Khrushchev's
political style and the thrust of his policies, most of the
other contributors prefer to treat his reign as overwhelmingly
the product of circumstances and Khrushchev's unique
personality. Indeed, Rigby, in highlighting certain important
distinctive features of Khrushchev's style, argues that the
latter's politics very much bore the stamp of his long
Stalinist apprenticeship. The only persons who apparently
accepted in toto the idea of Khrushchevism as a discrete
socio-political phenomenon were the Chinese communist leaders.
As Young and Woodward illustrate in their essay, Mao and his
supporters created a spurious 'straw-man' - a congeries of
stylistic and policy features which they entitled
'Khrushchevism' - for the purpose of castigating the Soviet
leader and his successors. The Chinese leaders frequently
used this effigy to condemn their Soviet counterparts for
alleged deviations from an undefined (probably not Stalinist,
but certainly 'Maoist') ideologically and politically
'correct' domestic and foreign policy line.

In his opening paper Ferenc Féher draws up a balance
sheet of positive and negative consequences of Khrushchev's
policies. While crediting Nikita Sergeevich with definite
achievements in struggling to repair and make amends for some
of the worst excesses of Stalinism, Féher demonstrates the
unviability and insubstantiality of the Leninist myth with
which the Soviet leader tried to replace it. And he traces
the different social elements whose opposition to Khrushchev's
policies and style ultimately caused his downfall.
Interestingly, among them Féher places the broad Soviet masses
themselves, whom Khrushchev strove so mightily to uplift.
For, in addition to undermining the order and grandeur of
Stalinist authority, Khrushchev simply failed to 'deliver the
goods'. The collapse of his extravagant promises of general
affluence made him appear merely ridiculous to the principal
objects of his search for legitimacy, the Soviet people.

T.H. Rigby demonstrates Khrushchev's failure to 'deliver
the goods' politically as well - a far more serious
shortcoming in the game of political survival whose rules
Rigby thoroughly analyzes. In the elaborate nexus of
patron-client relationships which have come to dominate Soviet
politics since the early days of the regime there have arisen
certain mutual expectations of performance on both sides.
Khrushchev's unusual zeal and enthusiasm in playing this often
dangerous game allowed him to bend the rules on numerous
occasions. But when, in the latter part of his reign he
became increasingly arbitrary in doing so - and failed to

'deliver the goods' (for example, by thwarting the expectations of security and protection among his supporters) - he was inevitably forced to pay the penalty and, to continue the metaphor, was ultimately 'sent off'.

Dr A.M. Nekrich provides an eloquent inside view of the transformation of Soviet intellectual life during the Khrushchev years. He recounts how, at first timidly, but later with increasing boldness, Soviet scholars and literators resumed the critical traditions of the old Russian intelligentsia, which had been so mercilessly suppressed for two decades by Stalin. Yet many Soviet intellectuals, especially among the literary and academic bureaucrats who had managed to make satisfactory careers under Stalin, were far from enthusiastic over their new-found freedoms and remained ambivalent - or even hostile - toward their main benefactor and his policies. In tracing the tortuous evolution of the reawakening of the intellectuals, Nekrich mentions several interesting events and personalities whose importance has perhaps not been fully appreciated in the West.

In his essay on Khrushchev's economic policies and style of administration, Bob Miller argues that the stylistic and decision-making modes evidently preferred by Nikita Sergeevich can be interpreted as comprising a distinct pattern, similar to what has come to be known in Western organisational literature as the 'organic model' of administration. This model has been found propitious for technological innovation and adaptability to changes in the organisational environment and its requirements. The author stresses Khrushchev's talent for 'lateral thinking' in devising alternative ways to attain his reform goals. Yet Khrushchev's ultimate fate illustrates some of the disadvantages of the 'organic model': namely, the intra-organisational tensions and redundancies to which it often gives rise. The analysis suggests some additional perspectives on the nature of the bureaucratic opposition to Khrushchev and his reforms.

Part II of the book deals with the impact of Khrushchev's style and policies on selected countries of the socialist world and their leaders. Professor Bill Brugger begins the section with an interesting comparison of the political styles and policy impulses of Khrushchev and Mao Zedong. Brugger demonstrates that despite the radically different official and popular images of the two leaders, they were in fact remarkably similar in temperament, in their attitudes toward bureaucracy, and in their basic policy orientations. Ultimately Mao proved to be the more astute politician: even if he could not 'deliver the goods' to repeat Rigby's felicitous expression, Mao was careful not to antagonise too many of his supporters in the process of casting about for alternative strategies - before the Cultural Revolution, that is.

The content and underlying purpose of the Chinese conception of Khrushchevism are directly addressed by Graham Young and Dennis Woodward. They argue that the Chinese dispute with Khrushchev was not so much over his repudiation of Stalinism - to this the Chinese leaders had tacitly assented - but over his failure to draw the proper lessons from the mistakes of the Stalinist model and over the policies he devised to rectify them. By the 1960s the Chinese leaders were openly ridiculing, as 'Khrushchevism' or 'Khrushchev revisionism', the entire syndrome of policies emanating from what they regarded as Khrushchev's incorrect and unsystematic understanding of Stalinism, errors they claimed to perceive not only in the USSR and other East European countries, especially Yugoslavia, but embryonically in China herself. Whether or not the revisionist label actually suited Soviet conditions under Khrushchev is highly dubious, but from the Chinese standpoint that was not really relevant.

Turning to the particular bête noire of the Chinese critique, Yugoslavia, Bob Miller traces the course of the peculiar love-hate relationship which developed between Khrushchev and Yugoslav President Josip Broz Tito. Khrushchev placed great symbolic political significance on bringing Yugoslavia back fully and formally into the international communist fold. The saga of the attempts of both communist statesmen to play upon each other's vanity to obtain commitments which neither was willing to fulfill in good faith is extremely revealing of their respective political styles and the nature of politics in the international communist movement.

In another essay Ferenc Fehér explains the impact of Khrushchev's de-Stalinisation policies on the Hungarian political system before and after the 1956 uprising. He presents evidence of the formative influence of Khrushchevism on the early development of Janos Kadar as a political leader. The subsequent evolution of what Fehér calls 'Kadarism' is described as a product of Khrushchevism and Machiavellian politics and the peculiarly vulnerable geographic and economic circumstances of the Hungarian state.

Zdenek Mlynář analyses the impact of the atmospheric changes introduced by Khrushchev in the USSR on the policies of the Communist Party of Czechoslovakia in the run-up to the 'Prague Spring'. In his essay Mlynář argues that the rule of CPC leader Antonin Novotny has too often been incorrectly characterised in the West as a period of undifferentiated Stalinism. Once Novotny had become convinced that

Khrushchev's reforms were serious and durable, he opened the door to various reformist projects within the CPC. This opportunity was eagerly seized upon by reform communists to formulate liberal social policies and systemic changes which went far beyond anything contemplated by Khrushchev in the USSR. In Mlynar's view the CPC thus showed itself to be a forerunner of what would come to be called Eurocommunism, influenced by the strong residue of the party's Central and West European traditions, rather than a typical East European copy of the CPSU.

In these introductory remarks I should like to pay tribute to the valuable contributions of the principal commentators on the papers presented at the symposium. Their observations provoked a good deal of fruitful discussion and influenced not only the successful outcome of the symposium but also the ultimate shape of the papers themselves. Dr Marian Sawer (Political Science, Faculty of Arts, ANU) introduced some useful data and argumentation to illustrate the egalitarian social tendencies in Khrushchev's domestic policies, which had been only implicit in Feher's opening essay.

Dr Graeme Gill (Department of Government, University of Sydney) raised, in his discussion of Rigby's paper, the important distinction between the 'normative' and 'prudential' rules of the Soviet political game. Fred Teiwes subsequently used this distinction as the basis for a companion analysis of Chinese politics during and after the Khrushchev era not included in this volume.

Rosh Ireland (Slavonic Languages, Arts, ANU) noted the relatively greater constancy of support for Khrushchev and his memory among intellectuals, as compared with other strata of Soviet society. Ireland stimulated additional discussion by prompting Dr Nekrich to provide further justification for the selection of particular figures and occurrences as significant for the progress of the literary 'thaw'.

Dr Stephen Fortescue (Political Science, Research School of Social Sciences, ANU), in his comments on Miller's essay on Soviet economic developments under Khrushchev, offered the useful reminder that in the end there has been surprisingly little difference between the programmatic objectives of Khrushchev and those of his successors. He argued that Khrushchev's most enduring legacy has been as a negative example of administrative techniques.

Dr Fred Teiwes (Government, University of Sydney) and Professor Bill Brugger (Discipline of Politics, Flinders University) combined their comments on both the domestic and foreign policy sides of Chinese politics in the Khrushchev era. Both commentators stressed the reinforcing role of ideology in aggravating the Sino-Soviet dispute, which had its real origins in substantive differences over policy. Teiwes noted specifically that issues of foreign policy vis à vis the West and appropriate strategies and tactics for the international communist movement comprised the initial matter of the dispute. It became 'ideological' only in 1961, when the purported evidence of Khrushchev's revisionism was viewed by Mao as conclusive and a potential source of contagion for China itself. Once the dispute had reached the level of actual and potential military conflict, ideology tended to become increasingly irrelevant, according to Teiwes. For Brugger, on the other hand, ideology has remained a significant feature of the contention between the two main communist powers.

The essays presented in the following pages certainly lend support to the argument that Khrushchev was a major Soviet historical figure, not the 'un-person' he became at the hands of his official successors, and that his influence far transcended the boundaries of the Soviet Union itself. Owing to the thematic limitations suggested by the title of this book, the editors have not sought to address the questions of Khrushchev's undoubtedly great impact on the course of East-West relations or the development of Soviet involvement with the non-communist nations of the Third World, which really began under his aegis. Just how important and enduring his influence was, even in the communist world, which is the focus of this book, must ultimately be left to the judgment of the reader - and of History.

NOTES

1. See, for example, George Paloczi-Horvath, <u>Khrushchev: The Road to Power</u> (London: Secker and Warburg, 1960), esp. chapter XV, where the author argues that Khrushchev, although not personally a Stalinist, is far from the liberal of the spirit of the Secret Speech.

2. Intellectual dissidence assumed an organised form, of course, only after Khrushchev's fall, once it became clear that opportunities for further, or continued, liberalisation had been precluded. The landmark trial of Siniavskii and Daniel took place in February 1966. The use of confinement in psychiatric prison-hospitals for political deviance also became systematic only under Khrushchev's successors. For a devastating critique of the economic ineptitude and rigidity of the Brezhnev

regime see Igor' Birman, 'Ekonomicheskaia situatsiia v SSSR', <u>Kontinent</u>, No. 28, (1981), pp. 259-300.

3. For example, Carl A. Linden, <u>Khrushchev and the Soviet Leadership, 1957-1964</u>. Baltimore: The Johns Hopkins Press, 1966; and Merle Fainsod, <u>How Russia is Ruled</u>, Revised edition, enlarged. Cambridge, Mass.: Harvard University Press, 1963.

4. This tendency is quite noticeable in two of the most prominent recent works on the Soviet political system: Jerry F. Hough and Merle Fainsod, <u>How the Soviet Union is Governed</u>. Cambridge, Mass.: Harvard University Press, 1978; and Seweryn Bialer, <u>Stalin's Successors: Leadership, Stability and Change in the Soviet Union</u>. Cambridge: Cambridge University Press, 1980.

5. Roy A. Medvedev and Zhores A. Medvedev, <u>Khrushchev: The Years in Power</u>. Translated by Andrew R. Durkin. New York: Columbia University Press, 1976.

6. Roy Medvedev, <u>Khrushchev</u>. Translated by Brian Pearce. Oxford: Basil Blackwell, 1982.

7. Jeremy R. Azrael, 'Khrushchev Remembered', <u>Soviet Union</u>, Vol. II, No. 1, (1975), pp. 94-101.

8. George W. Breslauer, 'Khrushchev Reconsidered', <u>Problems of Communism</u>, Vol. XXV, No. 5 (September-October 1976), pp. 18-33.

9. Roy Medvedev (1982), op.cit., p. 260.

PART I: KHRUSHCHEV'S IMPACT IN THE USSR

Chapter One

THE SOCIAL CHARACTER OF KHRUSHCHEVISM:
A TRANSITION OR A NEW PHASE?

Ferenc Féhér

I. IMAGES OF KHRUSHCHEV

Who was Khrushchev? Or in a somewhat more pointed
formulation: What was Khrushchev? What did the period
hallmarked by his name represent? In order to reply to this
question, easier put than answered, we first have to set the
time limits of the period that can appropriately be called the
Khrushchev era. Speaking accurately, and despite the fact
that he was First Secretary of the Central Committee (but, due
to the very confused state of post-Stalin affairs, only the
fourth man on the nomenklatura) already in 1953, the period
which can, with many qualifications, be described as his
'rule', certainly did not start earlier than 1955. Its
symbolic initiating acts were the fall of his great rival,
Malenkov (mainly engineered by him with much cunning and
Stalinist demagoguery) in February 1955, and his dramatic
appearance at the Belgrade airport to rehabilitate the
Gestapo-agent Tito and his ideologically newly 'resocialised'
Yugoslavia: a most emancipatory deed as far as East European
history is concerned, in May 1955. (I fully agree with
Crankshaw that the never-to-be-repeated peak of Khrushchev's
rule and influence came very shortly afterwards, with the 20th
Congress of the CPSU, and the world-historic 'Secret Speech'.)
To indicate the end of the period is a seemingly simple act
indeed: apparently, it would suffice to point to the coup in
October, 1964. But, in actual fact, and despite the reality
that literally nobody awaited Khrushchev's demotion (Soviet
First Men died, were not demoted, and since Khrushchev was
vigorously alive, he could have only been murdered which would
have been out of tune with his regime), nonetheless
unmistakable signs on the wall indicating the imminent
collapse of the whole edifice were already visible in 1963.
To cut a long story short, these early signals were his
incapacity to restore the order and unity of the communist
world movement under Soviet domination, (the public break with
Albania, and subsequently, and incomparably more important,
the public break with China), and his insincere but vulgar and
clamorous attacks against the rebellious Soviet intelligentsia
of the 'thaw', which apparently did not convince the apparatus
but unmistakably convinced a good many Communist reformers in
the Soviet Union and abroad that not much was to be expected
of Khrushchev. The coup de grace certainly was Togliatti's

famous <u>Memorandum</u>, his testament, an unmistakable withdrawal of confidence by a politician who would have been a natural ally had Khrushchev really delivered the goods promised at the 20th Congress. All these events between mid 1962 and early 1964 indicated the slow agony of a period which can then be characterised as having lasted not more than 7-8 years, in fact, not even half the time of the Brezhnev era. Its very brevity indicates rather a transition than a new phase.

A further puzzle to be resolved is presented by Khrushchev's many and radically divergent images, the practically total absence of even a minimal consensus on his assessment, both during his rule and after. This was not the case with either Lenin or Stalin. Both evoked a manichaean dichotomy: they were either adored or hated: the faith in, or the rejection of, them was absolute. (Which, of course, does not at all mean that their adorers had to lionise both of them. As is documented by the classic case of Trotsky and his followers, an idolatry of Lenin, not less uncritical than that of the Stalinists, at best stylistically more sophisticated, could still go hand in hand with a hatred of Stalin.) Furthermore, Brezhnev, to speak of the aftermath, presents a hermeneutically simple case as well. Firstly, under his reign, with the considerable assistance of a total lack of personality on the part of this skilful but insignificant and malevolent <u>apparatchik</u>, the 'cult of personality' died peacefully indeed. There could be really no reason at all to cultify Brezhnev's so-called personality. What was happening around him was just the usual base court flattery. Secondly, the Soviet Union is for the first time in its history fairly transparent at least in one respect: the post-Khrushchevian state does not inspire any kind of pseudo-religious beliefs or expectations; it simply attracts certain very pragmatic interests. One made, if one was interested, a simple and straightforward deal with the Brezhnevite Soviet Union; one did not invest cultic adoration in it or in its leaders. This, of course, could happen under two conditions: by following Soviet strategic interests, and by importing the Soviet ways of government. All this needs Machiavellian determination (as imitating the Soviet example always did) but no longer elements of <u>enthusiasm</u>. Therefore Brezhnev's image, in marked contrast with that of his historical predecessor, was a matter of a very simple interpretation indeed.

But here I would make very clear what I mean by the term 'image': certainly not the sort of amateurish psychological attempts at decoding an enigma with which so many works on Khrushchev, otherwise knowledgeable and interesting, are so ardently preoccupied. I am in perfect agreement with Dostoevsky's statement that psychology is a stick that has two ends. Every deed, even if it is not wrapped up in veils of

deliberate camouflage to the extent that Khrushchev had always
had to camouflage his actions, on pain of perishing, is at
least ambivalent. The term 'image' indicates here a <u>socially
relevant ensemble of opinions and assessments</u> of the First
Secretary on the part of pertinent human groups, which
influenced the actions of these groups towards the Soviet
Union and communism. Therefore, what these people - so
divergent amongst themselves - <u>believed</u> of the Khrushchev
enigma was an organic part of the Khrushchev era itself and
inseparable from its aftermath, its posterity.

The first representative image of Khrushchev is that of
the <u>reformist</u> communist (a category to which I myself
belonged, with certain ups and downs, for a long period). As
internationally known and acclaimed last mohicans of this once
so numerous type and now so much diminished, one can mention
the courageous Medvedev brothers, Roy and Zhores, or that
monument of heroism in the face of Nazism and Stalinism,
Robert Havemann, inmate of a Hitlerite prison awaiting (and
miraculously escaping) his execution, practically under house
arrest for years in the 'real socialism' of Ulbricht's and
Honecker's 'German workers' state'. It is appropriate to sum
up that reformist communist's image of Khrushchev with his
words (a verdict basically identical with that in Zhores
Medvedev's book: <u>Khrushchev - The Years in Power</u>).

> The disbandment of the archipelago Gulag was a
> courageous act worthy of our admiration. Although
> it was not directed against any external enemy of
> the Soviet Union, it was directed against its most
> evil and dangerous enemy in the inside, against the
> domination of the 'system', against the distortion
> of socialism and the international discrediting of
> the communist world movement stemming thereof.
> Khrushchev deserves our deepest recognition and
> respect. It was for the first time after Lenin that
> with him, a great and courageous revolutionary got
> to the top of Soviet society'.(1)

The main terms of this remarkably dense and comprehensive
characterisation are the following: 1) On the whole, Soviet
society remained socialist but with remarkable 'distortions'
or 'perversions'. 2) These distortions can be repaired by
certain system-immanent reforms (the abolition of the system
of terror, party democracy - whatever that term may mean - and
the like). 3) Khrushchev was the actor, or rather the
world-historic protagonist of this work of reparation; this
is his main claim to glory before history. He was certainly
no <u>chevalier sans reproche</u> (and both Havemann and the Medvedev
brothers criticise him repeatedly); the ineffectual character
of his reforms is exemplified by his very downfall, but his

policies, if socialism has a future, should be restored to their full rights. (Let me remark here in parenthesis that the reformist communist Khrushchev image is the only one which hopes and predicts a comeback of the First Secretary's allegedly consistent social options). 4) Finally, and clearly visibly, this logic is circular in that it regards the mass crimes of Stalinism, not a bit less horrendous than those of Hitler, as an atrocity against humanity; but their recompense is treated as a profit accruing to the account of reformed communism which asserts, even if with many provisos, a historical continuity with Stalin's period as socialist. While the representatives of this image are rapidly dwindling, some 25 years ago they constituted a major social force. For instance, during the preparation of the Hungarian revolution they were the protagonists of social changes par excellence.

The opposite pole of the Khrushchev image, that of the militant anti-communist, can again be exemplified by a literary work, George Paloczi-Horvath's Khrushchev – The Road to Power. But this exemplification does not at all mean that such an image was the distinguishing feature only of certain biased literary circles. For all practical purposes, this was also a view widely shared by the policy-making bodies of the Western powers, which had undoubtedly good reasons for their aversion. Nonetheless, their Khrushchev image was just as one-sided as that of the reformist communist if not more so. According to this view Khrushchevism was nothing but a new chapter in the long history of fraudulent communist strategies, a new Trojan horse. Khrushchev himself was a younger member of the generation of the purgers (a fact which has now been profoundly documented by Crankshaw's excellent biography, as well as by Markland's book). His main aspiration to become the new dictator had only been blocked and frustrated by his equally jealous colleagues who dreaded the axe of a new Stalin. The exposition of the crimes (to a great measure: his own crimes) was imposed on him by his colleagues; he only snatched their historical merits to display himself as the liberator.(2) Finally, this view regards Khrushchev as a) a dictator under whom the essence of the regime did not change, and b) as a Soviet imperialist tout court, against whom the West had to brace itself in exactly the same way as it did against Stalin. A blatant example of the results of this short-sighted attitude has been analyzed in our book written with Agnes Heller, Hungary, 1956 Revisited. The militant conservative took just as extremist a view of the Khrushchev period as the biased reformist communist. While for the former nothing had changed, and Khrushchev's period was not even a transition to something new but a simple continuation of the old, for the latter the system had become unperverted socialism again (to be sure with

certain minor blemishes), at least for the time of the rule of
Khrushchev.

The liberal image of Khrushchev represented by such
journalists and historians as Crankshaw or historical
protagonists like Sakharov has a far more objective and
differentiated view of our hero than any partisans of the
former two positions. No doubt, Khrushchev epitomised a
social force totally alien for them, but within its limits the
First Secretary had two immense merits. The first was the
moderation and relative tolerance of his regime as compared
with that of Stalin; the second, its capacity for occasional
rational bargaining and discussion. Since I have given a
summary of the reformist communist's image of Khrushchev by
one of its morally outstanding adherents, it is only fair to
proceed in a similar manner on the liberal side and listen to
the testimony of the both scientifically and politically
representative personality of Sakharov. His list of
'Khrushchev's contributions' to a more liberal turn of Russian
history is remarkably (and let us add: deservedly) lacking in
enthusiasm or even sympathy, which only enhances its value as
objective. To his contributions belong the release of the
prisoners of Stalin's times, the increase in the payment for
the labour of the kolkhoz peasants, a remarkable rise in
pensions, a growing proportion spent on housing, a quest for
new methods in international relations, attempts at improving
the style of leadership, attempts at restricting the
prerogatives of the nomenklatura and at reducing the enormous
military budget. The last two ventures were the main reasons
for Khrushchev's fall.(3) The main terms of the liberal
assessment are the following: a) while Khrushchev's regime
had obviously never questioned the principles of the Leninist
dictatorship, it was an incomparably more humane edition of it
than the phases under both Lenin's and Stalin's rule. (The
liberal analysis is visibly uninterested in the problem,
fundamental to Khrushchev's self-understanding, whether and to
what extent Khrushchevism was dependent on its historical
predecessors.) b) The liberals also emphasise the relatively
more peaceful character of the Khrushchev era, primarily in
terms of a reduced military budget. And finally, c) all this
adds up to the verdict that Khrushchevism was a short period
in Soviet history which, alas, turned out to be only a
transition towards a more rigid and conservative, and also
much more expansionist rule. Whether or not Khrushchev's
policies can return, and if so, with what changes in form, the
liberals generally do not care to predict.

A distinct and directly hostile image of Khrushchev
appears in the Chinese view of his leadership. For all
consecutive Chinese leaderships, however divergent, Khrushchev
and his policies inaugurated in the Secret Speech appear as

Thermidor (even if they do not use the terminology), as a treason against the 'correct proletarian line' whose patron saint was Stalin, the loyal continuer of Lenin's work. In this regard, not even the Chinese version of Khrushchevism, Deng's rule, abandoned the unmitigated hostility against Khrushchevite 'revisionism'. The explanatory value of these theories is necessarily very limited. First of all, and for good reasons, the official Chinese theorists who patched together the idea of the 'Khrushchevite Thermidor' have never taken up the question of the cause of such a traitorous turn. They particularly did not touch upon the responsibility of their adored Stalin's mass murders for triggering a response in the form of a liberalising turn. (There was some vague mention by Mao of the fact that Stalin was 'unjust' to a few innocent people in exactly the same vein as Deng's mention, in the form of a mild rebuke, of Pol Pot's responsibility for 'offending' the Kampuchean people in his interview with Oriana Fallaci). The Chinese propagandists are equally hesitant to enter the minefield of discussion whether the Soviet Union has remained, under Khrushchev's and his successors' traitorous rule (the latter are not better for them in this respect than Khrushchev was), a 'socialist' country or whether capitalism, pure and simple, has been restored there. Since theory for the Chinese party theorists (except for the case of Chen Boda, who was a genuinely fanatical, Babeuvian-egalitarian theorist and the creator of the Mao Zedong idea) is a matter of purely pragmatic considerations to the same extent as for their Soviet colleagues, they are not dumb enough to walk into the trap Yugoslavia presented for Soviet propagandists in the 40s and declare the Soviet Union capitalist, which may later prove embarrassing. Therefore the more verbose their 'theory' is, the more it suggests that Khrushchevism is a distinct and fatal new phase in Soviet history, the less actual explanatory value it has.

A certain image of Khrushchev on the New Left has to be briefly scrutinised here as well, actually a somewhat arbitrary merger of several theories from the 60s. On the whole, none of the new leftist trends was infatuated with Khrushchev and his regime, and of course the lack of affection was absolutely mutual. Soviet observers found the new leftists at best superfluous. If they were new editions of a pro-Soviet policy, why did they not join the communist parties, the observers logically asked: and if not, then they were evaluated in Soviet files and articles along a continuum which ranged from 'muddle-headed' (sputannik) to 'agents of the class enemy'. The aversion of the average new leftists to Khrushchev generally had a twofold motivation. On the one hand, they found his regime still too oppressive for their liking, and on the other hand, very conservative, which reproduced bourgeois prejudices mobilised against them at home on a much higher and a far more intolerant level. The terms of this - mostly negative - evaluation displayed a certain affinity with the Chinese polemics, even in the case of non-Maoist interpreters; and since the New Left had a far greater theoretical freedom than the Chinese theoretical apparatus, it evinced an incomparably wider and more convincing explanatory power. First of all, most new leftist observers grasped the causal nexus between the excesses (errors, distortions and the like) of the Stalin era and the emergence of Khrushchevism. Further, they perceived at least one fundamental aspect of Khrushchev's period: its involuntary 'Bukharinism', the (limited) rehabilitation of the consumer in the Soviet citizen. And since they also grasped its deeper implication, the partial rehabilitation of market relations, they condemned it. (They had to do so, as they were opponents of the so-called 'affluent society' and blamed everything on the market economy). Finally, the whole idea of 'peaceful co-existence' was a most suspicious sign for a generation inspired by Guevara's 'hundred Vietnams'. This seemed to be an outright betrayal of the revolutionary impetus, especially as implemented by the First Secretary during the Tonkin-Gulf Crisis. In sum, most of them believed Khrushchevism to be a transition which could be superseded not by any relapse to Stalinism but by the 'healthy regenerative forces' resurrecting 'proletarian democracy'. Needless to say, here we have arrived at the main weakness of all new leftist theories of the 60s: their verbal vehemence on behalf of a non-existent proletarian democracy turned into a most ambiguous and half-hearted discourse when they had to answer the main question, whether or not the Soviet Union represented socialism for them.

Finally, there was a hostile popular view of Khrushchev, created and spread by some legendary social protagonist, the 'man in the street', even the cursory analysis of which presents exceptional methodological problems. Already the previously mentioned ideal types of my typology have been drawn up like a police composite picture, with the aid of the utmost enlargement of very scanty empirical data. But in this case, I can only rely on hearsay evidence, on no written document at all. Nonetheless, I am absolutely convinced of the existence of this fluid but unambiguous opposition to the de-Stalinising First Secretary. I too often heard its arguments, or rather, emotional outbursts of indignation, via friends living in, or visiting, the Soviet Union, or from Soviet tourists in Hungary. The social identity of this vaguely located subject can best be understood from its opinions.

The main accusation against Khrushchev coming from this quarter was a melange of <u>disillusionment</u>, an <u>offended sense of great power chauvinism</u> and and <u>irrascibility caused by the insecure atmosphere</u> of Khrushchev's social improvisations. The proportions varied from person to person. Even if I can understand all three elements and feel a limited sympathy with some (not all) of its aspects, I regard the whole melange as the expression of a <u>conservative, antidemocratic</u> position. Further, even if many of its advocates were party members, and occasionally some of them mobilised traditional demagogic communist arguments against Khrushchev, this opposition was not identical with the Stalinist (let us say: Albanian) denigration of the de-Staliniser. Basically, it had very little to do with communist doctrinal tenets at all.

Among its elements, the disillusionment was related to the well-known fact that Khrushchev did not deliver the goods; and this was mostly expressed in a narrow-minded, totally philistine manner. Its main charge was that, instead of fulfilling the promise of overtaking America in affluence, his regime could not solve fundamental economic problems; progress in terms of real income proved to be, in fact, very slow. This was a true statement. In addition, it reflected a social grievance which had great moral relevance in a country which had borne the brunt of the war. But the accusation preserved in its structure a behavioral pattern which had been constantly criticised by the few genuine representatives of Russian democracy: the unreconstructed humility <u>and</u> the slanderous bad faith of the born servant. The advocates of this view never questioned the privileged position of the Master: they never expressed any resolute will to take their own affairs in their own hands. Instead they remarked, with glee and strictly behind the back of the Master, that he was not a good Tsar, but an undignified blunderer.

Even less appealing was the second feature of the composite portrait: the preference given to Stalin, who had created national <u>grandeur</u>, who had not only won the war but could behave like a ruler. This second aspect was a strange mixture of deliberate forgetfulness (both about the Gulag and Stalin's monumental blunders at the beginning of the war) a forgetfulness which disliked being awakened by Khrushchev's revelations about the 'good ruler' and the 'great warlord', of a traditional Great-Russian chauvinism against all alien elements who would be treated, if Khrushchevite norms were observed, with more tolerance and deference than they, as aliens, deserved, and of a newly emergent 'imperial consciousness' which was disturbed when its partisans saw the First Man publicly singing or pounding the table with his shoe at the UN. The third aspect, irrascibility caused by chaos and insecurity, was felt mostly by middle-level and low-level apparatchiks, but not only by them. The negative result of the wild impromptu measures, decreed one day, revoked the next, afflicted as well people whom they had originally been intended to assist.

On the basis of this vague description the subject can perhaps be identified. Representatives of this position were, first of all, strata which were politically vocal, at least to some extent and in the typical Soviet underground way of circulating views through jokes and confidential gossip. This fact, by definition, excludes very large groups (perhaps the majority) of industrial workers and kolkhozniki. The latter simply suffered the events, with somewhat less burden and considerably less danger than under Stalin but in an equally mute and passive way. Secondly, this subject was to be located in urban strata and groups, among people who lived where 'things happened' (in a country with still very limited available information) who could have an at least distorted and distant view, but nevertheless a view, of the actual events. Further, even if elements of this popular, or rather populist, disaffection expressed the interests of certain groups within the apparatus, the whole syndrome did not present either a communist, or an anti-communist position. With its readiness to serve the authorities, especially if they were capable of instilling a satisfactory amount of respect and fear, but with its traditional and unaltered system of Great-Russian prejudices, our populist subject was the closest thing to what can be called the Soviet middle-classes.

Were these many interpretations, so irreconcilably at variance with one another, simply mistaken - all except for one? If so, which is the one to choose? My answer to this question is as follows: none of them was a total misunderstanding, even if they obviously do not contain equal explanatory value. Even a superficial glance at the Memoirs (Khrushchev Remembers), that amazingly inconsistent and at the same time dramatically revealing document, will find smaller or larger chunks of evidence for each standpoint. Was our hero then a hopelessly confused man, a dilettantish, accidental protagonist who just stumbled upon the stage of a world-historic drama, mixing in his policies the most contradictory options? My answer is decidedly in the negative: Khrushchev was undeniably one of the great statesmen of modern Russia, ineffaceable from its annals, but at the same time, the repository of all the options facing the war- and Stalin-ridden country after the despot's death. He frantically strove for a unified and coherent policy of his own to put an end to the long martyrdom of his people, the target of various sorts of forces of action and reaction impinging from the top and from the bottom of the social order. It was the 'fault', if one may state this in an unhistorical way, of these forces to the same extent as it was Khrushchev's that he could not forge a coherent policy and remained the repository of so many conflicting options. To understand this unique situation, we have to cast a cursory glance at the options the Soviet Union faced in 1953-55 when Khrushchevism was in statu nascendi.(4)

Every successor of Stalin faced an inevitable task in 1953: consolidation, including the more or less open admission that under Stalin's rule (or at least after a certain period of Stalin's rule) 'Lenin's work' had undergone a crisis inside and outside the Soviet Union. But Khrushchev was decidedly the man for the job, since for him only three versions of consolidation were excluded outright from the start: a total abrogation of the party's primogeniture, its prerogative to steer and control social life; the continuation of the government by methods of mass terror; and military dictatorship. But plastic and 'poliphonic' as he was, he was open to the following courses of consolidation. Firstly, as a man of authoritarian habits, he was most favourably inclined towards a simple swap of Stalin's terroristic totalitarianism for a non-terroristic but autocratic and repressively conservative paternalism. Such a state of social affairs would have needed a leader with great authority, a wide power of command without glorification and the physical elimination of the Neinsager, and such a position would have suited him fine. But, secondly, he would also have found acceptable a situation characterised by 'party democracy'; in other words, a repressive liberalism in the methods of party administration, a complete recognition of the rights to increased consumption of the Soviet citizen without the slightest recognition of his or her rights to free political action. Thirdly, under certain circumstances (to which I will return later), even a gigantic edition of the Yugoslav alternative would not have been impossible. The leading role of the 'emancipating upper stratum' would have been preserved but, instead of favours, actual and legally stipulated concessions to the populace would have been granted while the satellite states would have been granted the status of 'Findlandisation'. To that end, it would have, of course, been necessary not to crush the Hungarian Revolution but to negotiate with its leaders along the lines of the many draft compromises, in principle highly acceptable for the Soviet Union, worked out by Hungarian politicians. Having missed this historical bus, they missed, or rather miscarried, important internal Soviet social options as well.

It is no puzzle for the expert, or perhaps even for the incisive non-professional observer, why an oligarchic conservative paternalism became the winning option after

Khrushchev's fall. Therefore, I shall mention the causes only briefly. Firstly, the regime had an apparatus with not only an iron hold over the whole societal life but also with the self-confidence of half a century of rule and a great victory in war. Secondly, the fact that they had already passed through the stage of forced extensive industrialisation, required options different to those of both Stalin and Mao. Finally, a special factor should be mentioned which very rarely appears in the list of causes: the Soviet masses themselves. It is fashionable to make retroactive reproaches to certain leaders on the grounds that they, as subject, had their freedom to act otherwise and did not. But the unanimous masses also have different options and a freedom to choose among them, for they, too, are after all constituted of individuals. And had the millions of petitioners mentioned by Zhores Medvedev, on first hearing of the Secret Speech and anticipating the rehabilitations, taken to the streets and demanded, instead of supplicating for, the release and the rehabilitation of the inmates of the Gulag, and also the publication of the Secret Speech, Soviet history might have taken a different turn. I emphasise: it might have, and it was far from excluded that Khrushchev would have put down the rebellion by armed forces. But, poliphonic as he was, other options were equally not impossible for him. Thus, I have answered the question raised in the title: Khrushchev's regime was a transitory period, not a lasting new phase in Soviet history, and it had to be so because of the collision of contradictory options. What future, if any, his promises have for Soviet history to come will be answered in the conclusion of this paper.

II. THE SECRET SPEECH AS A HERMENEUTICAL CLUE FOR THE
     UNDERSTANDING OF KHRUSHCHEV'S REGIME

Khrushchev's Secret Speech to the 20th Congress of the CPSU, which was actually held under mysterious circumstances after the Congress had completed its formal duties - destined to be secret but leaked out immediately to the world press, is one of the most important documents of our century. It became the source of inspiration for my generation of reformist communists (even George Lukacs remarked that under the spell of the speech he expected a Blitzkrieg-like self-purification of socialism), but an object of hatred and fear for the ruling apparatuses, as well as for many doctrinaire communists outside the apparatus who never forgave Khrushchev for this 'traitorous' act. In the West, perhaps with the exception of the most important recipient, the US State Department, it was generally taken as the sign of a possibly new Soviet Union in the making. Regarding the explanation of its genesis, there are in the main three versions. The first version has already been mentioned: this is Paloczi-Horvath's militantly anti-Khrushchevite explanation which attributes the speech to mysterious and, I think, unidentifiable, protagonists who allegedly coerced Khrushchev to speak under duress. Apart from Crankshaw's important evidence to the contrary, one simply has to remark: even had it happened so, which is almost impossible and contradicts the whole body of knowledge about the period, the fact still remains that the mask grew on Khrushchev's face, and from then on he was the man of the Secret Speech. But let me mention a piece of additional and, in my view, cardinal evidence, since it comes from a man of irreproachable character, Imre Nagy. This later victim of Khrushchev's 'legality', then still a favourite of all 'consolidators' in Moscow, mentioned in his Memoirs that Khrushchev complained to him on the 1st of January, 1954 (!) that in Hungary the work of rehabilitation could not even be started because of the sabotage of Rakosi and his apparatus. This certainly reveals the author of the Secret Speech, not its enemy. The second version appears in Medvedev's book on Khrushchev and describes the speech as a coup de theatre improvised by the First Secretary, sensing the general anti-Stalin tide of the congress after Mikoyan's stormily applauded attack. This is an improbable version given the whole character of the text of the speech, which showed unmistakable signs of having explored the archives and shrewdly judging the possible limits. The final version is one of Khrushchev's typical self-apologetic lies in his Memoirs. According to this story, even if the Pospelov committee, which actually gathered the material and in all probability wrote the main draft of the speech, had the text completed before the Congress, there was no decision to address the delegates in a secret session; and he, Khrushchev, in a way foisted this option on the reluctant members of the Presidium. Whatever the truth may have been, one thing seemed to be undeniable: Khrushchev was the initiator of the whole report, and the text offers the best clue to understanding his politics.

After the first shock of consternation or relief, the speech was generally mistreated, as far as both its intellectual-moral level and emancipatory content are concerned. There were four objections made against it (not counting the fifth which regarded it as material evidence of Khrushchev's treason). the first was the charge of shallowness and superficiality. What sort of social explanatory category is the 'cult of personality', many people asked. What does it explain of all the horrors which happened in Soviet society, in what way does it account for their structural causes? The adherents of the second position simply called Khrushchev a cheat and a liar who pretended in the speech to be a democrat and immediately after the Congress suppressed all voices calling for actual social changes. The third remarked, with understandable moral contempt, that after such a holocaust, which can be compared only with Hitler's deeds, the First Secretary mentioned only the communist (and from among them, overwhelmingly the Stalinist) victims and gave a total of less than 8,000 people who had been rehabilitated up to the time of the 20th Congress. Finally, other observers remarked that the speech displayed a cynical morality since it distinguished between necessary and unnecessary murders, and it condemned Stalin only for having committed the latter.

To some extent, all these critics are justified, even if not to the same degree, except those who termed Khrushchev's position fraudulent. The remarkable feature of the Secret Speech in Khrushchev's career, so full of lies and tricks, is that it was 'strictly Weberian' in the sense that Khrushchev (who had obviously never heard the name of Max Weber) clearly identified his leading values and stuck to them. He <u>never</u> called himself a democrat in the speech. If my textual inventory is correct, he made only one, and even then a very perfunctory, reference to inner-party democracy, by which he meant that leaders should preferably not be butchered if they disagreed on the priority of winter or spring wheat (hardly an exaggerated conception of democracy). But gallows humour aside, he unrepentantly and very sincerely identified with <u>Lenin's system of terror</u> when and where such 'harsh measures' are necessary (by which he clearly meant: when and where the leaders deemed it to be inevitable and useful). As in his <u>Memoirs</u> (except for one remark where he quite unexpectedly questioned Stalin's horrendous collectivisation policy) he approved retroactively not only the terror practiced in the Civil War but all those wars of extermination against wide strata of the population (mostly during the fatal years of 1929-1932 in the countryside) which led to the consolidation of Lenin's shaky edifice. For him, <u>negative</u> history starts <u>ab urbe condita</u>: when the 'socialist' bases were already solid, cemented by the blood of millions, and when Stalin's fury turned against the builders. Roughly, then, it started with the symbolic act of Kirov's assassination and with the 'Lex Kirov', the dreaded formula of terror whose last practitioner (against Beria, Bagirov <u>et alii</u>) was Khrushchev himself. This is a cynical and in many respects a brutal view of history indeed, but certainly not a fraudulent one.(5)

But the obverse side of the coin, Khrushchev's great deed before History for all eternity must be mentioned here in all fairness: while he spoke of thousands, he immediately released millions. (According to Medvedev, Havemann and other sources some 10 to 12 millions were released and an at least similar number of dead inmates of the Gulag received a posthumous document of rehabilitation.) This was not only an act of humanity and audacity of the first order, which will always shield his reputation against even justified charges, it meant a general moral turn in a world which was on the brink of losing all moral norms whatsoever and sinking into that social situation which Marx had foretold in the remarkable phrase: relapse into barbarism. I fully agree with Mlynar's assessment (and will later come back to expand on it): 'Khrushchev's critique may have been more primitive on a national scale, but it did highlight whether intentionally or not, the question of guilt and responsibility of the individual'.(6)

The deep inherent ambiguity of the Secret Speech, its most 'ideological feature' (in the sense of a 'false consciousness') is not to be found in its alleged democratic promises. No such promises were made. Therefore all those who left the historical scene in disillusionment should have blamed it on themselves in the first place. The ideological, and thus false, claim in the speech is its main slogan: 'back to Lenin'. It is sociologically impossible to return to Lenin because Lenin was and is dead in the simple sense that his unconsolidated Jacobin dictatorship, whose many options did not even totally exclude a return to political democracy (and thereby the impugning of the relevance of the very period of dictatorship), was consolidated through Stalin by the cataclysmic exclusion of practically all its earlier options. Lenin had indeed introduced the system of la permanence de la guillotine but, together with his party, was most reluctant to admit its permanence and regarded his rule as an emergency phenomenon — a most Jacobin feature indeed.(7) Stalin had no scruples here whatsoever. His famous formula of the 'necessarily sharpening class struggle in socialism' parallel to the progress of 'constructing socialism' heralded precisely this permanence of the terror without much ideological disguise. After Stalin the 'historical innocence' of Lenin's government is no longer possible. Anyone with moral responsibility who intends to establish a Jacobin regime based on the actual permanence and the illusory short-term use of terror must (as for instance, the original Cuban Jacobins, Castro, Guevara and others did initially, but with an adequate historical consciousness) be perfectly aware of one fact: that the actual permanence will remain and the illusions evaporate, leaving a hangover of greed for power and cynicism after them.

But why did Khrushchev need the myth of 'return to Lenin'? Was it simply paying lip-service to the ideological continuity of the regime, or did it reveal his incapability of thinking a theoretical problem through to the end? This latter was certainly a character trait of the First Secretary who combined elements of the great statesman and the simpleton in cultural and ideological questions. The insistence on ideological continuity certainly played some role in this decision but it, equally certainly, does not account for the central, maniacally repeated role of the slogan: return to Lenin. As to the second explanation, intellectual simplicity is no answer here, since a thinker like Lukacs, who had no match in his culture since the death of Karl Marx, hatched the same universal panacea in his capacity as the representative theorist of the Khrushchev period. Khrushchev, as all reformist communists, was caught up in an inextricable dilemma. On the one hand, he wanted to preserve untouched the whole structural network of the Stalinist regime (one-party dictatorship, command economy, totalitarian homogenisation of society), remaining totally uncritical towards its essence, and at the same time he wanted to eliminate Stalin (in other words: regularly practiced mass terror) from it as dangerously dysfunctional: Stalin, through whom alone the regime had achieved its final shape and become consolidated. This impossible task could only be fulfilled under two conditions: firstly, by declaring Lenin's period as having elaborated the 'correct' solutions to all problems of 'socialist construction' which were later 'to some extent distorted' by Stalin (to what extent, it always remained a mystery, not only for Khrushchev but also for Lukacs). Secondly, by raising the scholastic and totally misleading pseudo-dilemma that, granted all this was true, was Stalin 'necessary' or 'only accidental' in Soviet and world history? The first statement is the greatest ideological lie of the whole Khrushchev period. Lenin's regime was, after the moment the Civil War was won, absolutely confused and undecided regarding its own options; the leaders were without the faintest idea whither to go. As a first aspect of this very complex situation, it has to be mentioned that this mystical entity, 'History', meted out a just punishment to 'Maximilien Lenin', the Jacobin, who during the bitter struggle of a quarter of a century had forged a social force capable of 'snatching' from triumphant revolutionary crowds the fruit of their own deed, a free and victorious revolution itself, and had preached uninterruptedly that there is one single revolutionary duty and problem: seizing state power. It had finally achieved its goal through a system of unprecedented terror, whereupon it had found itself in a historical and social vacuum without the elementary social options. The range of Lenin's choices covered no smaller social territory than the one extending from the abolition of money and the introduction of direct exchange (at least in principle in the system of war communism) to a restoration of market relations and the principle of 'enrichissez-vous' (in the system of NEP) – a remarkable distance to travel even in fantasy. Contrary to historical legend, under Lenin there was no system of

planning, not even any central idea of how and in what forms
it ought to be introduced. Even a general socio-economic
strategy was absent. Lenin's lamentations about a single
sentence which ought to have been passed down by the
'classics' to their unhappy grand-children but which they had
failed to do, his self-contradictory ideas to cure
bureaucratism through new super-bureaucratic institutions, the
platitudes and inner confusion of his so-called testament,
relaying only one message, namely that the revolution had been
frozen, might have aroused an understandable contempt towards
him in Stalin, who must have increasingly seen in Lenin a
mummy better put into his mausoleum rather than the leader and
paradigm he publicly mourned.

Secondly, Lenin's inability to opt for the permanence of
the terror, under any theoretical justification he might have
chosen to that end, must have appeared to Stalin, and justly
so, a very inconsistent and a very dangerous politics. It was
inconsistent because Lenin had earlier most generously
administered mass terror against whole social groups. This is
a type of activity, as Stalin knew all too well, which cannot
be stopped until terror is internalised. As we all know, it
is easier to mount the tiger than to get off it. It was a
very dangerous inconsistency as well: as long as the populace
only senses that there is not an iron determination on the
part of the terroristic authorities to go to literally any
lengths to preserve their power, not short even of the
magnitude of demographic catastrophes, the spirit of rebellion
is never quelled. People understand that the murder of their
father, mother, children and brother was the 'necessary
byproduct' of a beneficiary world-historical necessity only if
a simple inner doubt and the slightest external sign of it
implies a similar fate for them as well.

Therefore, thirdly, Stalin, whose intellectual
capacities, as a comprehensible reaction to his Byzantine
cult, are now systematically underestimated, conceived
correctly that Lenin's emphatic advice given to Rykov when he
first thought he might be dying: 'Let no blood flow among
you', was a false piece of advice. More precisely, it was a
classic instance of false learning from history: the
representative Russian Jacobin wanted to avoid at least one
spectacular fiasco of the original. It was his inner desire
that the Russian Revolution must not devour its children. But
Stalin grasped correctly that this was a formalistic learning
from history (obviously without consulting Michelet, who
proved why, for similar reasons, it was a practical necessity
for Robespierre to embark on the gradual extermination of
precisely his own faithful, but much too independent and
critical, Montagne). Stalin was determined that blood should
be let - precisely in the ruling apparatus - and - from the

viewpoint of the survival of the regime which was a joint
venture with Lenin - he was far more consistent than 'Ilyich'.
The Bolshevik Old Guard, seemingly a barracks under military
discipline for European socialists, was a much too
freedom-loving, quarrelsome, interdependent lot with which to
implement a totalitarian system, where the spirit of terror is
so deeply entrenched that all other options vanish from the
membrane of social imagination, and resistance itself becomes
self-censored. There is no need to point to the Trotskyites'
half-hearted demonstration in 1927: they were anyhow an alien
body in the party, barely tolerated. It was not even
necessary to think of Zinoviev and Kamenev's letter before
October; it was enough if one had in mind no one else than
Lenin himself, who, as is well known, threatened to leave the
Central Committee and agitate against it publicly during the
Brest-Litovsk debate. Stalin understood quite correctly that
a party where behaviour like Lenin's can occur, where, in
other words, the Leader is the head of a dictatorship but not
a personal dictator or despot, is no tool for a totalitarian
dictatorship to realise its mission. Stalin was, therefore,
adamant on two points. Firstly, the party must be subjected
to the iron will of one leader whatever this may cost in human
lives; and this despotic leader of a dictatorship now aware
of its permanence was, of course, to be he himself, Stalin.
The second point related to the 'general line':
collectivisation and industrialisation. It was too often
emphasised that Stalin snatched, as it were, these ideas from
the so-called Leftist Opposition. In actual fact, this was
mentioned so often that in the heat of the copyright debate
people tended to forget that Stalin did not and could not
steal any random programme. For the purposes of his regime,
Bukharin's policy was totally inadequate, because only
militarily enforced collectivisation plus a military order in
the factories (complemented by the more than 10 million slave
labourers of the Gulag) guaranteed the total control of the
society he, Stalin, aimed at.

This is also an answer to the pseudo-philosophical
problem of Stalin's 'necessity' or 'contingency' in
history.(8)

If we start from the above analysis, the whole sophistry
can indeed be reduced to the following simple propositions.
For all those who wanted to transform Lenin's system of
Jacobin terror into something permanent, which could not
happen except through the self-conscious permanency of
Stalin's dictatorship with adequate - anti-capitalist but
non-socialist - institutions, Stalin was a logical conclusion
of Lenin's premises. In that sense, Stalin was a necessity.
For all those who wanted to revise the very idea of a Jacobin
dictatorship, Stalin represented a causally well established,

but unacceptable and monstrous, as well as eliminable, system.
Stalin was certainly not contingent, but he was not necessary
either. Nikita Sergeevich Khrushchev certainly did not belong
to the latter type of interpreters, however.

Since he did not belong to those who became critical of
Lenin's Jacobinism to the slightest degree, but rather to
those who understood that Stalin had performed, in terms of
Leninism, something 'very positive' and since he wanted to
keep the results without admitting the necessity of the
methods leading to it, he needed a new historical mythology.
This was the widely accepted idea of 'return to Lenin', to the
legendary but never existing 'perfected' institutions and
solutions of the Lenin period. Needless to say, the Soviets
never again enjoyed even those miserable remnants of their
freedom of action which Lenin most reluctantly had temporarily
to grant them. The adherents also referred to the
non-existent 'Leninist norms of legality'. Lenin's legality
had one single principle, a very doubtful one if it stands
alone without a penal code, formalised procedures of law
enforcement, rights of the defendant, and, at least formal
independence of the courts: this was the Roman maxim salus
rei publicae suprema lex est. There is only one aspect in
which the Khrushchevite mythology of the return to Lenin
proved to be a realistic description of the state of affairs:
he and his colleagues really renounced bloodshed in their own
circles. This is, of course, a statement which needs a
certain qualification. The moment a Bolshevik was ready to go
so far as to relinquish the primogeniture of the party, to
abrogate the usurped prerogatives on behalf of the much
neglected masses as Imre Nagy did, the principle of 'no
bloodletting' was no longer applicable.

But the fact that Stalin's system outlived its usefulness
could not be restricted to the leading stratum. It was, first
of all, a problem of broad masses, outside the Soviet Union in
the East European countries often in the form of open
rebellion; inside the Soviet Union (and within it: inside
the Gulag) in fermenting discontent, in a state of gathering
storm. The only solution could be, and it was Khrushchev's
political genius to have understood this without ever having
formulated it, the closure of the period of destructive
'revolutions from above'.(9) In this sense, the Chinese
theorists were wrong in picking their simile. It was not
Thermidor but Brumaire that could be, with the necessary
vagueness and inexactitude of all historical analogies,
applied to Khrushchev.

It cannot be emphasised too strongly here that history
cannot be 'inferred' from the psychological make-up of a
representative protagonist. In the given case, Khrushchev was

anything but a peaceful man, a champion of methodical and liberal government. He was of a violent and cruel, even if not sadistic, nature, a born improviser, and a statesman of authoritarian leanings. Here is the vivid description of his work style during his first spectacular action, the construction of the Moscow Metro in his role as Moscow Party Secretary in the early 30s given by Crankshaw:

> The task of tunnelling was a job after Khrushchev's heart: it called for boldness amounting to recklessness, sacrificial toil, vast operations based on insufficient forethought, a standing disregard of the limitations of human flesh and blood and the facts of nature. Speed was of the essence. Immense risks had to be taken to keep up to schedule: nobody knows how many died as a consequence of the inevitable catastrophes'.(10)

As a viceroy of the Ukraine for 13 years he not only had more than his usual share of terror and oppression, as all Stalin's emissaries everywhere had in the gigantic country: his was the privilege to perform the round-up and mass deportation of more than a million Poles from the 'liberated' Western Ukraine under the methodical guidance of his crony, the later hangman of Hungary, 1956, General Serov, who was just a 'jolly good fellow' to Nikita Sergeevich. As is evident from his Memoirs, written after being driven out of office and when, to hear Khrushchev, he might have invented democracy, he did not feel the slightest remorse for this not particularly brilliant episode of his career. His much discussed figment of a particularly feverish Stalinist voluntarie fantasy, the plan of agrotowns - which would have transformed, preferably overnight, a much too dispersed Soviet kolkhoz peasantry into city-dwelling agricultural wage-labourers, also testifies to a man of violent and irrational impromptus. Quite irrespective of the theoretical merits or demerits of such a plan, the war-ridden Soviet Union was lacking in just about everything such a new 'transformation of social nature' required.

And yet he was the only one in a leadership who understood the imperative of the historical hour: to terminate the revolutions from above. All those who describe him as just another ambitious politico ruthlessly jockeying for supreme power or who remind us of the unsophisticated character of his 'sociological' descriptions of his adversaries' positions miss the important point. In marked contrast to 30 years of Soviet history, Khrushchev at least tried to give explanations instead of the usual labels: 'wrecker', 'enemy of the people'. Initially, in his fight against Malenkov, he did resort to the old technique of referring to 'the belching-up of Bukharinite-Rykovite rightist

deviationism' and, whenever he had antagonists he could not
cope with, he immediately relapsed into Stalin's vocabulary:
Imre Nagy's entourage was for him 'Nagy's gang', as it was
earlier his de dernier cri to speak of 'Tito's gang'. But he
did try to account for what had happened to 'Lenin's work' to
provide a rationale for his, and the Party's, future plans as
best he could, ensconced, of course, in the Procrustean bed of
his neo-Leninist mythology with an accompanying, often
meaningless and always doctrinaire vocabulary, and also
impeded by his own ineptness at genuine theoretical thinking.

The theoretical formulation of the exigencies of the
'Brumaire-period' of the Soviet Union started with a
discussion to which practically all Western observers (who
generally consider everything expressed in Marxist vocabulary
as just so much rubbish) attributed only a factional and
personal importance: with forcing Molotov to recant his
'erroneous statement' that the Soviet Union had not yet
accomplished the phase of constructing socialism. Molotov had
to admit that the Soviet Union had accomplished this phase and
was then 'constructing communism'.(11)

But there was much more to this than an empty exercise in
the Stalinist blend of Marxism-Leninism. Given that, for a
quarter of a century, socialism in Stalin's authoritative
interpretation was still a phase in which there was class
struggle, and this class struggle had perforce constantly to
sharpen, and given that the constantly sharpening class
struggle was but the code name for the permanence of the
terror, this sterile debate meant (as the shrewd Molotov
understood perfectly well) that an end must be put, not only
tacitly but also publicly, to the reign of terror. The second
step was taken immediately afterwards. In his anti-Stalin
campaign at the 20th Congress Khrushchev declared the
principle of constantly sharpening class struggle in socialism
erroneous; this meant the abrogation of the rationale for
mass terror and the undermining of Stalin's theoretical
authority in uno actu. The third and parallel step was
wrapped up in the fairly meaningless demand of the transition
from Stalin's cult of personality to 'collective leadership'.
This meant the important step of the closure of the wars of
extermination from above against the leading apparatus.
Behind the facade of an infantile psychology, as presented in
the Secret Speech, and the hackneyed phrases of Pravda
editorials this was equivalent to a return to the Lenin
recipe: no blood should flow between you. Khrushchev, who in
his truly polyphonic Memoirs finds a good word even in defence
of the Stalinist purges of the late 30s, which he had so
emphatically condemned in the Secret Speech (true, in the form
of a recollection of his then position but without having the
slightest guilt feeling for it), was fully aware of the fact

that the purges in the leading stratum were no longer needed.
Now no one would have the crazy idea that Lenin had had during
the Brest-Litovsk crisis: to leave the Central Committee and
take to the streets to agitate publicly against party
resolutions. There is no stronger proof of this than
Khrushchev himself, who accepted without hesitation his
post-coup confinement to a polite form of house arrest and
prudently did not say a single word about the colleagues who
had ousted him from office.

Two subsequent steps of terminating the period of
revolutions from above are closely interconnected: these are
the 'restoration of the Leninist norms of legality' and
announcing the advent of the 'all-peoples' state' in place of
the dictatorship of the proletariat. Of the first, we have
seen that there are simply no such norms; of the second, it
must be stated that this is one of the phoniest formulations
of the Khrushchev period, because the First Secretary
certainly did not intend to renounce the party's prerogatives,
in other words: the one-party dictatorship. Nonetheless,
behind the ideological double-talk, they had a definite and
definable meaning. They contained the firm, and in the main
kept, promise of Khrushchev's Brumaire government: a) not to
launch again any campaign of mass extermination like the
collectivisation (and the concomitant mass execution and mass
death by starvation of millions), b) not to use one stratum of
the population as a weapon against others, for intance during
the collectivisation when the alleged interests of the working
class were mobilised against 'greedy kulaks' and well-off
middle-holders. This theoretical declaration was complemented
by the already mentioned truly historical deed, the
disbandment of the Gulag empire which, apart from its obvious
primarily humanistic aspect, had a general practical economic
importance as well. I do not accept the theories so widely
circulating (especially in the German leftist discourse) of
the Stalin period according to which Stalin's regime was - by
virtue of the 10 million or more regular slave workers of the
Gulag - an 'Asiatic mode of production'. But it is undeniably
true that during the whole Stalin period there had always been
a sufficient number of slave workers at the disposal of the
'planners' to realise any lunatic or unnecessarily costly
project. And, at least in principle, the number of slave
workers could easily be reproduced, even increased, at any
given moment. It is very important therefore to emphasise
that the system of mass terror did not only serve directly
political purposes, but was a vigorous reinforcement of the
total and uncontrolled economic voluntarism of the system.
The moment Khrushchev put an end to this state within a state,
to this separate but immense realm of slave labour he reduced
the socio-economic space of <u>total</u> irrationality.

A further step was the announcement of the era of peaceful coexistence. Whatever the truth and sincerity behind this declaration, whatever the merit of the principle for a radical global strategy, one salutary effect was imminent: the power centres lost their legitimation for stepping up terror with reference to the 'encirclement of the Soviet Union' by world capitalism, a constant excuse for any action of mass terror touched off by any reasons. The encirclement theory was, of course, untenable in the whole post-war period of the Stalin leadership despite the short time span in which the United States had, and the Soviet Union did not yet possess, nuclear weapons. But it was for good reason that Stalin remained silent on this subject. He did not want to relinquish this comfortable principle of justification for any action of mass round-ups. An important aspect of the Secret Speech related to this was his description of Stalin's methods of wartime leadership which became a general laughing-stock for both Khrushchev's Stalinist and liberal critics. The story may abound in childish elements (even though the most dramatic part, the tragic collapse in the fateful year of 1941 is wholly substantiated by Nekrich's excellent and important book), but it had two important social consequences, both pertaining to the closure of the revolutions from above. One of them was the collective rehabilitation of all Soviet soldiers and officers who had been POWs because of Stalin's lunatic and criminal unpreparedness for war. These were people who were reluctant to commit collective harakiri for the greater glory of the Vozhd and over whom, even if they were not deported to Siberia, the Damoclean sword constantly hung. A second constituent was the rehabilitation of whole nations, the 'punished nations' whom Stalin, on the basis of a truly Fascist principle, namely collective punishment for collective crime, sent to deportation because of alleged or actual collaboration of some groups within them with the Nazis. Even if Khrushchev did not keep his word and these nations could not return to their proper domicile (Medvedev gives quite a credible account of this: the Volga-Germans for example, were an excellent agricultural workforce needed for the virgin land programme), the verdict of their innocence was an important and enduring deed.

Two additional theoretical and practical gestures completed the programme of closing the revolutions from above. The first was the well-known (and much ridiculed) slogan of 'overtaking America in per capita production', and the second, the 'scientific thesis' that the Soviet Union and its brother countries would simultaneously enter the phase of communism around 1980. Now, in spite of the capitalist world crisis, it will suffice to make a quick comparison between Moscow and any Western shops to derive a sardonic view of the predictive value of the first; and just to look at the Polish shopwindows to have a much grimmer view of the same with regard to the second statement. And yet, they were not so much balderdash as merely two positive promises of Khrushchev's government which he did not keep or kept only very partially. At least he honestly intended to deliver the goods. Ironically enough for such an ardent anti-Bukharinist, Khrushchev drew ever closer to the original project of the designer of the NEP, and while he did not have the slightest intention of creating a politically free citizenry (at best, he could have been pushed into Yugoslav-type concessions), he certainly wanted to respect the consumer in the Soviet man. His 'gulash communism' became the stumbling block of the Chinese theorists and the New Left and was scorned even by those liberals who have nothing against consumerism in their own society. But it simply has to be stated that Khrushchev's consumerism, shabby as its result turned out to be, was a policy with beneficial effects in a country whose populace had been systematically ravaged by artificially created famines and had been lacking in elementary consumer goods for decades. As to the second promises, even if we disregard the Marxist-Leninist 'wisdoms' displayed in all the discussions on whether East-European countries had already built socialism or only laid its foundations, the Khrushchevian slogan contained a promise to them which also had a reasonable content. It is a debatable point whether or not the Soviet-East European economic interrelationships during Stalin's lifetime were based on a simple exploitation of the latter by the former (Sartre, for instance, denied it and he had arguments) but this much is beyond any doubt: an economic system and strategy were imposed on these countries which was disadvantageous for them economically and advantageous for the Soviet Union, at least politically, (by making them dependent on Soviet imports, energy sources and the like). Now, one of the possible shades of interpretation of the Khrushchevian dictum of arriving simultaneously at the promised land was precisely the intention of abolishing this economic dependence of East Europe on the Soviet Union and replacing it by a mutually profitable 'cooperation'. At least certain countries, so very different to each other in their general policies as Romania and East Germany, interpreted it in this manner and got away with it. The real face of these allegedly so harmonious relationships under both Khrushchev and his successors was another question. But the very promise formed an integral part of the Khrushchevite Brumaire: the policy of closing the period of revolutions from above.

Up to this passage, I have constantly pointed out the inconsistencies of this policy and I could easily add other important aspects. Khrushchev solemnly promised to restore Leninist norms of collective leadership but continually tried to impose his arbitrary will on his colleagues, if necessary by breach of promises and dirty tricks; this is why his downfall became a necessity for them. He also promised, even if indirectly, to respect the inner peace of the <u>nomenklatura</u>, but by the constant and <u>deliberate</u> reorganisations which were aimed at weakening the power of the bureaucracy, he made their life hell, and, more importantly, he disrupted social bonds between them which were simply necessary for the functioning of this particular society with its irrational command economy. Even if no formal promises were made to rescind the policy of population transfer, as we have seen, it very logically followed from his whole general line. Nevertheles, there can be hardly any doubt that the majority of those 500,000 who were mobilised for the cultivation of the Virgin Lands did not leave their domiciles and accustomed milieux voluntarily. On the one hand, he consolidated Stalin's work through the mythology of returning to Lenin, eliminating at the same time the gravest horrors and the genuine dysfunctions; on the other hand, he thus provoked the appearance of a comeback of 'Soviet democracy' which did not belong to his objectives but which appeared as a logical conclusion of his own exposure of the Stalinist horrors. And the list of inconsistencies could be further expanded.

However, the really important question is the following: should a closure of revolutions from above be assessed positively or negatively? There are only two clear-cut answers. One comes from the conservative who regards terminating <u>any</u> revolution as a beneficial deed in the main. It was this conservative audience that was ready to applaud Khrushchev during his visits abroad. Without a theoretical framework for understanding Soviet affairs they sensed, as it were, the protagonist of a Soviet Brumaire in Stalin's successor. The other unambiguously negative answer to the question comes from the Maoist, for whom the crux of the matter was precisely this closure of revolutions. The Maoists regarded Khrushchev as a traitor precisely in that they no longer regarded Khrushchevite Russia as a revolutionary country. Here I do not have either space or time to criticise the mythological elements of the Maoist conception of revolutions based on 'contradictions within the people'; therefore a simple statement of the fact of condemnation will suffice.

To speak for myself, I have an ambivalent relation to the Khrushchevite Brumaire, an attitude, I think that all democratic but radical socialists should adopt. On the one hand, he was indeed a liberator of his own people from the unmitigated pestilence of the Stalinist mass terror, an unavoidable corollary feature of all revolutions from above. Here once again, I have to emphasise, against shallow interpreters of a complex historical development, that Stalin, one of the most horrible phenomena in human history ever, was not a lunatic half-wit but an evil genius, the designer and realiser of one of the most important social projects: <u>a society living in permanent revolution</u>. I have to repeat that both collectivisation and forced industrialisation were <u>means</u>, not <u>ends</u>, for him: partly, but not overwhelmingly, they were means to defend his revolutionary Russia from the adversary, a task which he very incompletely fulfilled. Overwhelmingly they were means to keep society under <u>total control</u> and <u>constant military mobilisation</u>. The latter two features were for Stalin identical with 'revolution', these were his genuine policy objectives. It is very hard to speak of the unwittingly positive yields of such an horrendous period. Nonetheless, it has to be said in summary that Stalin's period put a world-historical end to the delirium of enthusiasm, that halo of magnificence surrounding the very word of revolution since 1789 (or more precisely: since 1793) on the left. The results of a sobering realisation, a state of mind which accepts revolution as a <u>last resort</u> against tyrannical regimes but is most suspicious of the working of the instrument, are dawning upon us, of course, very slowly. But this undeniably happens, and the somnambulist but energetic push with which Khrushchev drove his country beyond the orgy and mythology of permanent revolution was an emancipatory deed precisely in this sense.

On the other hand, the task has remained uncompleted, and when one looks at his successors, the Brezhnevite and Andropovite Soviet Union with its threatening military might, expansionism, unbroken and ever increasing inner oppression, the total silence of graveyards which replaces the Khrushchevite promises of a cultural renaissance, the unquestioned and haughty rule of an ignorant, brutal and oppressive apparatus, one should say: the First Secretary did not have Mao's resolution (nor did his followers who, in a good Russian manner, invested their hopes in authority and did nothing for themselves) to launch <u>a revolution</u> from above. Undoubtedly, it could not have been a <u>democratic</u> revolution: no revolution from above is democratic. But, somewhere in the middle of the road it might have met social forces released by the impetus from above which had genuinely democratic intentions. <u>In this sense</u>, and irrespective of the mainly psychological question of the extent to which it accorded with the potentialities of his personal make-up, Khrushchev's renouncement of the revolution from above has a negative final balance sheet.

NOTES

1. Robert Havemann 'Die DDR in den zwanzig Jahren nach Stalins Sturz', in: R. Medvedev, R. Havemann, J. Steffen u.a. Entstalinisierung - Der XX. Parteitag der KPdSU und seine Folgen, Frankfurt/Main: Suhrkamp, 1977, p. 67.

2. To cut a matter of party history as short possible, let me quote Crankshaw's most convincing remarks: 'Nothing was ever said about a speech which Khrushchev made in Sofia on his way back from Belgrade in June (1955 - F.F.). Here, it was later discovered, only ten days after he had invited Tito to join him in blaming everything on Beria, he for the first time attacked Stalin openly...' Edward Crankshaw: Khrushchev, London: Collins, 1966, p. 211. Apart from the fact that this is a practically irrefutable proof of Khrushchev's intentions, the position hostilely biased against him also cannot account for the actors who had allegedly imposed their reformist will on him. Who were they? Perhaps Kaganovich or Molotov?

3. Quoted in R. Medvedev, R. Havemann, S. Steff, Entstalin-isierung, op.cit., p. 308.

4. A cursory glance will do as we have, in our book with Agnes Heller: Hungary, 1956 Revisited (The Message of the Revolution - A Quarter of a Century After, in manuscript) analyzed these options in somewhat more detail.

5. I would explicitly like to avoid calling the interpretation of Khrushchev's text as democratic a misinterpretation. It was a social project of one representative social actor, the reformist communist, who read Khrushchev's mind in this way and who succeeded in imposing this way of reading on a wide audience, spreading their later disillusionment to equally wide spheres of reception.

6. Zdenek Mlynar: Night Frost in Prague, London: Karz Publishers, 1978, p. 31.

7. In my The Frozen Revolution (forthcoming in Spanish, German and Italian) I have analysed the social character of Jacobinism. In The Dictatorship over Needs (A Structural Analysis of East-European Societies) written with A. Heller and G. Markus we have analysed how and in what respects Stalin was indeed the 'continuator of Lenin's work', how Stalin alone, the man, dreaded by Lenin himself, was the only possible safeguard of his

regime. And when I mention names, I certainly mean social tendencies.

8. I term it a pseudo-problem because there is no reasonable answer to it, especially not in terms of the theories of those who raised the question. If one deems Stalin's emergence necessary, one has first to account for the nature of this generative necessity, which is, philosophically speaking, practically always an impossible task; and, secondly, if Stalin was a necessity how does the de-Staliniser know that he is no longer necessary? And if he still is, the de-Staliniser commits a crime against 'historical necessity' which, in the form of Stalin, metes out very harsh punishments. Should, however, Stalin be declared a 'contingency', a sizeable and most palpable contingency indeed, then the whole view of history of the observer collapses immediately and no phase of Soviet development can be explained any longer.

9. Stalin's Trotskyite enemies tend to forget that Stalin also filched the idea of the permanent revolution: the Soviet Union, from the late twenties until his death, did live in such revolutionary permanence.

10. Crankshaw, op.cit., p. 90.

11. Needless to say, at a certain level all this is so much rubbish for me as well. The Soviet society is <u>not</u> socialism and the theoretical hairsplitting about the differences between socialism and communism have always served the purposes of the dirtiest pragmatism.

Chapter Two

KHRUSHCHEV AND THE RULES OF THE SOVIET POLITICAL GAME

T.H. Rigby

Politics in any country will always present the foreign observer with both familiar and unfamiliar aspects. There are certain conditions of success that he will be likely to encounter in almost any system, though they may appear in varied guises. Can you make good in any political system without being seen to 'deliver the goods' by those able to influence or control your fortunes, whether these be factional colleagues, hierarchical superiors, or electors? Can you do without 'friends', without supporting those who help you and helping those who support you? Can you avoid forming shorter or longer-term alliances or coalitions with others standing outside your friendship circle, on the basis of compromised or shared or complementary goals? And in doing all these things, will you not sometimes need to exercise initiative, to take risks, and to have an active rather than a passive approach to the structures and written or unwritten rules of the system, not just sitting back and expecting them to work to your advantage, but _making_ them work to your advantage, if necessary tinkering with them in the process? Only, perhaps, if and when you achieve the absolute power of an Octavian become Caesar Augustus, a Henry VIII, or a Stalin, can you afford to neglect these basic requirements of the successful politician.

RULES OF THE SOVIET POLITICAL GAME

Now let us glance briefly at the form these requirements take in the Soviet case: and incidentally these remarks apply on the whole to other Leninist systems as well. I believe they all strongly condition behaviour at each stage of making a political career in the USSR, although they manifest themselves in somewhat different ways at different hierarchical levels. At lower levels 'delivering the goods' means for the most part effectiveness in performing tasks assigned from above. This, however, involves far more than just obeying orders, for it is frequently impossible to carry out all the tasks assigned you while maintaining all the standards demanded, and difficult decisions have to be made about priorities in the employment of limited resources and in obedience to various rules and instructions.(1) At higher levels policy advice and policy responsibility form increasingly important components of the political role, and here too one must show initiative and willingness to make hard priority decisions if one is to succeed. What is common to all levels in the Soviet system is that 'delivering the goods' means satisfying the priority demands of your hierarchical superiors. It is only at the very top that, at periods when there is no strongly dominant individual leader, it is the assessment of your peers rather than of 'the boss' that counts.

Turning to the question of 'friends', there is no doubt that you need a patron if you are to get started on a political career in the Soviet Union. But you also need clients if you are to go very far with it. The initial patron-client relationship is usually formed between hierarchical superiors and subordinates, and as in any hierarchical system the client has valuable resources to offer in the form of information that can be provided or withheld and in the lengths he is prepared to go to in the patron's interest. As Konrad and Szelenyi have put it, 'if you are to advance rapidly your superiors must be convinced that you would put your hand in the fire for them'.(2) Two factors specific to Soviet-type systems are of particular importance in this connection. The first stems from what was said earlier about 'delivering the goods': at local levels this will frequently involve superiors and subordinates in shared complicitly for actions which violate official policies or norms. And this is probably a factor in the often remarkable durability of clientelist bonds in the USSR. The other is the operation of the nomenklatura system, which puts the main weight in personnel administration on superiors' evaluation rather than objective criteria, and places particular power in the hands of certain dominant figures in the party hierarchy. The clientelist network formed around First Secretaries of a regional or republican party committee is of particular importance, since if he should go on to a top position in Moscow it is from this source that he is likely to staff many key posts within his sphere of control. But at this point the successful politician will also experience the need and opportunity to diversify his clientele beyond the narrow circle of his old cronies, and he would be wise to do so if he wishes to reinforce his position. Two new sources of clients in particular present themselves: 'victims' of his rivals (Stalin was adept at making supporters out of prominent bolsheviks aggrieved at the treatment by Trotsky or Zinoviev) and relatively junior figures generously promoted (again Stalin made ample use of this gambit in the later '1930s and on the eve of his death). But a leader would be imprudent to draw too much on these additional sources of clients at the expense of his older cronies if these are currently occupying most of the key positions, unless he already enjoys a very high level of personal authority and coercive power.

At lower levels coalition-building is found in both weaker and stronger variants. The weaker variant consists of the exchange of favours in the form of services and information with officials standing outside your immediate organisation, and is of much the same order as the networks of mutual favour which citizens of Soviet-type societies are obliged to build up and rely heavily upon in managing their everyday lives. The stronger form of coalition consists of alliances within one's own organisation, and like all alliances implies someone to be allied <u>against</u>, i.e. rivalry or conflict. Within the bureau of a local party committee (the key decision-making body for the district, city or region and the usual training-ground for the budding Soviet politician) the dominant First Secretary will seek to weld his colleagues into a loyal and harmonious team, but the latter may be pushed by conflicting ambitions or by conflicting needs arising from the demands of higher echelons in their respective chains of command into taking sides among themselves. At higher levels policy elements become more important and especially so at the summit, for obvious reasons. Since alliance and conflict must always be played out in terms of <u>issues</u> on which decisions must be made, while conversely conflict over issues must always take the form of conflict between <u>people</u>, the question whether it is power or policy that is at the root of leadership coalitions and their rivalries is as much a chicken-and-egg problem in the USSR as it is in other political systems. However in the case of some individual leaders we may find out enough about them to hazard a guess as to the balance between power calculations and policy commitments in their particular coalition behaviour. Coalitions can vary of course along a durability continuum that runs from the single-issue alignment to the stable faction. Since the latter is anathema to the organisational principles of the CPSU, leadership coalitions are typically informal and shifting, and considerable political skill is called for in adjusting one's coalition tactics to the changing context of power and policy. The classical example is Stalin's successive alliances, first in the <u>troika</u> with Zinoviev and Kamenev, then with the 'Right', and finally against the 'Right'. As in all such cases, there was an interplay here between coalition politics and patronage politics, and the latter grew in relative importance so that by the time of Stalin's final coalition switch it was supporters rather than allies of Stalin that had come to dominate the Politburo.

The need for initiative, risk-taking, and an active and manipulative attitude towards institutions and rules is apparent at all levels of the political hierarchy in the USSR. The ambitious young party official will learn at the outset of his career that he has to play this game and that whether he

sinks or swims will depend largely on his boldness, judgement
and luck in playing it. As we have seen, he will scarcely
'deliver the goods' if he is unprepared to bend the rules or
illegally switch material or institutional resources from
low-priority to high-priority targets. If he does 'deliver',
which may mean for example in the case of a rural raikom
secretary managing to get in a good grain harvest, then he is
unlikely to be called to account; but if he fails, he has
provided ample grounds for his dismissal or worse. The same
applies as our politician climbs to higher echelons.   But as
he nears the summit he must also accept the risks involved in
making policy recommendations and policy decisions and
accepting responsibility for the results – unless he is strong
enough or wily enough to unload his sins on a scapegoat in the
case of failures. Under Stalin, the high costs of failure or
of being scapegoated for the failures of others were
compounded by the possible costs of <u>succeeding</u> in some
operation which the dictator now wished to repudiate.

The risks attendant on your political 'friendships' are
also obvious: if you are called upon to put your hand in the
fire for your patron, it may get burnt, while the sins and
failings of your clients, if you cannot cover them up, may
compromise you dangerously. And, of course, if your patron
falls, you are likely to fall with him. Coalition politics
are by definition risky, since there must always be losers, a
point again amply illustrated by the experiences of Stalin's
successive allies in the 1920s.

MAKING OF A STALINIST POLITICIAN

The Donbass mine-worker Nikita Khrushchev was no
revolutionary. The Bolsheviks were already in power when he
joined them in 1918, at the age of 24 (by which age such
near-contemporaries as Kaganovich, Molotov and Mikoyan had
spent years in the revolutionary movement).(3) He was,
however, clearly ambitious, and his acts of joining the party
and then the Red Army, in which he took on (perhaps not
immediately) the highly compromising job of a 'political
worker', suggest a willingness to take risks on behalf of his
ambition. He was rewarded on demobilisation with appointment
as political deputy manager of the Ruchenkov mines in Yuzovka
(later Stalino) where he had earlier worked and in which a
'close friend' was now manager (a coincidence?). Almost
immediately, however, he showed his penchant for raising the
stakes, giving up this promising job in order to repair his
lack of a secondary education, with some difficulty obtaining
party permission to take a full-time course in a 'Workers'
Faculty', where he studied from 1922 to 1925.(4) What,
however, did an ambitious young communist do in these times

when he 'studied'? Khrushchev immediately became secretary of his party cell and the following year was made politruk or 'political guide' of the school. The period 1923-24 was the highpoint of Trotsky's challenge to the Stalin-Kamenev-Zinoviev troika, a challenge that won its greatest support among young communists doing study courses. There can be little doubt that Trotsky's attacks on the 'bureaucracy' found at least some resonance among Khrushchev's fellow students, or that the thirty-year old politruk dealt with them effectively, thereby 'delivering the goods' to the Stalin machine that was firmly in control of the Yuzovka party organisation. The latter showed its appreciation on his graduation in 1925 by making him secretary of a district party committee. Khrushchev had now taken a crucial step on the ladder of political success, and he had also found a patron in the person of that stalwart Stalinist, the regional party secretary K.V. Moiseenko.

As luck would have it, it was precisely at this point that Stalin sent one of his closest supporters, Lazar Kaganovich, to take over the leadership of the Ukrainian party machine, of which the Stalino organisation was one of the major components. Khrushchev claims to have met Kaganovich early in 1917,(5) but whether the raw young miner had made much of an impression on the seasoned revolutionary seems doubtful. Now, however, with Moiseenko's sponsorship, Khrushchev gained access to settings where he could catch the great man's eye. His first opportunity occurred at the 9th Ukrainian Party Congress late in 1925, at which he gained inclusion as a non-voting member of the solidly Stalinist delegation to the 14th All-Union Congress, where he no doubt joined the chorus howling down the supporters of Stalin's former allies Zinoviev and Kamenev. In 1926 he attended the 1st Ukrainian Party Conference at which he delivered a blistering attack on an opposition delegate who had challenged Kaganovich's defence against charges of suppressing intra-party democracy. The following year, at the 10th Ukrainian Party Congress, he likewise distinguished himself in expressing a more uncompromising attitude towards oppositionist communists than the Stalinist leadership of the Party was at this point willing to adopt publicly, however pleased they were to have them manifested by their supporters. It was Khrushchev who was chosen to propose certain organisational changes which had the effect of further tightening the power of the apparatus over the Party. Khrushchev thus continued to raise the stakes, but by this time he could have little doubt that he was backing a winning horse. At the end of 1927 his services were rewarded by selection as one of the eleven voting delegates from the Stalino Region to the 15th All-Union Congress.

By this time he had earned a further promotion, to a 'leading position' in Stalino, evidently as Head of the Regional Organisation and Assignment Department. But this landed him in his first sticky patch. In the winter of 1927-28 the Ukrainian Central Committee and Control Commission commissioned an investigation of the Stalino Party Organisation, which came up with a report condemning the regional leadership for encouraging widespread corruption, drunkenness and other abuses. There was a large-scale purge, from which, however, Regional Secretary Moiseenko escaped with a demotion to a less important region.(6) Khrushchev, whose own account suggests he may have played some part in his former patron's disgrace, emerged unscathed. He had now clearly been taken up by Kaganovich, whom he 'trusted and respected one hundred percent', and who at this point offered him a job as deputy chief of the Organisation Department of the Ukrainian Central Committee. After some hesitation he accepted the offer, but (at his own request, he claims, in order to escape total involvement in the paper work) he soon obtained a transfer to Kiev as head of the Organisation Department of the Regional Committee.(7)

In 1928 Kaganovich returned to Moscow and resumed his pre-1925 post of Central Committee Secretary, with primary responsibility for internal Party affairs, including personnel. It is clear that Stalin intended him for a key role in the struggle against the 'Right Opposition' and indeed his official biography in the first edition of the Great Soviet Encyclopedia states that he now 'carried out great work in the reconstruction of the Party's ranks and all organs of the proletarian dictatorship'. The following year Khrushchev also came to Moscow and evidently with some difficulty obtained permission to study in the Moscow Industrial Academy, one of the country's most prestigious educational institutions intended to train mostly mature persons for senior positions in the industrial administration. The Academy posed a delicate problem for the Moscow Regional and Central Committee party officials to whom it was responsible: it was a hotbed of 'Rightist' criticism of the effects of Stalin's collectivisation and forced industrialisation policies, but meanwhile its student body included Stalin's wife Nadezhda Alliluyeva, who was herself becoming increasingly distressed with the consequences of these policies. A problem of such delicacy must have been drawn to Kaganovich's attention, and he may well have decided that he needed a man in the Academy whose Stalinist zeal and loyalty were beyond reproach and in whom he had personal confidence. This may be what lies behind the statement in one of Khrushchev's official biographies that he was 'sent by the Central Committee' to the Industrial Academy, though Khrushchev himself claims that the initiative was entirely his and that he had difficulty in persuading the

Ukrainian party authorities to release him. In any case it was Kaganovich who overruled an early attempt to remove him from the Institute on the grounds of his inadequate preparation.(8) The Party Organisation in the Academy had been purged of its 'Rightist' leaders in September 1929, on the eve of Khrushchev's arrival, but in the following May the new Party Bureau were in turn replaced for 'tolerating' the persistence of 'Rightist' dissent, and their successors, now headed by Nikita Khrushchev, were charged with the task of removing dissident students from the Academy 'in the shortest possible time', their actions being subject to direct approval by the Central Committee.(9)

Khrushchev must have completed the task to the 'Central Committee's' satisfaction, for eight months later he was promoted to be First Party Secretary of the Bauman District, in which the Academy was located. He had spent only 14 months at the Academy, which supports the inference that it was for political purposes, rather than for purposes of study, that he had been assigned there.

As a raikom (district committee) secretary in Moscow, he now worked directly under Kaganovich, who had meanwhile added the post of First Secretary of the Moscow Committee to his Central Committee Secretaryship. It is almost certain that by now his name had already been brought favourably to the attention of Stalin. Certainly both Kaganovich's sponsorship and Stalin's approval would have been necessary for the successive steps in his meteoric rise during the next four years.(10) After a mere half year heading the Bauman raikom and a similar period in charge of the Krasnaya Presnya raikom, he was made second secretary of the Moscow City Committee (in January 1932); by 1934 he was First Secretary of the City Committee and simultaneously Second Secretary (under Kaganovich) of the Moscow Regional Committee; in 1935 he took over as First Secretary of the Regional Committee as well. There is sufficient evidence that he owed these successive promotions not just to the goodwill of the masters of the party machine, but to his demonstrated capacity to 'deliver the goods'; as Khrushchev himself puts it, 'apparently my performance justified the trust and responsibility that had been invested in me when I had been promoted from the district level'.(11) The Moscow press for this period reveals him as a man of exemplary energy, imagination, and 'Bolshevik toughness' in imposing discipline and sacrifice on the Moscow workforce and population in the carrying out of party policies.(12)

Khrushchev's entry into the top party leadership coincided with the most difficult and dangerous phase in the establishment of Stalin's dictatorship. By 1935 the mounting

frenzy of expulsions, dismissals, 'unmaskings' and arrests
that constituted the 'Great Terror' had already begun, and
within three years four-fifths of the members of the Central
Committee were under arrest or already dead. What was it that
saved Khrushchev? Evidently not Kaganovich's protection, for
the latter was not even prepared to stand up for his brother
Mikhail, also a Central Committee member, on his arrest some
years later.(13) The answer probably lies in one aspect of the
Great Purge that has been little noticed, namely that whereas
nearly all 'ordinary' members of the Central Committee
perished, those of them who were in the Dictator's inner
circle did not, unless they actually <u>had</u> opposed Stalin.(14)
Although Khrushchev was not made a candidate member of the
Politburo till January 1938,(15) from 1934-35 his leading
party role in Moscow would have kept him constantly under the
General Secretary's eye. He must also have won the latter's
approval for the relentless drive he displayed in pushing
through the ambitious plan for the reconstruction of Moscow in
this period.

While the help of powerful 'friends' evidently played a
major part in Khrushchev's rise, little evidence has yet been
brought to light on his own exercise of patronage to this
point. However, as boss of the Moscow regional and city party
machines he could scarcely have avoided it, and his later
record showed no tendency to do so. One clear case from this
period is that of D.S. Korotchenko, who first worked closely
with Khrushchev in the Bauman district in 1931, when the
former was Chairman of the Executive Committee of the District
Soviet (<u>raiispolkom</u>) and the latter First Secretary of the
District party Committee (raikom). As Khrushchev rose to the
top in the Moscow Party organisation, Korotchenko received a
series of promotions, becoming by 1937 his second secretary in
the Regional Committee (obkom). He emerged unscathed from the
Yezhov purge, being sent to Smolensk as First Secretary of the
Western Obkom. It was, of course, the holocaust of 1937-38
that explains the paucity of survivors among those who had
served under Khrushchev in the preceeding years, and if he
felt moved to intercede for them, prudence evidently
restrained him: otherwise, in the unlikely event of his
living to tell the tale, we should no doubt have heard of it.
There were limits to what a 'principled Bolshevik' could do
for his 'friends'.(16)

The same reason helps to explain the shortage of evidence
as to the coalitions he formed in this period. There was
perhaps no great call for the 'stronger' type of coalition,
owing to the dominance of the Moscow organisation by his
patron Kaganovich, but one man he seems to have formed an
alliance with was Nikolai Bulganin, whose own links with
Kaganovich evidently went back to the Civil War period and who

was Chairman of the Executive Committee of the Moscow City Soviet from 1931 to 1937, when he became Chairman of the Council of Ministers of the Russian Federal Republic. In order to meet the rigorous demands being made on them, not least by Stalin himself, the two men would have had to establish a close working relationship within the Bureau of the Moscow Committee.(17) Another rising leader who became a good friend of Khrushchev during this period was Georgi Malenkov, also a protege of Kaganovich and an official of the Moscow Obkom in 1930-34. This link must have been a valuable one for Khrushchev in the years that followed, when Malenkov served as deputy chief of the Leading Party Organs Department of the Central Committee, although it exposed him to danger when Malenkov came under suspicion following the arrest of his former boss Yezhov.(18) As for the 'weaker' type of coalition, Khrushchev must have built up a considerable network of contacts within the central party and Government machines during this period, but many of those concerned must have perished in the Yezhovshchina, and Paloczi-Horvath's assertion that these contacts proved useful to him in the political struggles of the post-war years seems to be based on no more than supposition.(19)

IN STALIN'S POLITBURO

In January 1938, simultaneously with his promotion to candidate membership of the Politburo, Khrushchev was sent to Kiev to take charge of the Ukrainian party organisation. The following year he was made a full member of the Politburo. Although the worst of the Terror was already over in the Ukraine, Khrushchev could not have avoided complicity in its final stages.(20) It was Khrushchev's main task, however, to put the pieces together again as the whirlwind passed, and in the first instance to restock the party and state apparatus. Here he evidently did not have a free hand, as he was accompanied to Kiev by M.A. Burmistenko, one of Malenkov's subordinates in the Central Committee's Department of Leading Party Organs, who was made Second Secretary, with responsibility, inter alia, for party cadres.(21) Nevertheless Khrushchev would have had the major say over the more senior appointments, and several of the officials who now came into prominence were to serve under him for many years to come, both inside the Ukraine and beyond. His chief Moscow protege, Demyan Korotchenko, was meanwhile transferred from Smolensk to Kiev, to take over the key position of Chairman of the Council of People's Commissars.

Khrushchev must have performed to Stalin's satisfaction in directing the important Ukrainian segment of the great industrial drive of 1939-41, in Sovietising the new territories acquired from Poland, Czechoslovakia and Romania in 1939-40, in his wartime role as 'Member of the Military Council' (i.e. chief party representative) on a series of southern fronts, and in the reconstruction of the devasted Ukraine after 1944.(22) In 1946-47, however, he came under an ominous cloud. In July 1946 a Central Committee decision was issued strongly criticising the work of the Ukrainian leadership in training, selecting and assigning leading party and Soviet cadres.(23) Amongst the more serious charges was the tolerance of Ukrainian 'bourgeois nationalism'.(24) Then in February 1947 the Ukraine was criticised for its poor performance in a Central Committee resolution on agriculture, an area to which Khrushchev had devoted great personal effort and attention.(25) There can be little doubt that certain of the Moscow-based Politburo members, including Malenkov and probably Andreev and Beria, were resentful of the authority Khrushchev was accumulating in the Ukraine and of his assertiveness in policy-areas under their jurisdiction, and were anxious to discredit him in the eyes of Stalin. Their task would have been made all the easier by Stalin's hostility to the Ukrainians over what he saw as their wartime treachery(26) and the continued widespread activity of the Ukrainian Insurgent Army (UPA) in the Western provinces. Khrushchev had angered Stalin by his efforts to secure relief for the Ukrainian population during the catastrophic famine of 1946, and Malenkov and Beria had allegedly exploited this situation to weaken his position. It reached the point, as he reports, that 'some people were spreading the rumour that I was giving in to local Ukrainian influences, that I was under pressure from Ukrainian interest groups, and that I was already becoming a Ukrainian nationalist myself'.(27)

These moves heralded the most serious setback in Khrushchev's political career.(28) In March 1947 he was stripped of three of his posts - First Secretary of the Ukrainian Central Committee and of the Kiev Regional and City Committees - remaining only Chairman of the Ukrainian Council of Ministers. His chief party post was taken over by none other than Kaganovich. Although no personal accusations were publicly made against Khrushchev, it must have been as obvious to others as it evidently was to him that a large question mark had been placed against his past record and future fate. For four months, from May to August, he did not appear in public (though he was convalescing from a serious illness for part of this time). Precisely what Kaganovich's terms of reference were we cannot be sure. The fact that he was accompanied to Kiev by N.S. Patolichev, a protege of Andreev (and today Minister for Foreign Trade) who took over as Agriculture Secretary tends to confirm the view (supported by Khrushchev's own account) that agricultural issues were indeed among the sins being laid at Khrushchev's door, but that

Kaganovich was free to exercise a more general role. He did become personally involved in the farm production drive and also in industrial matters, but seems to have concentrated much of his effort on that other shortcoming that was being laid at Khrushchev's door, namely 'Ukrainian bourgeois nationalism', especially in the newly incorporated Western regions and among intellectuals.(29) One of the few concrete achievements of the Kaganovich episode in 1947 was the accelerated collectivisation of most of the West Ukrainian peasantry. He seems to have had an open brief to assess the situation on the spot, take such drastic immediate action as was necessary, and report to Stalin on the adequacy of Khrushchev's leadership. That Kaganovich was chosen for this role - a man unaligned with Khrushchev's critics but unlikely to 'put his hand in the fire' on his old protege's behalf - suggests that Stalin was genuinely undecided what to do at this point. At the very least the operation should correct any inclinations to hubris on Khrushchev's part. If part of Stalin's intention was to sow hostility between Khrushchev and his erstwhile protege, in this he was eminently successful.(30) The first sign that Khrushchev was passing the test was Patolichev's removal from Kiev in August 1947 (in Khrushchev's account, Patolichev himself took the initiative in order to escape from Kaganovich). The following month Khrushchev appeared again in public, and in December he regained the First secretaryship and Kaganovich returned to Moscow. He did not resume his other posts, but his old associate Korotchenko again became his Chairman of the Council of Ministers. How far he owed his restoration to Stalin's renewed trust and how far to changes in the constellation of power in Moscow (in which Malenkov himself suffered a setback at the hands of Zhdanov and his 'Leningraders') it is impossible to say.

It is noteworthy that the Kaganovich episode brought no major changes in the second-level leadership of the Ukraine. Khrushchev himself had undertaken a few replacements in the wake of the July 1946 decision on defects in Ukrainian cadres administration, but the Ukrainian political elite, as it was formed under him at the end of the war, consisting mainly of men initially recruited in 1938-39, remained largely intact for the rest of his period in Kiev, despite numerous switches of posts. For instance, of the 23 first secretaries of Ukrainian obkoms replaced in the four years 1946-49, only four failed to receive other senior posts.(31) In other words, wherever possible Khrushchev looked after his clients, and many bonds forged in this period were to assume great political importance in later years (see Appendix).

In December 1949 Khrushchev left Kiev to become a Secretary of the Central Committee and First Secretary of the Moscow Obkom. The political background to this shift needs to be briefly sketched. By the end of the war Kaganovich and Andreev had lost their earlier dominance of the central machinery of the party and two younger Central Committee Secretaries, Zhdanov and Malenkov, had come to the fore. In 1946, however, Malenkov had to withdraw from the CC Secretariat, remaining a Deputy Chairman of the Council of Ministers, and for the next two years Zhdanov was riding high. Zhdanov's death in August 1948 gave the kaleidoscope another sharp wrench, and shortly afterwards Malenkov and Beria secured Stalin's approval to launch the 'Leningrad case', in practice a bloody purge of Zhdanov's supporters in the central party and government machine as well as in his Leningrad stronghold itself. Beria's role was evidently to manage the police aspects, through his protege V.S. Abakumov, who headed the Ministry of State Security, and that of Malenkov, now back in the Central Committee Secretariat, to initiate the personnel replacements.(32) One effect of these developments was sharply to increase the weight of these two men within the leadership, and it is likely that Stalin's chief motive in moving Khrushchev to Moscow was to provide a counterweight to the Malenkov-Beria alliance.(33) From being the only Politburo member other than Stalin in the Secretariat, Malenkov now became just one of two. Further, Malenkov's dominance (through his protege V.M. Andrianov) of the Leningrad Party machine was offset by Khrushchev's dominance of the even more important Moscow machine. Stalin's intention was evidently not to substitute Khrushchev for Malenkov as the dominant figure in the Secretariat, but to set them at loggerheads. An additional example is his investing of both with policy responsibilities in the sphere of agriculture. This led to some sharp encounters, from at least two of which Khrushchev emerged with a bloodied nose. In one of these, arising form his 1951 proposal to move the peasants from their villages into 'agro-towns' (a term which Khrushchev himself actually repudiated), it is noteworthy that the public criticisms of the proposal (but without naming its initiator) emanated from Malenkov (at the 19th Party Congress) and from two of Beria's principal henchmen in the Caucasus.(34)

Before looking further at Stalin's machinations during the last two years of his life and considering how Khrushchev may have fitted into them, let us briefly glance at the latter's 'work with cadres' during this, his second incumbency as boss of the local party machine in the city and region of Moscow. Within a brief period he had made almost a clean sweep of those officials who had been prominent under his predecessor G.M. Popov. In seeking replacements for them he did not (could not?) bring in many protégés from the Ukraine.

Among those he did were Z.F. Oleinik, who became his Second Secretary in the Moscow Obkom, but who died in 1951. Most of his new team, however, were recruited locally by the rapid advancement of younger officials or promotion of others who had been languishing in relatively minor posts under Popov. As in the case of Khrushchev's Ukrainian 'cadres', these included many whose names were to become familiar in the post-Stalin years,(35) (see Appendix).

Back now to the high drama.(36) In his 1956 'secret' speech Khrushchev was to allege that on the eve of his death Stalin had made the first steps in what was to be a major purge, in the course of which he would 'finish off' his 'old guard', and there were, indeed, indications at the time that suggested to some observers that something of the kind was afoot. The most important of these were, first, the abolition of the Politburo after the Nineteenth Party Congress in October 1952 and its replacement by a much larger 'Presidium of the Central Committee', which included many recently promoted younger officials along with former Politburo members, and, secondly, the 'vigilance campaign' which began almost simultaneously and rose to new heights with the 'doctors' plot' allegations in January 1953. But there were certain earlier moves which went relatively unnoticed at the time and which suggest, inter alia, that Beria was not to be the chief instrument of Stalin's new purge (as was later suggested) and indeed was probably its first major target. Chief among these were the removal (evidently in 1951) of Beria's protege Abakumov as Minister of State Security and his replacement by S.D. Ignatiev, the purging of Beria's supporters from all leading party and government positions in Georgia, and the arrest of some of the latter for alleged participation in a Mingrelian nationalist conspiracy - Beria himself being a Mingrelian.(37)

As for Malenkov, although he was ostensibly anointed as dauphin by being entrusted with delivering the main report to the Nineteenth Congress and continued to receive favourable press treatment up to Stalin's death, there were reasons for thinking that he, too, was not privy to Stalin's machinations and that his position was beginning to be undermined. For instance, in 1952 he lost control of one of his chief levers of power, the Party Organs Department, which was transferred to a new Central Committee Secretary, A.B. Aristov, who later emerged as a protege of Khrushchev's. Moreover, the accusation against the arrested Kremlin doctors that they had contrived the death of Zhdanov clearly carried the seeds of danger for Malenkov, in view of his earlier rivalry with Zhdanov and his gains, along with Beria, from Zhdanov's death and the subsequent purge of his supporters.

If it is fair to assume that neither Beria nor Malenkov was involved in Stalin's new purge preparations and that certainly the former and probably the latter felt threatened by them, there is no reason to doubt that the same applied to other older members of the leadership, particularly Molotov and Mikoyan.(38) It is important to make this point, for although it seems likely that in conducting his manoeuvres Stalin was dealing directly with officials further down the line, it is improbable that he failed to involve at least one or two of his senior lieutenants by either giving them a direct role in his moves or at least encouraging them to see themselves as likely beneficiaries of them. Khrushchev is the most likely candidate for such involvement, although it must be stressed that there is no more than circumstantial evidence for this view. An important fact is that in addition to Aristov, several other second-level officials who were on the offensive in the Mingrelian nationalism and Kremlin doctors cases and/or the accompanying vigilance campaign, including State Security Minister S.D. Ignatiev, Central Committee secretary for propaganda M.A. Suslov, and F.R. Kozlov, Second Secretary of the Leningrad Obkom (and from his history already a cuckoo in this particular Malenkov nest) were all to figure as allies or proteges of Khrushchev during the period of his post-Stalin rivalry with Malenkov. It may also be pertinent that it was Khrushchev who gave the report to the Nineteenth Congress on the amendment to the party rules which opened the way for the reorganisation of the top leadership organs which he himself was later to connect with Stalin's moves against the 'old guard'. If, however, he was probably encouraged to see himself as a likely beneficiary of whatever Stalin was up to, we have no way of knowing whether he was personally implicated in any of Stalin's moves. Further, Khrushchev was canny enough to realise that once Beria, Malenkov and other early targets were eliminated (with or without his direct help), Stalin might well then turn his attention to him.

Can anything be said about Khrushchev's alignments within the leadership in this period? Obviously, no dictator can tolerate groups of his lieutenants forming close coalitions among themselves, and there seems no reason to reject the conventional view that Stalin took considerable pains to prevent this by giving them overlapping and conflicting responsibilities, sowing mutual distrust, and so on. Nevertheless, it is clear that some cleavages were deeper and more lasting than others, and some leaders shared broader or more vital interests with some of their colleagues than with others. The situation in which Khrushchev found himself on the eve of Stalin's death evidently thrust him into a posture of rivalry with Malenkov and antagonism to Beria, and gave him little common ground with the older leaders, even his old patron Kaganovich, whom he had long since outrun. The men

with whom he now found himself in the same boat were those
more junior officials whom Stalin was evidently setting up
against the 'old guard' on the eve of his death.

STALINIST WITH A DIFFERENCE

If this account of Khrushchev's political career up to 1953 is
not too far off-beam, it reveals him as in many respects the
quintessential Stalinist. No revolutionary intellectual, but
a shrewd and ambitious lower-class provincial, he elbowed his
way up the party hierarchy using the standard methods of
displaying exemplary zeal and energy and not a little
brutality in carrying out the asignments of his superiors in
the Stalin machine, and ultimately of Stalin himself, while
taking care to buttress his position with good patronage
connections and alliances and with supporters who understood
that their fate and prospects depended on his.

And yet if we were to leave it at that, we would miss
that something extra without which Khrushchev's career after
1953 becomes difficult to comprehend. In identifying this
'something extra' I do not offer any penetrating new insights
or interpretations. Its ingredients were, I believe,
precisely those that became the cliches of scholarly and
journalistic comment on our hero from the middle fifties on
(even though not all would agree with the terms I use to
describe them or the relative weight I accord them): an
earthiness and folksiness along with a seeming compulsion to
talk with people at the 'grass roots' and talk them around, an
evidently related capacity to empathise (though not
necessarily to sympathise) with the subordinate officials and
'masses' under his command, a close interest in practicalities
rather than generalities or abstractions, innovativeness and
daring in furthering his objectives and those of his
superiors, and finally a certain streak of naive utopianism.
What is perhaps not sufficiently realised is that these
characteristics did not suddenly blossom in the more benign
atmosphere of the post-Stalin years: they were apparent in
his early career as well, justifying our characterising him
even then as a 'Stalinist with a difference'.

Pistrak discerns the first of them - the earthiness and
taste for the 'grass roots' - even at the outset of his
political career, when he was a mere raikom secretary near
Stalino,(39) although the evidence is slight and it is not
clear how far this approach was unusual at that time. More
striking and convincing evidence emerges when we look at the
style and content of some of Khrushchev's speeches in the
post-war period, by which time no other leader would deign (or
dare?) to express himself in terms of other than dead

stereotyped phrases and vague and pompous generalisations.
Here, for example, is Khrushchev rebuking Ukrainian party
officials for the sin normally discussed in terms of standard
formulas of 'supplanting' (podmena) of government
administrators, of obsession with 'petty details', and so
on.(40)

> Certain leaders of soviet and economic organs try to
> remove responsibility from themselves and shift it
> onto the party organs. At the same time some soviet
> and economic officials are not beyond flattering the
> party officials and emphasising their extreme
> respect for them. 'No-one can think out a problem
> better than you,' they say, 'no-one can do it
> better'. 'Give us a directive,' they say, 'and
> we'll carry it out'. Some of our insufficiently
> experienced leaders take this as their due. It's
> the accepted thing, you know, to say to the
> secretary of the party committee: You, Ivan
> Ivanovich, see all and know all. How can one reply
> to such an economic official that you don't see
> everything? But this economic official will make
> capital out of this. He brings the secretary or the
> head of the department of the regional committee the
> draft of a decision or a telegram and asks for his
> signature on it. And having obtained the decision
> or telegram, the economic official breathes a sigh
> of relief, counting on the fact that the district
> party committee will now be doing his job for him.

Those who have read Khrushchev's speeches from 1953 on
will immediately recognise the style; the remarkable thing is
that this dates from 1948, when it stood out in startling
contrast to the wooden utterances of other leaders. No wonder
he aroused the suspicion and hostility of some of them.

Early examples of the boldness and inventiveness he
brought to the task of 'delivering the goods' range from the
purely political through the organisational to the technical.
At the political end of the spectrum one can mention the
radicalism of his proposals for combatting oppositionists in
the mid-twenties. Pistrak gives some good examples of his
organisational inventiveness from the period a few years later
when he was a raikom secretary in Moscow, concluding that 'he
not only faithfully followed Kaganovich's orders and the party
decisions in general, but also displayed initiative in
inventing new methods and devices for better and speedier
fulfilment of these ...'.(41) Further, there is no difficulty
in spotting early manifestations of his energy in seeking out
and promoting technical innovations in the economy, so
familiar to us from the post-Stalin period, for example the

various devices he espoused on the eve of the war to stimulate Ukraininan agriculture.(42)

It is only when he is well established in Stalin's Politburo that his innovative zeal begins to develop a Utopian strain. The best example is the 'agro-town' proposals mentioned earlier. The point to note here is that these were grafted onto a practical, down-to-earth scheme initiated by Khrushchev (possibly at first experimentally in the Ukraine and then on a wider scale in the Moscow region in 1950 before being applied nationwide) to consolidate the smaller collective farms, which in the first three years reduced their number from a quarter of a million to about 100,000. Not satisfied with achieving this important reorganisation, Khrushchev was emboldened to present it as the basis of major social changes in the village, which (though he avoided saying so explicitly) were to constitute a giant stride towards 'liquidating the gap between town and country' - one of the acknowledged basic 'tasks' in the 'building of communism'. In doing so he needlessly made himself politically vulnerable, and suffered an embarrassing rebuff. Did his Utopian streak cloud for once his usually impeccable political judgement? In any case, the comparison with Khrushchev's later ill-fated 'hare-brained schemes' is unavoidable.

FROM ONE OF TEN TO NUMBER ONE

The climax and denouement of our hero's tale can be related somewhat more briefly. Some of what for the purpose in hand constitutes background detail constitutes the subject-matter of other chapters in this book, and some factual material can be relegated to appendices. This will allow me to depart somewhat from a chronological presentation and to set out the argument more schematically, assuming readers will have a reasonable familiarity with the context. My central proposition is that the particular blend of political skills and personality traits that made Khrushchev a superbly successful 'Stalinist with a difference' were what carried him to victory in the post-Stalin 'succession struggle', but then his inability to adapt and apply them successfully to his new role of personal dominance led him to failure and defeat.

During his rise from a relatively junior member of the oligarchy that took power in 1953(43) to a position of <u>primus inter pares</u> by 1955 and then to one of personal dominance by 1957, Khrushchev displayed exceptional acumen and energy in applying himself to those conditions of political success which I summarised at the beginning of this chapter: the need to 'deliver the goods', to make use of 'friends', to form effective alliances, and to creatively adapt the rules and structures to his purposes.

In doing so he employed methods strikingly similar to those used by Stalin in the 1920s, but the style was different: Stalin's was cautious, ponderous and conspiratorial, Khrushchev's was bold, imaginative and populist. Like Stalin he used the powers over personnel available to him as dominant figure in the Central Committee Secretariat to reward his friends and punish his enemies. Like Stalin he built up a basis of support among provincial officialdom to offset and ultimately to swamp the support of his rivals, which lay mainly in the central institutions in Moscow. Like Stalin he fostered the authority of the Central Committee, increasingly packed with his own supporters, vis-à-vis the Politburo (called Central Committee Presidium 1952-66) where at first his personal supporters were few. Like Stalin he formed successive and changing alliances within the leadership, enabling him to bring down now one, now another, of his principal rivals. Like Stalin he threw his weight behind policies acceptable to his allies of the day and turned them to his own purposes. For convenience of analysis I will expand separately on each of these aspects of Khrushchev's political tactics, but it goes without saying that in practice they occurred more often in combination than in isolation.

As suggested earlier, there are three main sources of patronage available to a Soviet leader near the summit of power: old followers who had worked under him at lower levels, 'victims' of his rivals, and relatively junior officials generously promoted. In the early post-Stalin period, it was the first of these that Khrushchev chiefly relied on. In the period 1953-55 many officials selected and nurtured by Khrushchev when he was party leader in the Ukraine (1938-49) and Moscow (1949-52) were promoted to leading positions in the provinces and at the centre. But he made early use also of the second source of clients: officials who had suffered at the hands of Malenkov and Beria, several of them associated with the Leningrad party organisation, and (overlapping with the latter) certain of the younger officials who had been advanced to prominence shortly before Stalin died only to be relegated to minor posts after his death. By the time of the Twentieth Congress early in 1956, Khrushchev's Ukrainian and Moscow supporters plus the 'victimised' Leningraders he had since taken up occupied about a third of the posts senior enough to warrent election as voting members of the Central Committee. By the end of 1957, following Khrushchev's victory over the 'anti-party group' (on which more below), supporters of Khrushchev drawn from these sources constituted the overwhelming majority of voting members of the

Central Committee Presidium. But meanwhile Khrushchev had also been enlarging his network of supporters from the third source, promoting a number of relatively junior officials to high positions, in particular as first secretaries of obkom, kraikom (territorial committee) and Republic central committees. It is noteworthy that, presumably in accordance with understandings arrived at within the post-Stalin oligarchy, Khrushchev's sphere of patronage in this early period seemed to extend beyond the party apparatus to include republic and provincial government leaders, senior police officials, and officials of agricultural ministries, but not to the bulk of senior positions in the central government apparatus. Details of the spread of Khrushchev's patronage network in the period 1953-57 summarised in this paragraph are set out in the Appendix.

Khrushchev's efforts to foster a support-base among provincial officialdom had two main components. The first was a direct consequence of the spread of his patronage network: the old associates he installed as first secretaries in a number of regional and republic party committees and the local officials he elevated to the leadership of others quickly gathered around them new teams of leading party and government cadres, thus converting their areas into strongholds of the Khrushchev cause. The second was his commitment to administrative decentralisation. This can best be illustrated from the field of industry, where the process went through a series of stages. In 1954-55 some 11,000 enterprises were transferred from Union to republican jurisdiction.(44) In May 1955 responsibility for a large number of decisions relating to planning and finance, previously vested in various central government agencies, was devolved on the republic governments.(45) In May 1956 enterprises administered by twelve central government ministries were transferred to the full operative control of republic agencies.(46) Then in May 1957 came the abolition of most of the central industrial ministries and the shift of focus of industrial administration to the hundred or so new economic councils (sovnarkhozy), most of them based on the territories of the various oblasts, krais and smaller republics.(47) During this period Khrushchev made the cause of decentralising economic administration peculiarily his own, and although the earlier measures must have been undertaken with the willing acquiescence of the majority of his Presidium colleagues, it is clear that there were growing misgivings, especially on the part of those whose base lay within the central government machine, and this culminated in their opposition to the sovnarkhoz reforms of May 1957. One thing on which there can be little doubt is that leading republic and regional officials set great store by these measures, which enlarged their powers and importance,

and that they saw Khrushchev as the political driving-force
behind them.

A further consequence of economic decentralisation sprang
from the supervising, coordinating, problem-solving and
conflict-resolving role of the provincial party apparatus.
This meant that the transfer of administrative
responsibilities from central to republic and regional
agencies automatically enhanced the powers of party
officialdom at this level and therewith the importance of
party lines of control and communication, which converged on
the Central Committee apparatus, Khrushchev's principal power
base. Like any skilful practitioner of the arts of
bureaucratic politics, Khrushchev fully grasped how even a
small organisational change can produce a re-routing of
communication flows and thereby bring about sharp changes in
the effective control and decision-making powers of different
top-level bodies. Another example deserves mention.

In September 1953, when he launched his program of
agricultural renewal, Khrushchev contrived to have the main
responsibility for supervising the collective farms entrusted
to groups of party officials stationed in the
machine-and-tractor stations (MTS), and the agriculture
departments in the raion (district) soviets were subsequently
abolished.(48) The effect of this was to weaken at the base
the line of communication between the farms and the
agricultural agencies in the republic and central governments
(in which at this time his influence was limited) and to
concentrate communications within party channels (which he
controlled). This was of vital importance to Khrushchev in
ensuring direction over the on-the-spot implementation of his
measures and over reporting to the centre on their results.
Five years later, incidentally , by which time Khrushchev
himself headed the central government machine, the party MTS
zone groups came to an end (along with the MTSs themselves)
and 'agricultural inspectorates' were set up in the raion
soviets, which, according to the then Minister of Agriculture
I.A. Benediktov, enabled his ministry to resume the
organisational role vis-à-vis the kolkhozes which had lapsed
in the intervening period.(49)

Let us now turn to the role of the full Central
Committee, which convened only twice in Stalin's last six
years and membership of which seemed by now to confer nothing
more than a symbol of status within the political elite. The
supplanting of the Central Committee by the Politburo as the
party's chief decision-making body goes back to the Civil War
era, and the mutually linked trends towards larger membership
and diminished powers were well under way before Lenin left
the scene. In the mid-twenties, however, the decline of the

Central Committee was partially and temporarily reversed, and there were clearly two reasons for this. On the one hand, lacking the authority of Lenin for their decisions, the ruling oligarchy saw the advantage of imbuing them with greater legitimacy by having them endorsed by the full Central Committee, constitutionally the supreme executive organ of the party. On the other hand, conflicts within a leadership now lacking any stable internal authority structure provoked appeals against Politburo decisions to the Central Committee, and along with this the use of the latter by currently dominant groups to humiliate and discipline Politburo opponents. At the time this seeming revival of the Central Committee's role was lauded as a 'further flowering of intra-party democracy', but its consequences were more like the reverse, because of the way Stalin contrived to exploit it. By virtue of his control over party personnel administration Stalin was able to stack the Central Committee more and more with his own supporters and to use its meetings to constrain, overrule, discipline and ultimately remove his rivals. Once his personal dominance was assured, the process of decline in the Central Committee's power and significance resumed with a vengeance.

Something similar happened in the post-Stalin years.(50) The group of older leaders who succeeded in concentrating power in their hands at the time of the dictator's death immediately saw the need to legitimate this fait accompli by having it endorsed by the full Central Committee, and they repeated the procedure each time their internal rivalries led to further changes in the leadership: when Malenkov was obliged to withdraw from the Central Committee Secretariat, when Beria was arrested, when Khrushchev became First Secretary, and when Malenkov was ousted from Chairmanship of the Council of Ministers.(51)

But meanwhile the meetings of the Central Committee began to take on a policy content, and the initiative here was predominantly if not entirely Khrushchev's. In this early period his main area of policy responsibility was agriculture, and instead of simply having the measures for which he had secured the agreement of his colleagues promulgated in the established fashion through published or unpublished decrees, he launched them with considerable publicity at specially convened meetings of the Central Committee. Such meetings were held in September 1953, Feburary-March 1954, June 1954 and January 1955. At these meetings he spoke with a frankness and directness unknown since the 1920s, taking pains to explain the reasons for the measures proposed and evincing a seeming sense of responsibility towards the assembled Central Committee members for the work under his jurisdiction. There can be little doubt that many Central Committee members felt gratified and flattered at thus being taken into the First Secretary's confidence. For two years no other Presidium member followed suit, so Khrushchev went unrivalled as the protagonist of thus 'restoring Leninist norms in party life'.

At the same time, just as in the mid 1920s, matters at issue within the leadership began to overflow into the full Central Committee, and their discussion there was used to discredit Presidium opponents: and again Khrushchev seems to have deliberately encouraged the process. Among those of his policies that he referred to meetings òf the Central Committee for ratification some at least are known to have been opposed by certain Presidium members, e.g. the 'virgin lands' program (February 1954 meeting) and the rapprochement with Yugoslavia (July 1955 meeting). Thus it seemed that Khrushchev was seeking to establish the Central Committee's right to the last word on major issues in dispute within the Presidium. The pay-off was to come in 1957, but we shall look at that a little later.

Let us go on now to Khrushchev's coalition tactics in the early post-Stalin years. The first coalition was of course the one that constituted itself as the voting membership of the Central Committee Presidium in the days following Stalin's death, but there is little we can say about how it was formed and its boundaries set, apart from noting that it corresponds exactly neither with the Politburo on the eve of the Nineteenth Congress nor with the Bureau of the Presidium that in effect succeeded the latter.(52) Clearly, however, it was essentially an alliance of older leaders who had managed to sink the sharp differences that their conflicting ambitions and Stalin's machinations had fostered among them, in order to concentrate power in their own hands and exclude the younger men that Stalin had been raising up to replace them. If I am right in thinking that Khrushchev had been pushed into at least a tacit alliance with these younger leaders at the end of the Stalin period he probably found himself rather isolated at first within the new 'collective leadership'. This is, indeed, the impression conveyed in his memoirs, which suggest that his only confidante in the Presidium was his old croney from the early 1930s, Bulganin, now Minister of Defence.(53) This alliance proved to be important to him, however, especially in the showdown with Beria, because of the military's role in the latter's arrest. Khrushchev tells us that he made an early attempt to get Malenkov on side, but was rebuffed owing to the latter's alliance with Beria.(54) It was only many weeks later, by which time, if we accept Khrushchev's account, Beria's push for personal dominance was unmistakable, that Malenkov agreed to join with Khrushchev (who had already assured himself of Bulganin's support) in recruiting other Presidium members for a coup against

Beria.(55) Khrushchev's claim that he took the initiative in forming this anti-Beria coalition which came to include all the voting members of the Presidium except an ambivalent Mikoyan, is intrinsically plausible, expecially as it was Khrushchev, of all the leaders, who was most directly threatened by Beria's mounting power. His success in this quarter increased both his security and his standing within the leadership, but he had risked all to achieve it, displaying a boldness in raising the stakes which we have observed at several critical junctures in his earlier political career.

Khrushchev had now substantially advanced his position within the pecking order of the ruling oligarchy, which was reflected both in the changed order of official listings and in his election a few weeks later as First Secretary of the Central Committee.(56) But he was still junior to both Malenkov and Molotov, and in the wake of Beria's arrest the former's primacy was temporarily enhanced, accompanied by a mild 'leadership cult' as 'head of the Soviet Government' (glava sovetskogo pravitel'stva). From the latter part of 1953, however, Khrushchev's authority gradually grew while Malenkov's declined, and by the middle of 1954 the replacement of seniority order by alphabetical order in official leadership listings signalled that it was no longer clear who was primus inter pares. Half a year later Malenkov was obliged to give up the Chairmanship of the Council of Ministers to Bulganin, and it was Khrushchev who was now clearly primus inter pares (but still no more than this!). How had he done it? While this time we have no inside stories, it seems that part of the explanation was his success not only in undermining Malenkov's credibility but also in forming a conservative coalition against the latter's continued primacy.

There are several good reasons why Khrushchev should have taken up the agriculture issue with particular energy during this period. As the only Soviet leader with much practical experience in agricultural administration, Khrushchev seems to have been given primary responsibility for it in the allocation of policy areas within the post-Stalin leadership. At the same time food production was indeed a major area of Soviet weakness, and there was probably agreement that strong measures were needed to improve it. As we have seen, it could also be exploited by a resourceful First Secretary to enhance his organisational position and the weight of the party apparatus in the structure of power. But the fact that Malenkov had borne prime responsibility for agriculture at the end of the Stalin era and had gone on record at the Nineteenth Congress as stating that the grain situation was 'basically solved' made it a winning card in Khrushchev's hand. By revealing how disastrous the food production situation actually was and initiating effective measures within the existing system to deal with it Khrushchev both discredited Malenkov and gathered kudos for himself.

But increasing food production was only one side of the drive rapidly to improve living standards which the leadership had evidently agreed was necessary to bolster the output of manufactured consumer goods, and this objective Malenkov made peculiarly his own, beginning with the August 1953 meeting of the Supreme Soviet. In doing so he aroused misgivings in many quarters, including those responsible for heavy industry and the armed forces, who resented the diversion of resources to light industry, as well as ideological conservatives, who saw in Malenkov's willingness to allow the growth of consumer goods production to outrun the growth of capital goods production a violation of the principles of Marxist-Leninist political economy. In December 1954 Khrushchev signalled his solidarity with such positions by publicly stating that 'only on the basis of the further development of heavy industry shall we manage successfully to promote all branches of the national economy, constantly raise the well-being of the people, and ensure the inviolability of the Soviet Union's frontiers'.(57) By this time a conservative coalition capable of unseating Malenkov was evidently in place, and the coup de grace came three weeks later at a meeting of the Central Committee.(58)

Almost immediately, however, Khrushchev again moved to readjust his alliances, and this time it was Molotov, the most respected and authoritative older member of the 'collective leadership', who found himself isolated. The central issue area now was foreign policy, and the main skirmish was fought, as noted, at the July 1955 meeting of the Central Committee. By this point Mikoyan seems to have joined Bulganin as one of Khrushchev's firmest allies, and his coalition was further strengthened with the elevation as voting Presidium members of A.I. Kirichenko (one of his Ukrainian supporters) and M.A. Suslov (an old opponent of Malenkov and one of the 'vigilantes' of the 'doctors' plot' era with whom Khrushchev had evidently found himself in alliance). At the same time three new Central Committee secretaries (Aristov, Belyaev and Shepilov) were elected, all tied to Khrushchev.

Following the Twentieth Congress eight months later two further Khrushchev supporters (Furtseva and Brezhnev) were added to the Secretariat, strengthening the First Secretary's hold over this body. At the same time, although four out of the five new candidate members of the Presidium were also Khrushchev adherents, there were no more changes in the full (voting) members at this time. Thus, although Khrushchev's

clientele now predominated in the outer circles of the ruling
oligarchy, it was still a distinct minority within its inner
core, and he could not yet dispense with the business of
seeking accommodations with other leaders. In the latter part
of 1956 the leadership seems to have pulled together to
confront the crises in Poland and Hungary and their domestic
and international ramifications, but insofar as these troubles
sprang from Khrushchev's 'secret speech' they must have placed
severe strains on his alliances. At the same time the
leadership was faced with serious difficulties in industrial
performance and administration, and the decisions made on this
at the December 1956 meeting of the Central Committee are
indicative of an uneasy compromise between Khrushchev and
other Presidium leaders: on the one hand there was to be a
shift of administrative responsibilities to the regional
level, but on the other the powers of the central ministries
were to be increased. At the same time, one might speculate
on why this issue was moved to the fore at this particular
juncture: the issue was genuine, but could the way it was
brought on have represented a diversionary tactic by
Khrushchev? Be this as it may, it seems reasonable to suppose
that, had it not been for the support Khrushchev had now
amassed in the wider circles of the political elite, the
events in Hungary and Poland could have precipitated a
Presidium-level revolt against his leadership at this point,
i.e. half a year earlier than it actually occurred. The shift
of attention to the economic 'crisis' certainly gave
Khrushchev a breathing spell as well as a platform from which
he could later counter-attack. But I shall come back to this
point later.

I have been arguing that Khrushchev's political tactics
in 1953-57 followed the same main lines as Stalin's in the
1920s, and displayed a similar wiliness and skill. And here
the final dimension to mention is that of policy.(59) We have
already seen from a number of examples how Khrushchev (like
Stalin before him) exploited policy issues to cement changing
leadership alliances and isolate rivals, to spread his
patronage network, to shift business into administrative
channels which he could more effectively control, to foster
support among provincial officialdom, and to court the full
Central Committee while enhancing its authority vis-à-vis that
of the inner leadership. Other illustrations could be added,
but perhaps the point is sufficiently made. This does not
prove, of course, that he was simply being cynical and
opportunistic in the policy positions he took, for politicians
anywhere must constantly harmonise the demands of power and
policy if they are to be effective. Nevertheless the
similarity of Khrushchev's tactics with Stalin's is striking,
and must raise the question whether this was simply due to
their having operated in much the same structural and ideo-

logical context of constraints and opportunities, or whether there was an element of imitation involved.

It would be misleading, however, to leave it at that. Khrushchev's earlier career had already revealed him, I have suggested, as indeed a Stalinist, but a Stalinist <u>with a difference</u>, and in this post-1953 period this difference was most clearly manifested in his style and orientations in the sphere of policy. The components of this are already familiar: the close interest in grass-roots practicalities, the folksiness, capacity to empathise with subordinate officials and ordinary people and to communicate with them in relatively realistic and down-to-earth fashion, the penchant for technical and organisational innovations within the established parameters of the system and boldness in promoting them, and the streak of utopianism. This is not the place for a close examination of Khrushchev's contributions in various policy areas - some of which receive careful attention in other chapters. A question we must ask here, however, is why it was that Khrushchev managed to impart so much of his personal style and orientations to the development of Soviet policy in this early post-Stalin period. The most obvious explanation lies in the political resources available to him as the leading figure in the Central Committee Secretariat and the vigour, skill and experience in operating the rules of the Soviet political game which he brought to the exploitation of these resources. If my earlier analysis is not too wide of the mark, this is indeed a large part of the answer, but is it the whole answer? I suggest there was something else as well: Khrushchev's policy style and orientations met the perceived needs of the Soviet political establishment at this time. While this proposition is far from original and may command fairly widespread assent, it is probably impossible to prove, and may forever remain no more than an untestable hypothesis. With apologies to those who might consider it therefore unscientific to discuss it at all, let me outline the argument.

Stalin's death faced the regime not just with a leadership crisis, but with a legitimacy crisis and a policy crisis as well, for a number of fairly obvious and related reasons: political legitimation needed a new focus in place of the cult of the living 'great father and teacher'; the vast and arbitrary powers of the political police, built up to support Stalin's personal dictatorship, would have to be curbed if 'collective leadership' was to be viable; given their uncertain legitimacy and reduced coercive capacity the regime needed to rely more on credible promises of material improvement to ensure the compliance of the population; the uncertain authority structure within the leadership called for a neutralisation of potentially divisive domestic and foreign issues; and the last two considerations necessitated a critical review of the established policies of the late Stalin era, one of the consequences of which was to reveal the scientific, technological and economic costs of repressive ideological controls and isolation from the West. There was probably something like a consensus within the ruling oligarchy and between them and the higher officials of the various bureaucracies that these matters must be confronted, and that they should be resolved in ways that did not shake the foundations of the system or of their own power and authority.

Alone of the Presidium members, Khrushchev possessed the requisite qualities for giving a lead in tackling these problems: the political boldness, the innovative drive, the capacity to address both officialdom and the population with a blend of practical sense and conviction in 'the cause', and the political and organisational skills needed to maintain effective central direction and control under conditions of change and uncertainty. Khrushchev <u>did</u> give such a lead (and here we might note that, unlike Stalin in the 1920s, he led from the front and not from the middle) most notably in taking on Beria and his police, in reducing international pressures on the regime, in the food production drive, in tackling the Stalin cult and substituting Leninism and the party as the foci of legitimation, and in opening windows to the West. Without Khrushchev how many of these crucial issues would have been resolved?

The argument then, is that Khrushchev was uniquely useful to the ruling oligarchy during these years, and that consequently, although particular leaders clashed with him sharply on individual issues, recognition of his usefulness disposed enough of them most of the time to give him his head. In other words, Khrushchev's rise to primacy within the leadership during this period was due not only to his political skills in deploying his patronage network, making effective alliances, building support in the provinces and the Central Committee, etc., of crucial importance though these were, but also to his success in 'delivering the goods', especially to those who mattered most, namely his fellow oligarchs. As we know, however, the latter eventually rejected his leadership and sought unsuccessfully to get rid of him, and it is to the circumstances of this that we must now turn.

FROM VICTORIOUS LEADER TO DICTATOR <u>MANQUE</u>

A further important difference between Khrushchev in 1953-57 and Stalin in the 1920s was that, having isolated and

discredited   successive   rivals   and   opponents,   he   did   not
proceed   to   have   them   removed   from   the   leadership   (the
exception being Beria, but here   the   situation   permitted   no
alternative).   Whether   the   failure   to attempt this should be
attributed to tolerance and generosity on   Khrushchev's   part,
to some kind of compact within the leadership which would have
been violated by any such attempt, or simply to a   realisation
by   Khrushchev   that   any   move   to do so would be seen by his
colleagues as evidence of Stalin-like   ambitions   and   provoke
them   to combine against him, we may never know.   In any case,
the   result was that   by   late   in   1956,   when   his   authority
suffered   such   severe   blows   from   the   Hungarian   and other
consequences of his attack on Stalin, the Presidium   contained
several   members,   chief   among   them Malenkov and Molotov, but
including in lesser degree Kaganovich, Saburov   and   Pervukhin,
whose   positions   had been damaged by Khrushchev's manoeuvres.
The   situation   was   potentially   dangerous   to   his   continued
primacy, and I have suggested that his tactics at the December
1956 meeting of the Central Committee might be interpreted   as
an   evasive manoeuvre.   If so, however, this was simply a case
of reculer pout mieux sauter.

His next move was   vintage   Khrushchev: he   drastically
raised   the stakes.   A second meeting of the Central Committee
to discuss the administration of industry   was   convened   just
six   weeks later and this time Khrushchev secured a resolution
entirely stressing the territorial principle   and   denigrating
the   central   ministries.(60)   This was followed at the end of
March 1957   with   the   publication   of   Khrushchev's   'theses'
envisaging   the abolition of the central industrial ministries
and the focussing of   industrial   administration   on   regional
economic   councils   (sovnarkhozy).   The public discussion that
followed,   while   containing   many   interesting   views   and
suggestions,   broadly   supported   Khrushchev's proposals - not
surprisingly in view of the grasp he now had   over   the   party
apparatus   and   through   it   the media.   On May 10 the Supreme
Soviet was   convened   and   duly   endorsed   a version of the
proposals   which   represented,   as   John Armstrong puts it, 'a
complete victory for Khrushchev and his territorial   apparatus
supporters'.(61)

The   losers   were   the   economic   administrators   in   the
Council   of   Ministers   and   their   overlords   in   the   top
leadership, who made up about half of the Presidium, and while
the   latter   were conspicuously silent on the issue throughout
the period from the February   Central   Committee   meeting   on,
there is no reason to doubt the later statements of Khrushchev
and   his   supporters   that   they   had   been   opposed   to   the
reorganisation.   The February meeting may, incidentally, have
been   the   first   occasion   on   which Khrushchev   secured   a
resolution   which   went   against the policy preferences of not

just one or two Presidium members, but of a large section of them, and possibly a majority. Be this as it may, it was plain to Khrushchev's fellow oligarchs that he was now prepared to impose his will in ways that made nonsense of 'collective leadership' and that if he were to be prevented from entrenching a pattern of personal dominance they would have to act soon.

And indeed it was to be only six weeks before they did act, obtaining a majority within the Presidium for Khrushchev's resignation. The story of how Khrushchev's supporters then managed to assemble the Central Committee and of how this overruled the Presidium majority and purged the would-be purgers, has been often told, and need not detain us here.(62) Khrushchev had the numbers, about one third of the Central Committee consisting of officials owing their career advancement to him and another third of regional and republic party and state officials whose institutional and personal interests were at stake in the issue that sparked the move to depose him. The other third saw which way the wind was blowing and voted with the majority. Thus, at this crucial point when Khrushchev could no longer rely on leadership alliances or his value in 'delivering the goods' to retain his position in the ruling oligarchy, he was saved by his achievements over four years in spreading his patronage net, currying support in the provinces, and building up the authority of the Central Committee <u>vis-a-vis</u> the party Presidium. Khrushchev won because he was a master of the Soviet political game.

The Presidium was now packed with Khrushchev's supporters. He further enhanced his power in October 1957 by removing Marshal Zhukov from the Presidium (despite his support for Khrushchev in the June crisis) and replacing him as Defence Minister by the more pliable Marshal Malinovsky, and in March 1958 by adding to the First Secretaryship the post of Chairman of the Council of Ministers. In a sense Khrushchev's personal victory in June 1957 had been a victory for the party apparatus as well, epitomised by the fact that Central Committee secretaries made up two thirds of the Presidium by the end of that year. However, after taking over direct leadership of the Government, Khrushchev proceeded to diversify the bases of his organisational support and lines of control, so that by 1960 neither the Secretariat nor the Government Presidium had a majority in the party Presidium, while he was the only leader with a seat (and the leading seat) in all three.

In their splendid book <u>Khrushchev: The Years in Power,</u> Roy and Zhores Medvedev write of our hero that in the period following the June 1957 showdown he 'became in effect a dictator, enjoying total power...'(63) They qualify this by adding that he based his dictatorial power not on coercion but on patronage, and later go on to show how his capacity to achieve his policy objectives subsequently declined. An alternative formulation might be that he was a would-be dictator who lacked the power resources of a real one. Stalin ensured his dictatorial power by means of a political police armed with arbitrary powers and of a 'cult' which became the focus of regime legitimacy and reduced the role of other leaders to that of mere servants of his will. Khrushchev did not seek the former, although one cannot be sure whether this was because he did not want it or because the de-Stalinising posture on which he rested his authority prevented him. Something of a Khrushchev cult did indeed develop, but this was in no way comparable with the Stalin cult and was far milder than the later cult of Brezhnev, whom few would describe as ever having enjoyed dictatorial power.

The policies of Khrushchev rampant are considered elsewhere in this book, and I propose to limit myself to a few general remarks. While the years 1957-64 were far from being the worst in modern Soviet history, broadly speaking Khrushchev's policies failed, and they failed largely because of those very characteristics that had stood him in such good stead in his rise to power. In this sense there was a tragic dimension to Khrushchev's political career. His boldness, lacking constraints on its expression, led him into foolhardy actions in both the international and domestic spheres, actions often costly both to his country and to his personal reputation. His folksiness and talent for talking horse-sense to his subordinate officials and the people at large degenerated into a demeaning boorishness and buffoonery and a hectoring banality. His penchant for technical and organisational innovation, again in the absence of constraints, tempted him into imposing a constant stream of technical panaceas and administrative reorganisations - the famous 'hare-brained schemes' of which he was later to be accused. His streak of utopianism, springing from his anachronistically uncomplicated conviction that the enterprise on which he was engaged was indeed the noble cause of Communism, led him into dubious and facile ideological reformulations (like 'the state of the whole people' and 'the party of the whole people'), into setting grandiose but unrealistic targets (as in the 1961 party program), and into practical measures designed to accelerate the march to Communism which were profoundly upsetting to those involved and ultimately counter-productive (like his vicious campaign against religion and the drive to have peasants sell their family cow to the collective). Trying to do too much too fast with the resources available, he did nothing properly.

Such policy failures would have been less damaging had he not proceeded - evidently now feeling secure in his power - to neglect the political arts that he had previously practised to such excellent effect. Supporters of sometimes several decades' standing were dispensed with as he raised up younger officials supposedly better equipped to achieve his new objective. For example, of the thirteen adherents with whom he had packed the Presidium by the time of the final consolidation of his power in 1958, only six were still there three years later, while by the early 1960s nearly two thirds of the RSFSR regional first secretaries installed under him in the mid 1950s had been replaced, and other changes continued thereafter. Naturally those newly elevated could feel little confidence that they would escape the fate of their predecessors. The interests of almost all major bureaucratic groupings were damaged by his policies. The government economic administration, never reconciled to the 1957 'regionalisation', were subjected to further reorganisations which totally confused lines of responsibility and fostered foul-ups for which they were then made to suffer; the military were deeply resentful of Khrushchev's cuts in conventional forces; ideological conservatives and the police were anxious and frustrated at what they saw as undue tolerance of heretical ideas and unorthodox behaviour; even the provincial party apparatus, Khrushchev's original support base, were seething with resentment at the effect on their standing and their capacity to perform effectively of his 1962 division of their structure into industrial and agricultural halves. As for the Central Committee, having relied so heavily on it to achieve power, Khrushchev quickly deprived it of its incipient 'parliamentary' role, turning its sessions into mass meetings at which he launched his latest schemes or pontificated on the successes and failures of his subordinates.

To combine with impunity such a record of policy failures and the alienation of all major institutional interests one would have had to enjoy the real dictatorial resources of a Stalin. Lacking such resources, Khrushchev was brought low. The irony was that, when his Presidium subordinates had conspired to remove him, they experienced no difficulty in having 'his' Central Committee unanimously endorse their action.

The system which Stalin bequeathed in 1953 had two components. The more basic was what I call its 'mono-organisational' character, the attempt directly to manage all social activities through a range of centralised administrative hierarchies, coordinated by the overarching machinery of the party. On top of this was imposed a second component, the devices of Stalin's personal despotism. It was the blend of these that we know as Stalinism, and which Arendt, Friedrich, Brzezinski and others characterised as totalitarian dictatorship.(64) In the aftermath of Stalin's death, it was by no means clear that these two components would - or could - be disentangled, and indeed some Western scholars seem to be unconvinced even today that they are fully separable. In my view, the main historical achievement of the Khrushchev era, and of Khrushchev himself, was to demonstrate that the mono-organisational society is viable without the additive of a personal despotism. Two decades later, this achievement remains intact. And one consequence is that the rules of the political game in the Soviet union remain much the same as those played so adeptly by Khrushchev in his rise to power.

NOTES

1. For an elaboration of this point, see T.H. Rigby, 'Politics in the Mono-Organisational Society', in Andrew C. Janos, ed., Authoritarian Politics in Communist Europe. Unity and Diversity in One-Party States, Berkeley: University of California, 1976, pp. 34-49.

2. George Konrad and Ivan Szelenyi, The Intellectuals on the Road to Class Power. A Sociological Study of the Role of the Intelligentsia in Socialism, New York and London: Harcourt Brace Jovanovich, 1979, p. 183.

3. However, he had been involved in strike activity both before and during the War, and in the course of 1917 became increasingly committed to the Bolsheviks who made him local chairman of the mineworkers' union after their takeover. See Roy Medvedev, Khrushchev, translated by Brian Pearce, Oxford: Basil Blackwell, 1982, pp. 5-6.

4. See Khrushchev Remembers, with an Introduction, Commentary and Notes by Edward Crankshaw, Translated and Edited by Strobe Talbott, Boston: Little, Brown and Co., 1970, p. 23. Unless otherwise indicated, basic biographical information on Khrushchev is drawn from official Soviet biographies. The most valuable accounts of Khrushchev's early career are to be found in Medvedev, Khrushchev and Lazar Pistrak, The Grand Tactician. Khrushchev's Rise to Power, London: Thames and Hudson, 1961. However, Khrushchev's memoirs were not available to Pistrak at the time his book was written.

5. Khrushchev Remembers, p. 31.

6. Pistrak, pp. 24-26.

7. *Khrushchev Remembers*, pp. 31-33. Medvedev (*Khrushchev*, p. 13), citing the testimony of A.V. Snegov, states that it was Kaganovich's successor as First Secretary in the Ukraine, S.V. Kossior, and the Organisation Department chief N. Demchenko, who were responsible for these transfers. If so, Khrushchev's circumstantial account of Kaganovich's involvement in both cases appears a very curious aberration.

8. *Khrushchev Remembers*, pp. 34-36.

9. *Pravda*, 31 May 1930. For Khrushchev's version of the background to this incident, see *Khrushchev Remembers*, pp. 40-42. There is a careful analysis of the evidence relating to this phase of Khrushchev's career in Pistrak, Chapter 5.

10. Khrushchev's version is that he had at first attributed his rise to Kaganovich's good offices but later realised that the initiative came from Stalin, influenced by his wife's enthusiastic reports. He states that he became a regular dinner guest at the Stalins', and since he refers to Alliluyeva's presence this must have begun before her death in 1932, believed to be by suicide: in other words *before* he became First Secretary of the Moscow City Committee. See *Khrushchev Remembers*, pp. 42-43. His memory may have been at fault here. Cf. Medvedev, *Khrushchev*, p. 15.

11. *Khrushchev Remembers*, p. 57.

12. See Pistrak, Chapters 7-8.

13. See Roy Medvedev, *Let History Judge. The Origins and Consequences of Stalinism*, London: Macmillan, 1972, p. 310.

14. The details are set out in my forthcoming paper 'Stalin: the Disloyal Patron?'. Khrushchev's own explanation is that Nadezhda Alliluyeva's warm and enthusiastic opinion laid the basis for a liking and trust towards him which Stalin never lost. See *Khrushchev Remembers*, p. 44.

15. This is the date cited by all official Soviet sources, but Khrushchev gives it as 1935. (*Khrushchev Remembers*, p. 49.) Despite the many slips in his memoirs (e.g. on p. 110 he gives the date of his arrival in Kiev as early 1939 instead of early 1938) there may be some factual basis to this apparent error. It is possible that with his assumption of the leadership of the Moscow party

organisation in 1935 it was considered desirable that   he
be regularly invited to attend meetings of the Politburo.

16.   Cf. Medvedev, Khrushchev, pp. 18-19.

17.   For indications of their closeness at   this   period,   see
Khrushchev Remembers, pp. 62-63.

18.   See Khrushchev Remembers, pp. 98, 127.

19.   See George   Paloczi-Horvath,   Khrushchev: The   Road   to
Power, London: Secker & Warburg, 1960, pp. 115-116.

20.   The purge of the Party elite was particularly   severe   in
the   Ukraine.   See   John   A. Armstrong,   The Politics of
Totalitarianism.   The Communist Party of the Soviet Union
from   1934 to the Present, New York: Random House, 1961,
pp. 68-69.

21.   See John A. Armstrong, The Soviet Bureaucratic Elite.   A
Case   Study   of   the   Ukrainian   Apparatus,   New   York:
Praeger,   1959,   pp.   72-74.   Khrushchev   (Khrushchev
Remembers, p. 107)   states that he got on very well with
Burmistenko.   The   latter   was   involved   in   directing
partisan   operations   during   the War, and disappeared in
unexplained circumstances.

22.   See Pistrak, Part   III,   Khrushchev   Remembers,   chapters
4-7.   Medvedev writes (Khrushchev, p. 41) that Khrushchev
stood very high in Stalin's esteem at the end of the War.

23.   The gist   of   this   unpublished   decision   was   given   by
Khrushchev in a report to the Ukrainian Central Committee
a month later.   See   Pravda,   23   August   1946.   Further
details   emerged   in the Ukrainian Party newspaper Pravda
Ukrainy in the following weeks and months.

24.   Shortly before the July decision Khrushchev attempted   to
anticipate   these   charges by himself launching an attack
on   Ukrainian   writers   and   historians   for   manifesting
nationalist tendencies.   See Pistrak, pp. 182-183.

25.   See Pravda, 7 March 1947.   The resolution was adopted   at
a   plenum of the All-Union Central Committee on the basis
of a report by Andreev: see Pravda,   28   February   1947.
The   seriousness of the occasion is indicated by the fact
that this was the   only   Central   Committee   plenum   held
between   the   end   of   the   War   and   1952.   Khrushchev's
involvement in agricultural management   and   policy   went
back   at   least   ten   years.   In 1939 it was cited as the
grounds of his award of the Order of the   Red   Banner   of

Labour. He was later (in <u>Teatr</u>, No. 6, 1961) stated to have initiated in 1940 the per-hectare basis for assessing collective farm grain deliveries. He was one of the foundation members of the post-war Council on Collective Farm Affairs (see <u>Izvestiia</u>, 9 October 1946).

26. In his 'secret speech' Khrushchev alleged that Stalin would have banished the whole Ukrainian people from their homeland if it had been physically possible.

27. <u>Khrushchev Remembers</u>, p. 235.

28. See Chapter 7 of <u>Khrushchev Remembers</u> for Khrushchev's own account of these matters.

29. However, Khrushchev's later allegations, that Kaganovich would have carried out on Stalin's behalf a much more drastic purge of Ukrainian intellectuals if Khrushchev (he actually used the Leninist equivalent of the royal plural - 'the Ukrainian bolsheviks') had not opposed it, need to be treated with caution.

30. See <u>Khrushchev Remembers</u>, pp. 240-243.

31. Based on personnel data culled from <u>Pravda Ukrainy</u>, 1946-49. In a number of cases new appointments followed courses in the Higher Party School in Moscow.

32. See R. Conquest, <u>Power and Policy in the U.S.S.R. The Study of Soviet Dynastics</u>, London: Macmillan, 1962, Chapters 4-5, Leonard Schapiro, <u>The Communist Party of the Soviet Union</u>, 2nd edition, London: Methuen, 1970, pp. 512-514, John A. Armstrong, <u>The Politics of Totalitarianism</u>, pp. 177-179, 199-203, and Werner G. Hahn, <u>Post-war Soviet Politics. The Fall of Zhdanov and the Defeat of Moderation, 1946-53</u>, Ithaca and London: Cornell University Press, 1982, chapters 1-4.

33. This view, which certain Western analysts had formed by the early 1950s, has since been lent further support by Khrushchev himself. See <u>Khrushchev Remembers</u>, p. 250.

34. See Conquest, Chapter 6.

35. Details of personnel changes in this period were culled from <u>Moskovskaia pravda</u>, 1949-1953. It may well be, as Medvedev claims (<u>Khrushchev</u>, p. 51), that it was largely to Khrushchev's credit that political charges similar to those in the 'Leningrad case' were not made against those who lost their jobs in the Moscow organisation when he took it over from Popov.

36. The best analysis of the murky politics of Stalin's last two years is to be found in Conquest, Part II, especially chapters 7 and 8, and the account that follows agrees in all essentials with this. See also Armstrong, *The Politics of Totalitarianism*, chapter XVII, Boris I. Nicolaevsky, *Power and the Soviet Elite*, London: Pall Mall, 1966, Part Three, Paloczi-Horvath, pp. 124-129, and Schapiro, pp. 547-551. Khrushchev's own account of the high politics of this period, although containing a few new points of information, is in general singularly patchy and evasive. See *Khrushchev Remembers*, pp. 276-87, 306-314.

37. Later Khrushchev was to confirm that Stalin was seeking 'to do away with Beria', but he cites only the Mingrelian nationalism affair in this connection. It is hard to escape the suspicion that he fails to link the other current moves against Beria because his own role in these was in some way discreditable.

38. See *Khrushchev Remembers*, pp. 278-281, 309-310.

39. Pistrak, p. 21. One might similarly interpret the unverifiable account of Khrushchev's participation in a *subbotnik* in Kiev in 1929.

40. *Partiinaia zhizn'*, No. 5, 1948, pp. 12-13. Other speeches of Khrushchev to the Ukrainian Central Committee and reported in *Pravda Ukrainy* contain similar passages of racy, down-to-earth comment.

41. Pistrak, pp. 76-78.

42. See ibid., pp. 229-230. Medvedev (*Khrushchev*, chapters 1-3) also mentions examples of Khrushchev's organisational and technical innovations.

43. His relatively junior status was reflected in his position in official listings of leaders (see note 56), and other public manifestations of status. Medvedev (*Khrushchev*, p. 58), cites him as already one of a dominant *troika* (with Malenkov and Beria) in the immediate aftermath of Stalin's death, but I remain unconvinced that he achieved such a position till some months later.

44. See S.R. Vikharev and I.D. Vetrov, *Rasshirenie prav soiuznykh respublik*, Moscow: Gosiurizdat, 1963, p. 55.

45. See <u>Direktivy KPSS i sovetskogo pravitel'stva po khoziaistvennym voprosam</u>, Vol. 4, Moscow: Gospolitizdat, 1958, pp. 400-417.

46. See <u>Spravochnik partiinogo rabotnika</u>, Moscow: Gospolit-izdat, 1957, p. 178.

47. The law embodying this reorganisation is available in a number of sources, e.g. <u>Direktivy KPSS i sovetskogo pravitel'stva po khoziaistvennym voprosam</u>, vol 4, pp. 732-38.

48. As a device for administering the kolkhozes, the party MTS groups were far from being an unqualified success. See R.F. Miller, <u>One Hundred Thousand Tractors</u>, Cambridge, Mass.: Harvard U.P., 1970, chapter 12. However, their <u>political</u> value to Khrushchev at this period was considerable.

49. See <u>Sovetskaia Rossiia</u>, 2 July 1958.

50. I have examined the developments outlined in this section in greater detail in my article 'Khrushchev and the Resuscitation of the Central Committee', <u>Australian Outlook</u>, Vol. 13, No. 3, September 1959, pp. 165—180.

51. In the first two instances, however, only a minority of Central Committee members were present when the relevant decisions were made. Such arbitrary procedures could scarcely have persisted in the rapidly evolving political conditions of the succeeding months, quite apart from the interest of Khrushchev in seeing that Central Committee meetings should actually become just that.

52. Membership of the Politburo on the eve of the Nineteenth Congress, October 1952, of the Bureau of the Presidium on the eve of Stalin's death, and of the CC Presidium immediately after his death was as follows:

Politburo to Oct. 1952	Bureau of Presidium*	Presidium 6 March 1953
Stalin	Stalin	
Molotov		Molotov
Malenkov	Malenkov	Malenkov
Beria	Beria	Beria
Voroshilov	Voroshilov	Voroshilov
Bulganin	Bulganin	Bulganin
Kaganovich	Kaganovich	Kaganovich
Andreev		

```
        Mikoyan                              Mikoyan
        Kosygin
        Shvernik
        Khrushchev          Khrushchev       Khrushchev
                            Saburov          Saburov
                            Pervukhin        Pervukhin
```

 * As reported by Khrushchev: <u>Khrushchev Remembers</u>,
   p. 281.

53. See e.g. <u>Khrushchev Remembers</u>, pp. 319-331.

54. ibid., p. 323. Khrushchev's old friendship with
   Malenkov, also dating from the 1930s, had been put under
   serious strain by the politics of the post-war years, but
   he claims that they were still on good terms personally
   at the end of the Stalin period (ibid., p. 314).

55. ibid., p. 330-338.

56. Since for some months Khrushchev had been the only
   Central Committee Secretary who was a voting member of
   the Presidium it was no more than appropriate that his
   designation should register his seniority over other
   members of the Secretariat, and the delay in his
   acquiring such a designation suggests the relative
   weakness of his standing with the oligarchy despite the
   great <u>potential</u> power of his office. From March to June
   1953 Khrushchev regularly appeared in fifth place in
   listings of Presidium members, following Malenkov, Beria,
   Molotov and Voroshilov. Beria's arrest automatically
   brought him into fourth place, and with his election as
   First Secretary he also moved ahead of Voroshilov. From
   then till mid 1954, when alphabetical listings became <u>de</u>
   <u>rigueur</u>, he always appeared third after Malenkov and
   Molotov.

57. <u>Pravda</u>, 28 December 1954.

58. Cf. Medvedev, <u>Khrushchev</u>, p. 71. There were, of course,
   other strands to the politicking that culminated in
   Malenkov's replacement as Premier. For a balanced brief
   account see Armstrong, <u>The Politics of Totalitarianism</u>,
   pp. 261-264.

59. For an extended thought-provoking examination of the
   matters considered in the following paragraphs, employing
   a different methodological approach, see George
   W. Breslauer, <u>Khrushchev and Brezhnev as Leaders:</u>
   <u>Building Authority in Soviet Politics</u>, London: George
   Allen and Unwin, 1982.

60. At the same plenum a further Khrushchev adherent, F.R. Kozlov, was elected a candidate member of the Presidium.

61. Armstrong, The Politics of Totalitarianism, p. 312.

62. See Conquest, Power and Policy, chapter 12, Armstrong, The Politics of Totalitarianism, chapter XXIII, Medvedev, Khrushchev, chapter 11.

63. Roy A. Medvedev and Zhores A. Medvedev, Khrushchev: The Years in Power, New York: Columbia University Press, 1976, p. 82. A similar evaluation is implicit in Roy Medvedev's recent book, Khrushchev, Part Five.

64. I develop this proposition in my article 'Stalinism and the Mono-Organisational Society', in Robert C. Tucker, ed., Stalinism: Essays in Historical Interpretation, New York: Norton, 1977.

APPENDIX

A. DEPLOYMENT OF KHRUSHCHEV'S PATRONAGE NETWORK 1953-57

Note: Former associates promoted to higher positions or to full or candidate membership of the Central Committee between Stalin's death and June 1957 crisis. Only principal move relevant to position before June 1957 is cited. Advancement to CC cited only when this is sole change in position. List seeks to include most important officials enjoying Khrushchev's sponsorship at this period. In certain cases heavy dependence on Khrushchev is contestable. For an attempt to quantify the different components of Khrushchev's CC-level support in 1957 see T.H. Rigby, 'Khrushchev and the Resuscitation of the Central Committee', Australian Outlook, Vol. 13, No. 3, September 1959, p. 174.

ABBREVIATIONS

cand.	candidate	CC	Central Committee
chmn.	chairman	ctte.	committee
dep.	deputy	dept.	department
mem.	member	min.	minister
Pres.	Presidium	sec.	secretary

1. Original Association in Moscow Early 1930s

Korotchenko, D.S.   Chmn. Pres. Supreme Soviet, Ukraine, 1954
                      Cand. Pres. CC CPSU 1957

2.   Original Association in Ukraine 1937-49

Brezhnev, L.I.	1st Sec. CC Kazakhstan 1955 Cand. Pres. CC CPSU 1956
Bubnovskii, N.D.	Sec. CC Ukraine 1954
Churaev, V.M.	Head Dept. CC CPSU Mem. CC Bureau for RSFSR 1956
Enyutin, G.V.	1st Sec. Kamensk Obkom 1954
Epishev, A.A.	(1951-53 1st Dep. Min. State Security) 1st Sec. Odessa Obkom 1953
Gaevoi, A.I.	1st Sec. Zaporozhe Obkom 1952 (to mem. CC 1956)
Grechko, A.A.	Commander-in-Chief Soviet Forces Germany 1953
Grechukha, M.S.	1st Dep. Chmn. Ukrainian Council of Mins. 1954
Grishko, G.E.	1st Sec. Kiev Obkom 1952 (to cand. CC 1956)
Gureev, N.M.	1st Dep. Chmn. Ukrainian Council of Mins. 1955
Ivashchenko, O.I.	Sec. CC Ukraine 1954
Kalchenko, N.T.	Chmn. Ukrainian Council of Mins. 1954
Kazanets, I.P.	1st Sec. Donets Obkom 1955
Kirichenko, A.I.	1st Sec. CC Ukraine 1953 Mem. Pres. CC 1955
Kirilenko, A.P.	1st Sec. Sverdlovsk Obkom 1955
Klimenko, V.K.	1st Sec. Lugansk Obkom 1951 (to mem. CC CPSU 1956)
Komiakhov, V.G.	1st Sec. Crimean Obkom 1955
Korneichuk, A.Ya	1st Dep. Chmn. Ukrainian Council of Mins. 1953

Korniets, L.R.	Min. Agricultural Procurements USSR 1953
Kucherenko, V.A.	Dep. Chmn. Council of Mins. USSR 1955
Markov, V.S.	1st Sec. Orel Obkom 1956
Matskevich, V.V.	1st Dep. Min. Agriculture USSR 1953 Min. 1955
Moskalenko, K.S.	Commander Moscow Garrison and Military District 1953
Mzhavanadze, V.P.	1st Sec. CC Georgia 1953
Naidek, L.I.	1st Sec. Odessa Obkom 1955
Podgorny, N.V.	2nd Sec. CC Ukraine 1953
Polianskii, D.S.	1st Sec. Crimean Obkom 1953 1st Sec. Orenburg Obkom 1955
Postovalov, S.O.	1st Sec. Kaluga Obkom 1954
Rudakov, A.P.	Head Heavy Industry dept. CC 1954
Rudenko, R.A.	Prosecutor-General USSR 1953
Rumiantsev, A.M.	Chief Editor Kommunist 1956
Semichastny, V.E.	Sec. CC Komsomol 1950- (to cand. CC 1956)
Senin, I.S.	Minister Ukraine (to cand. CC 1956)
Serdiuk, Z.T.	1st Sec. CC Moldavia 1954
Serov, I.A.	Chmn. KGB 1954
Siniagovskii, P.E.	Mining manager Ukraine (to cand. CC 1956)
Sokolov, T.I.	1st Sec. Smolensk Obkom 1956
Stakhursky, M.M.	1st Sec. Khabarovsk Kraikom 1955

Struev, A.I.	1st Sec. Perm Obkom 1954
Titov, V.N.	1st Sec. Kharkov Obkom 1953

3. Original Association in Moscow 1949-53

Andreeva, N.N.	Raikom Sec. Moscow (to cand. CC 1956)
Bobrovnikov, N.I.	Chmn. Moscow Soviet Executive Ctte 1956 (to mem. CC 1956)
Dudorov, N.P.	Head Dept. CC 1955 Min. Internal Affairs 1956
Furtseva, E.A.	1st Sec. Moscow Gorkom 1954
Grishin, V.V.	Chmn. Trade Union Council 1956
Ignatov, N.F.	2nd Sec. Moscow Obkom 1956
Kapitonov, I.V.	1st Sec. Moscow Obkom 1954
Leonov, P.A.	Head Dept. CC 1955
Lunev, K.F.	Dep. Chmn. KGB 1954 (probably personnel)
Marchenko, I.T.	2nd Sec. Moscow Gorkom 1954
Mylarshchikov, V.P.	Head CC Agriculture Dept. for RSFSR 1956
Prokhorov, V.I.	Sec. Trade Union Council 1955
Volkov, A.P.	Chmn. State Ctte. for Labour and Wages 1956
Ustinov, V.I.	Senior State Security post 1953
Yasnov, M.A.	Chmn. RSFSR Council of Mins. 1956
Zhavoronkov, V.G.	Min. State Control 1956

4. 'Victims' of Rivals

(Leningraders and 'doctors plot' era 'vigilantes' who suffered setbacks when Beria and Malenkov in ascendancy and 'rescued' by Khrushchev)

Aristov, A.B.   Sec. CC 1955

Ignatiev, S.D.   1st Sec. Bashkir Obkom 1954

Ignatov, N.G.   2nd Sec. Leningrad Obkom
                              1st Sec. Gorkom 1953

Kosygin, A.N.   Chmn. State Economic Commission
                                 1956
                              Cand. Pres. CC 1957

Kozlov, F.R.   1st Sec. Leningrad Obkom 1953

Shepilov, D.T.   Chief Editor <u>Pravda</u> 1954

Shtykov, T.F.   1st Sec. Novgorod Obkom 1954

Suslov, M.A.   (Sec. CC) Mem. Pres. CC 1955

Suetin, M.S.   1st Sec. Udmurt Obkom 1954

B.   KHRUSHCHEV PROTEGES IN CC PRESIDIUM 1953-1958

<u>Voting Membership of CC Presidium 1953-1958</u>

<u>March 1953</u>	<u>May 1957</u>	<u>Sept. 1958</u>
Molotov	Molotov	
Malenkov	Malenkov	
Beria		
Voroshilov	Voroshilov	Voroshilov
Bulganin	Bulganin	
Kaganovich	Kaganovich	
Mikoyan	Mikoyan	Mikoyan
*Khrushchev	*Khrushchev	*Khrushchev
Saburov	Saburov	
Pervukhin	Pervukhin	
	*Kirichenko	*Kirichenko
	*Suslov	*Suslov
		*Aristov
		*Belyaev
		*Brezhnev
		*Ignatov
		*Kozlov
		?Kuusinen
		*Mukhitdinov
		*Furtseva
		?Shvernik

*   Khrushchev Proteges

Chapter Three

THE SOCIO-POLITICAL EFFECTS OF KHRUSHCHEV:
HIS IMPACT ON SOVIET INTELLECTUAL LIFE

Aleksandr M. Nekrich

Before entering into my discussion of intellectual life under
Khrushchev I should like to make a few preliminary
observations. Under the heading of Khrushchev's reforms I
have in mind all his measures in the areas of internal social
policy and foreign affairs. It is very difficult to isolate
one reform from another when one is speaking of their
influence in a very short segment of time. Agreement with and
support for one reform did not necessarily mean support for
others. Gratitude to Khrushchev for rehabilitating the
victims of Stalinist terror was not infrequently accompanied
by condemnation and ridicule of him in connection with the
educational reform, with his anti-parasite measures, with the
corn-growing campaign, or with the moratorium on paying off
state loan obligations. The enthusiasm aroused by the
decisions of the 20th Party Congress was partially cancelled
by the events which followed. Many of those whose spirits
picked up after the death of Stalin tended to wilt by the end
of the Khrushchev decade. On the other hand, the 'thaw' of
1954-1956, with its still basically muffled criticism of the
regime, gave an impulse toward a deeper understanding of the
fate of Russia. In the wake of artistic works which were
still incomplete others appeared later which were more
profound. Everything had meaning, even short-term and
inconsistent support for the reforms by conservatives and
conformists who wished to pass for liberals. One can hardly
agree with those who in the eighties condemn the works of the
fifties for inconsistency or for the fact that they allegedly
fit completely within the framework of the Soviet regime and
socialist realism. The displacement of historical perspective
is often connected with a subjective personal attitude and is
unsuitable for the evaluation of an historical epoch.

By the time of Stalin's death the crisis in all spheres
of Soviet life had reached a critical point. The hopeless war
in Korea had a real chance of growing into a new world
conflict. The cold war threatened to become a hot one.

The process of formation of a modern Soviet society was
coming to an end. It was as if everything was ready for its
crystallisation. The individual classes and social strata
reflected the rules of social behaviour of this society in
their activities. But mass terror and the absence of a sense

of security created the greatest tension in the State. The transition from life under an extraordinary to a normal situation was becoming an historical necessity. All strata of society needed this - from the rank-and-file kolkhoznik to the highest party bureaucrat.

The intelligentsia was in a condition of almost complete prostration. The major part of it had obediently supported the most repulsive measures of the regime; this was especially true of the creative intelligentsia. Andrei Amalrik had maliciously, but accurately, characterised its condition as that of persons who think one thing, say another, and do yet another. Amalrik considered the creative intelligentsia as an even more unpleasant phenomenon than the regime which had engendered it. Hypocrisy and a readiness to take things as they were had become, as it were, a part of the conduct of the creative intelligentsia, and it regarded any attempt to act nobly as either a provocation or insanity.(1)

But this applied, perhaps, to the entire intelligentsia. The general line of the party since the time of the October Revolution consisted in the liquidation of the Russian intelligentsia as a social stratum whose chief function lay in criticism of the existing regime. The Russian intelligentsia had prayed for the revolution, appealed and prepared for it, created in the country the necessary psychological climate for the overthrow of tsarism and the winning of freedom. The new regime took this into account.

Yet the intelligentsia became the first victim of the revolution of 25 October 1917. Part of it was physically annihilated during the Revolution and the Civil War, another part fled abroad; those who returned achieved eternal peace here in the thirties during the Great Terror.

In order to find a replacement for the old intelligentsia the Bolshevik Party began to create a new, so-called 'proletarian' intelligentsia. Especially privileged conditions were created for persons of worker and peasant origin to enter educational institutions. Special high schools were established for them - workers faculties (rabfak). For the training of cadres with higher qualifications in the sphere of ideology there were established the Institutes of the Red Professoriate, party schools, and finally the Communist Academy, which ultimately merged with the Academy of Sciences, thus achieving the affirmation of party science in that citadel of non-partisanship.

N.I. Bukharin, around whom contemporary Western historiography and the unofficial Soviet loyal-oppositionist historiography have composed legends in recent years as an antipode to Stalin,(2) speaking in 1925 at the first meeting of the party leadership with representatives of the intelligentsia, promised that the party would henceforth turn out intellectuals the way they turn out parts in a factory.(3) One must say that the party fulfilled its promise and, perhaps, even over-fulfilled it. This overfulfillment related to the fact that very quickly the party leaders became convinced that the first edition of the Soviet (proletarian) intelligentsia had inherited some of the 'birth marks of the old Russian intelligentsia'. It was necessary to produce a replacement for them as soon as possible. A significant part of the proletarian intellectuals had begun critically to reassess the line of the party, which showed that the traditional function of the Russian intelligentsia - its capacity for a critical understanding of reality - was not alien to it. By this very act the first galaxy of the proletarian intelligentsia had signed its own death warrant. Stalin needed submissive implementers and not thinkers, least of all critical ones. Of course, I am stating the case here crudely and schematically. But it is sufficient to glance at Russian literature in the twenties and early thirties to understand what was going on. Not only Zamiatin, with his masterful tale We, or Boris Pil'niak, writers 'inherited' by the revolutionary epoch, but also proletarian writers (A. Arosev, A. Tarasov-Rodionov, and I. Makarov) could not, evidently did not desire to, conceal in their works the depths of the new moral conflicts called forth by the merciless fanaticism, cynical pragmatism, and uncontrolled despotism of the victors of the Revolution. But as Shakespeare said: 'Reason is the first step to treason'. The party leadership knew this, and proletarian writers began to disappear one after another.

Stalin correctly guessed that the most serious danger to the regime he had created came from doubting, critical people. A bit later Goebbels would put up the slogan: 'Down with fault-finders and maligners!' But Stalin arrived at this thought much earlier. The Great Terror of the thirties had 'rubbed out' the remains of the pre-revolutionary intelligentsia (we recall the executions by roster in Leningrad on the day after Kirov's assassination) and annihilated a significant part of the first levy of Soviet intellectuals. But by the time of the beginning of the German-Soviet war there had appeared a second generation of the Soviet intelligentsia. Its special characteristic consisted in the fact that it was nurtured in dedication to the regime Stalin had created. Before this generation there had been only echoes of the Revolution, its most general ideas. History appeared to people of this generation, born in the twenties and graduated from the Soviet school, in Stalin's interpretation, in the spirit of the well known remarks of Stalin, Kirov, and Zhdanov on the model of the textbook on the history of the USSR and the 'Short Course' on the history of the AUCP(B). The new generation had been brought up in the spirit of anti-fascism, covered in the romance not only of the civil war in Russia, but also in the more recent civil war in Spain. For them, Stalin embodied the Revolution. Only a few of them attempted to look into the real history of their country. At the height of the Great Terror they were about 15-20 years old. Stalin stood before them as the saviour of the Fatherland from the conspiracies of the Trotskyites, rightists, and international imperialism. And if anyone ever had his doubts, it was better to keep them to himself. They got the same advice at home. For many, the years of terror, when their parents were declared 'enemies of the people', were the first test. The second blow was the signing of the non-aggression pact and then friendship with fascist Germany. That was very difficult to understand. Probably future historians will find quite a bit of interesting evidence of the indignant reaction of youth at this unexpected turnabout. Of course, this applies mainly to the student youth, the same who in June-July 1941 went off voluntarily to the front. The second generation of the Soviet intelligentsia suffered cruelly during the war. Thus, Stalin at first didn't need to carry out a surgical operation on the second generation of the Soviet intelligentsia. The war did it for him.

By the end of the war the intelligentsia represented a rather ill-assorted social group. The war against Nazi Germany demanded of each, and not only of the masses as a whole, an internal mobilisation and an expression of both individual responsibility and activity, because responsibility for the common cause, that is, for victory over the enemy presupposed not only obligatory discipline for all, but also the full development of individual initiative. Those who returned from the front whole and unharmed, with their critical understanding of reality, represented danger number one for the Stalinist regime. The regime directed the activity, especially of the workers, kolkhozniks, the engineering-technical, and the rural intelligentsia, towards the restoration of the economy; to others it offered privileges for the resumption of their studies interrupted by the war. Beginning in 1943 the party undertook an ideological reconquest for the restoration of positions lost during the war. One of the most important tasks of the new ideological offensive was the struggle against the remains of the liberal intelligentsia and for the complete conversion of intellectuals 'gone astray' into submissive executors of the party's plans.

The war had been won by the Soviet Union with the active assistance of scientists and engineers. Already in the course of the war it had become evident that there was no sense in keeping scientists in the prison-laboratories, the so-called 'sharashki', which have been described by Alexander Solzhenitsyn in The First Circle, by N. Ozerov (Tupolevskaia sharaga) and in the recently published book of Lev Kopelev Utoli moia pechali (Soothe my sorrows).

After the end of the war the party resolutely changed its policy toward scientific workers, especially in the areas of the basic sciences, the technical and applied sciences, that is in that sphere of activity linked to the military potential of the USSR. Having created privileged groups among the intelligentsia, the party thus solved a basic social problem in this sphere - the disintegration of the intelligentsia, the destruction of emerging tendencies toward self-understanding and solidarity. Wages were markedly raised for all scientific staff members of academic institutions and for teachers and professors in higher educational establishments; measures were taken to improve their housing and living conditions, medical care, etc. Special privileges were established for scientists working in the fields of atomic weapons. Full and corresponding members of the Academy of Sciences were placed in the group of the most privileged. Stalin conferred on each of the academicians a personal gift - a villa with a block of land; and this property was transferrable as an inheritance.

But along with corruption the regime continued to carry out a policy of terror throughout the country. Stalin was preparing for a new round of the Great Terror. He dreamt of the conquest of capitalist Europe, and terror was to be a preliminary step towards a new war. This time the first victims were to be intellectuals of Jewish origin. Stalin needed this not only because of his pathological anti-semitism, but also in order again to mobilise millions, as in the thirties, for the support of the regime and to point out to them the concrete bearers of evil. Thus arose the 'case of the doctor-poisoners'. Several academicians were arrested in the USSR Academy of Sciences. Soon a pogrom was expected in the institutes of humanities. Lists of the next victims were being prepared. But on the eve of the beginning of the trial(s) Stalin died. The threat of a new wave of terror was thus removed from the agenda.

The triumvirate which came to power - Malenkov, Beria, and Molotov - hastened to calm the people, placed by the Stalinist regime on the verge of catastrophe. In the shadow of the first triumvirate Khrushchev gradually prepared himself for the seizure of power.

Already on the day after Stalin's death unprecedented confusion reigned in the state and party apparatus. This confusion was very well reflected in a Communique on reorganisation of the organs of power on 7 March 1953. In it were the notable words: 'for the avoidance of panic and disorder'.(4)

The tooth-shattering decrees prepared before Stalin's death still operated automatically, for example, the Decision of the Presidium of the Academy of Sciences of the USSR on the Institute of History. But it was obvious that neither the latter nor other decrees of the same character could be implemented. And if anyone still had any doubts about this, then the Communique of the Ministry of Internal Affairs on 4 April 1953 to the effect that the doctors accused of poisoning were innocent, that the whole case had been a provocation of the former leadership of the former Ministry of State Security,(5) and the liquidation of this ministry itself, signified the beginning of a new period. Generally, when we speak of 'Khrushchev's reforms' we forget about this decisive step, which laid the foundation for the new stage in Soviet history, called by Alexander Zinoviev 'the period of confusion'. In fact, it is more correct to call it 'the period of confusion and hopes'.

For the intelligentsia it seemed that a silver age had begun. Lead editorials in the newspapers condemned arbitrariness and lawlessness, demanded an end to silence and a return to 'Leninist norms'.

After the elimination of Beria the new leadership quickly transformed itself into a 'second triumvirate' (Malenkov, Molotov and Khrushchev), in which Nikita Khrushchev began to play the main role.

The cancellation of debts and the sharp decrease in taxes from the peasantry - the most resentful, most poverty-stricken class in Soviet society - the re-ordering of work in factories and institutions, the promise to uphold legality and restore justice, the declaration by the Government of its intention to normalise relations with the West and sign an armistice in Korea - all served as a powerful impulse toward the polarisation of forces of the intelligentsia. Very quickly it appeared that the Stalinists were on the defensive, and their enemies began an offensive wherever possible. The initial measures of the post-Stalin leadership had the greatest influence on the creative intelligentsia and on specialists in the humanities, who for decades had served the Stalinist regime in full faith and confidence, helping it to falsify history and apply a 'scientific foundation' for the most reactionary and anti-humanist measures. But it would be erroneous to assume that the scientific and technical intelligentsia remained deaf to the reforms. Here there were other kinds of problems - problems of technical progress, the use of science for the development of industry and agriculture. In one of his speeches Academician Peter Kapitsa - the only one among the academicians who had refused in the Stalin period to participate in the building of atomic weapons, on ethical grounds - likened Soviet industry to an ichthyosaurus, a pre-historic animal with a long body and a tiny head. For Kapitsa, the head was science. But it was the creative intellectuals who shaped public opinion, which was barely beginning to arise in the land of victorious socialism. And this was only natural; in their hands were the means of artistic generalisation. For Russia, with almost universal literacy, literature was obliged to answer the needs of everyday life.

In December 1953 the journal <u>Novy mir</u>, which was fated to become the centre of the literary renaissance, published Vladimir Pomerantsev's article 'On Sincerity in Literature',(6) which should to a certain extent be considered as a programmatic document. It was about the sincerity of the author in his work, about the refusal to varnish reality, to be hypocritical. From my point of view this sounded like a challenge to the well known formula of the writer as an 'engineer of human souls', although at the time no one wrote about this. But what is an engineer? He is a person who designs, invents, builds, or repairs. To call a writer an 'engineer of human souls' is equivalent to avowing that the writer creates these souls, contrives them, but does not try to penetrate to the depths of the human soul. By thinking up this formula, Gor'kii had done a great service to the party and a very bad one to the writers. He was also the originator of the formula, 'If the enemy does not yield, then he will be annihilated', which the Stalinist regime used to justify its multitudinous crimes.

The writers actually had created artificial heroes of the times. Their names were legion - for they all had the same face and repeated in the same truisms and acted according to the same pattern. It was natural, therefore, that Pomerantsev's article resounded like a challenge to the many-thousand-strong collective of the Union of Soviet Writers (USW). The thaw in literature really began with the article by Pomerantsev. Then appeared the artistically weak, but thematically important tale <u>The Thaw</u>, by Ilya Ehrenburg.(7) The title of this story was taken as the name of this whole period of Soviet history (and not only in literature) between the death of Stalin and the 20th Congress of the CPSU. In Ehrenburg's wake the emigre Turkish communist poet, Nazim Hikmet, living in the USSR, wrote a play under the title <u>Did</u>

<u>Ivan Ivanovich Really Exist?</u>(8) in which he spoke of the facelessness and anonymity of the Stalinist regime. The play was staged by the Moscow Satirical Theatre, but it lasted only three months. Its presentation was then banned. In January 1954, V. Vasilevskii, former colonel and member of the USW, came out with a ferocious reply to Pomerantsev.(9) He was seconded by Anatolii Surkov, one of the leaders of the USW. His article was published by the central organ of the CPSU, <u>Pravda</u>, and was full of accusations against Pomerantsev and some other writers attacking the principles of <u>partiinost'</u> in literature.(10) In December 1954, at the second Writers' Congress, there echoed speeches appealing, on the one hand, for consolidation, and on the other hand, upholding the Stalinist heritage. Later a physicist from Dubna, Dr Gera Kopylov, would have something to say about Stalinists in literature. In one of his poems of the sixties he would call them 'SS-men from the SSP' (ie. USW). Ferment bubbled up amongst student youth. There appeared the first semi-legal circles in the post-Stalin period. Probably the demands for deeper, more radical changes and not simply cosmetic ones, were quite widespread and encompassed not only the huge administrative and political centres, such as Moscow, Leningrad, Kiev and Tbilisi (although Tbilisi was regarded as a stronghold of Stalinism), but also the smaller cities and the countryside. Our attention should be drawn to the characterisation of the period given by Khrushchev in his memoirs:

> We were afraid, really afraid. We were afraid that the thaw might turn into a flood which we'd be in no condition to control and which would sink us. How could it sink us? It could escape the banks of the Soviet river-bed and bring forth a tidal wave which would wash away all the barriers and retaining walls of our society. From the leaders' point of view this would be an undesirable development. We wanted to direct the thaw in such a way that it would stimulate only creative forces, that would be a contribution to the strengthening of socialism.(11)

The thaw bred fear in Khrushchev's heart; later this fear would increase whenever it seemed to him that he was incapable of controlling the 'elements', and decrease when he believed himself to be in control. This almost schizoid feeling was reflected in Khrushchev's attitude to the intelligentsia. His irritation, which on occasion culminated in an explosion, was not only a function of his limited education and Stalinist training, but was also due to a sense of dependence on the intelligentsia. It perhaps reflected an inferiority complex born of a sense of interdependence. For who was it, if not the intelligentsia, who supported all of Khrushchev's reforms when he made his first steps in that direction.

The schizophrenia found expression at the time of the second Congress of the USW in mid-December 1954, when on the one hand, party bureaucrats were subjected to scathing criticism, while on the other hand, an attempt was made to restrain passions to some extent.

The years 1954-1955 saw the beginning of the process of rehabilitation of those arrested or who perished in the years of Stalinist terror. It can be stated confidently that no other measure, no other reform of the Khrushchev period dealt such a severe moral blow to the Soviet regime as a whole, and to Stalinism, as did the rehabilitation of the victims of Stalin's terror. The creative intelligentsia interpreted this as the removal of the muzzle from the most forbidden of themes. The intelligentsia, as a whole, began to feel freer. On a later occasion, Khrushchev would complain that the editorial staff of journals and publishing houses had been swamped by manuscripts on the labour camp theme.

The process of spiritual emancipation began, as I have already mentioned, at the instant of publication of the MVD communique, dated 4 April 1953. The truth, the half-truth, or the half-lie - however one wishes to regard it - began seeping through. The party leadership attempted to ration truth. However no-one had as yet invented a set of pharmaceutical scales accurate enough for weighing grains of truth. In 1954-1955, Stalin was still considered great, and his works were still in print. Authors continued to make references to him and to cite him in their writings. The number of quotations from Stalin did gradually begin to decrease. But the legacy of the Stalinist period still bore down on everyone and above all, on the intelligentsia, with somewhat lesser force. It was not so much fear, for this had begun to lessen, but the familiar instinct for self-censorship which tenaciously gripped the intelligentsia, forcing it every now and then to interrupt its forward movement to look around. But still, there was movement, from Stalinism towards the unknown.

The thaw was marked not only by the works of Pomerantsev, Ehrenburg, Nazim Hikmet and Leonid Zorin.(12) It also influenced the historians. In 1954-1955, the journal <u>Voprosy istorii</u>, published several articles by E.N. Burdzhalov and others, which to all intents and purposes refuted the official party version of the two leaders of the revolution - Lenin and Stalin. After long years of oblivion, the names of Kamenev and Zinoviev re-emerged without the accompaniment of the usual

abusive epithets. Burdzhalov not only wrote articles. He
began participating in public discussions. One of these
sprung up around the book by A. Likholat, The Victory of the
October Revolution in the Ukraine.(13) At its official
consideration by the Institute of Marxism-Leninism this book
received almost unanimous approval, although in it Likholat
repeated the accusations of the thirties against noted
communists condemned as nationalist-deviationists. However, a
few of these had survived, and were at liberty; and a fierce
struggle sprang up around Likholat's book. That there were
those who praised Likholat was no cause for astonishment.
After all, Likholat was the head of the history sector of the
CC of the CPSU, ie. one of those who exercised a decisive
influence over the fortunes of historians and over their
standing within the historical profession. The struggle
surrounding Likholat's book ended at the 20th Congress of the
party, when Mikoyan spoke out sharply criticising the
book.(14) Likholat had to quit his post in the Central
Committee and to remove to Kiev.

The thaw was also making itself felt in other areas of
life. Censorship weakened. The access to archives was
relaxed. In respect of the latter, it is impossible not to
recount a particular episode. In the Leningrad archives, a
large quantity of dossiers on the revolutionary movement in
Petersburg compiled by the Tsarist Okhrana, had been immured
for many years. At the time an official of the Tsarist
archives had stamped this material 'Top Secret'. After the
revolution, a Soviet official, seeing the stamp, added a
prohibition in the name of Soviet authority by stamping the
material a second time with 'Absolutely Secret'. As a
consequence Soviet historians were denied access to these
archives for many years.

In the history of social development in the Khrushchev
decade it is possible to note several turning points: the MVD
Communique of 4 April 1953; the 20th Congress of the CPSU,
February 1956; the 22nd Congress of the CPSU, 1961; and the
publication of One Day in the Life of Ivan Denisovich. The
intervals between these turning points were occupied by fierce
struggles between the progressive intelligentsia and the
Stalinists. Of course, when we say 'progressive' in reference
to the intelligentsia we are speaking in very relative terms,
for it is possible to include in its ranks a variety of trends
with a variety of final objectives - liberals, dreaming simply
of a mouthful of freedom (though it is true that even a
mouthful of freedom can frequently lead to drunkenness); the
'renewers' or 'ameliorators', Marxists-Leninists who believe
in all seriousness that a return to Lenin's precepts is the
only correct path to the future; and people who have become
generally disenchanted with socialism and feel themselves to

be the enemies of the regime but who, to begin with, have no clear conception of the path that they will finally select.

All these groups, tendencies and lone combattants were in agreement on one goal: not to allow a return to the past, to expose the crimes of the past, and to further the struggle against arbitrary rule and lawlessness. Questions of a social or political character were often coloured by emotional individual perspectives. The progressives experienced limited support from certain highly placed officials in the party apparatus, a rather small group of liberally minded officials from the middle and upper levels, mainly from those who dealt with international matters and, above all, with the international communist and workers movements. Their horizons were far broader. Of course they too had their own purely individual problems and they were far from indifferent to their personal careers, but walking step by step with Khrushchev and occasionally even running a little ahead, these people were concurrently also building their own careers. It should be noted that they nearly all managed to build careers for themselves, although of their progressiveness there remained only faint, pleasant memories. But not only memories. The position of these people at the time created the illusion of Marxists-Leninists within the country and for many Sovietologists abroad of the existence of practically a whole galaxy of young leaders who would replace the 'old men'. However, these 'young men' served the old men faithfully and continue to do so. The latter often use them in order to confuse western politicians and western public opinion as to the political goals and intentions of Soviet leaders. Such a transformation is not new to history. But then, Bernard Shaw was probably correct in remarking that history has never taught anyone anything.

Khrushchev's speech at the closed session of the 20th Congress of the party of 25 February 1956, was the second turning point.(15) By this time many thousands of innocent people who had been convicted were free. Those who had survived the camps now spoke out without fear, although some preferred to remain silent and immediately to wipe the past from their memories, for this was their only chance for a return to life - to forget, forget!

Khrushchev's address was read out in full at closed party meetings. Its fundamental propositions were also published in the press. Aside from this, Khrushchev's address was also read out at meetings of non-party people, sometimes in full and sometimes in a shortened form. The full text of the address did however appear abroad. Heated discussion followed its readings. Discussions in scientific and creative organisations assumed a particularly sharp character. In

Moscow, in the Institute of History of the Academy of Sciences
of the USSR, a conflict arose between two old bolsheviks -
both of them had served Stalin's regime faithfully - over
whether Stalin should properly be labelled a 'murderer' or a
'tyrant'.(16) In other words, things had reached a point where
it was now simply a matter of discovering the correct
qualification for the crimes of the 'father of Peoples'. In
the Institute of Thermal Engineering of the Academy of
Sciences of the USSR three young scientists demanded a
thorough investigation and the punishment of the guilty.
Among them was the future organiser of the Helsinki Committee,
Professor Iurii Orlov. All three were penalised, and Orlov
was forced to transfer to work in Erevan.(17) It was necessary
to restrict criticism to Stalin. It was also possible and
necessary to curse Beria, but as soon as an attempt was made
to criticise the Soviet system the cry went up: 'One should
not generalise!'. In fact, however, it was impossible to
avoid making generalisations. Proof of this lies in the
appearance of the work by Vladimir Dudintsev, Not by Bread
Alone,(18) which immediately became the subject of public
attention and the occasion for a bitter clash between the
Stalinists and the anti-Stalinists, a fact that is hardly
surprising. At the centre of the story there is a bureaucrat
(Drozdov) who is the embodiment of the entire Soviet
bureaucratic system which stifles any progressive idea and
numbs initiative. Party bureaucrats began to demand the
punishment of Dudintsev and the condemnation of his book.
Discussion of it in the Union of Soviet Writers took place on
22 October 1956, at the height of events in Hungary, a time
when the authorities and the Stalinists were exceptionally
frightened of the situation as it had developed. At the same
time the journal Voprosy istorii announced plans for a
conference of readers on the theme 'Historical Truth'.
However, due to the events in Hungary, this discussion was
postponed and did not in fact take place at that time. The
writer Konstantin Paustovskii expressed the general mood of
the liberal intelligentsia in his speech at the discussion of
Dudintsev's work. His speech was not printed in full in the
Soviet Union but appeared later abroad. However what was
reported by Literaturnaia gazeta gave a fairly clear
indication: Paustovskii stated that Drozdov did not represent
a single man but was the embodiment of a mass phenomenon, a
new social layer, ie. almost what Djilas wrote in his book The
New Class. According to the report of Literaturnaia gazeta,
Paustovskii said: 'This novel is the first battle with
Drozdov, whom our literature must attack until he is
annihilated'.(19) The position of Konstantin Simonov was
interesting; at the time he was editor-in-chief of Novy mir,
which had published Dudintsev's novel. Undoubtedly disturbed
that consideration of the novel had in fact turned into a
political discussion and foreseeing the undesirable

consequences that the discussion could have, not only for Dudintsev, but for himself as well, Simonov spoke out decisively against the main ideas permeating the entire course of the discussion and formulated by Paustovskii.

'There are quite a few people', declared Simonov, 'Who are prepared to use the term"Drozdovs" for no good purpose. They try to make it appear that whole strata of the party, social and state apparatus are being criticised in the novel. In reality, however, Drozdov is a certain type in the state apparatus, and everywhere all the healthy forces in that same state apparatus are carrying on an implacable struggle against him ... Dudintsev's novel is dear to me for the fact that in it resides a deep faith in the strength of Soviet power, in the strength of our people and society'.(20)

Later, similar arguments would be resorted to for the defense of one work or another containing criticism of the Soviet system - concealed, camouflaged, or overt. In the discussion of Dudintsev's novel there were established, so to speak, the general rules of the game. They would be applied later, too, in the discussion of One Day in the Life of Ivan Denisovich, but they turned out to be unsuitable for application to Doctor Zhivago.

Paustovskii's speech was greeted with warm approval by the overwhelming majority of those present at the discussion. Paustovskii went further than Dudintsev in condemning the 'Drozdovs', i.e. the ruling bureaucracy and their destruction of artists and writers such as Meyerhold, Babel, Artem Veselyi et al. In this way the emphasis was shifted from the crimes committed by Stalin to the crimes committed by the entire ruling stratum. This is the reason why in all his speeches, beginning with a meeting with the creative intelligentsia in May 1957, Khrushchev did not cease abusing Dudintsev and his book.(21) Nor was the abuse restricted to Dudintsev. Once again, as a reminder of Stalinist times, certain individuals were selected as subjects for criticism: these were those who sought to state something of their own, who spoke out against the embellishment of reality and those who, in all seriousness, had arrived at the belief that the silver age had begun. Some of these were rather uncompromising, like Dudintsev, and later Solzhenitsyn. Others attempted to take the right to speak further than was allowed - Yevtushenko, and Voznesenskii. And others again chose to create in silence - Pasternak. Among whom did Khrushchev seek his supporters, whom did he recommend as an example worthy of imitation? On the one hand, there was Dem'ian Bednyi - a poet who was first acclaimed, then forgotten and later abused. On the other hand, there were Stalin's former party cohorts in literature -

Sofronov, Kochetov, Gribachev, Sobolev, and in the fine arts - Vuchetich, Gerasimov and Serov.

In the course of the process of rehabilitation the names of many informants came to light. During rehabilitation, the investigators frequently made available to the ex-prisoners the materials associated with their cases, from which the latter discovered, to their horror, that they had been defamed or betrayed by their closest friends, and sometimes even by members of their families. As a result of these revelations a series of suicides rocked the intelligentsia in 1956. One of those who killed himself was A.A. Fadeev, the head of the Union of Soviet Writers, who was involved in the arrest and death of many writers. The previous editor of the journal Bolshevik, Aboltin, and the head of the Military Political Academy, Kovalevskii both shot themselves. Nor were these the only cases, although the press never revealed the real motives for the suicides. The leadership arrived at the decision not to reveal the names of the NKVD's secret collaborators - it is said they numbered about a million. There were cases of officers of the state security organs and the camps who had tortured prisoners, and who were punished for their lawlessness and brutality, but these were only exceptions. The majority were pensioned off to a 'well-earned rest', as the popular saying goes in the Soviet Union.

The events in Hungary altered the entire situation radically. The Stalinists took heart - this was what the encouragement of writers, artists and students had led to, WE TOLD YOU SO, WE DID WARN YOU!! They repeated the statements of the then Soviet ambassador in Budapest, Iurii Andropov, that if the Hungarian government had acted in time by taking strong measures against writers in Hungary, then there would not have been a Hungarian counter-revolution, ie. a revolution. From then on, and for many years, the ghost of the events in Hungary was to pursue Khrushchev relentlessly. His unwavering comrades reminded him of it on more than one occasion. This is why Khrushchev was so overly sensitive in his reactions to any significant events in literature, the fine arts and music which went beyond the bounds of his own perceptions, or required a higher level of understanding and talent from the conformist artists, who headed the creative unions, than they were capable of.

The picture, was, however, more complex. Divisions can be drawn between the literary generals and within the groups on which the party had relied in the past and on which Khrushchev intended to rely in the future. There was Aleksandr Tvardovskii, a poet enjoying enormous popularity for his poem about the soldier Vasilii Tiorkin, and Konstantin Simonov, a poet and writer who had also been extraordinarily popular during the war. They both stood for the party, but there was an enormous difference between them. Tvardovskii, the editor of Novy mir, was trying to open a way and to give support to these writers. A 'deviationist' writer did not frighten him. The best writers wrote for Novy mir - almost the whole constellation of 'rural writers' (derevenshchiki), Mozhaev, Abramov, Troepolskii. It was Novy mir which gave such wonderful writers as Iurii Dombrovskii, Victor Nekrasov and many others their first opportunities to publish. Simonov, at one time editor of Novy mir, which published Dudintsev's novel, and also of Literaturnaia gazeta, was a man of a different type, from a different environment. He tried to be on both sides at once, as we say in Russia, 'ours and yours'. He was an excellent courtier and he did not live badly under Stalin, even while having a reputation for being more of a liberal than officialdom would have liked. But when the moment of truth arrived and a choice had to be made, Simonov never erred. He was always on the side of those who had the real power in their hands. He backed only sure winners. To describe him you could use the words of a Russian poet of the last century: 'He's no fool in paying due respects to himself'. While the 'doctor's plot' trial was being prepared, a leading article appeared in Literaturnaia gazeta, of which he was the chief editor, with the title 'Murderers in White Coats'. Both of them, Tvardovskii and Simonov were undeniably part of the intelligentsia, and in the post-Stalin days they made different choices. Simonov refused, after his unfortunate experience with Dudintsev's novel, to publish Pasternak's Doctor Zhivago; Tvardovskii published One Day in the Life of Ivan Denisovich. Tvardovskii gave Solzhenitsyn to the Russian reader; Simonov took Pasternak away.

There were those who wanted to be in the present and the future, but who were still strongly rooted in the past, and they could not, despite their sincerest efforts, break away from it. Take Ilya Ehrenburg, with his evaluation of Stalin and Stalinism, with his support in the early 1960s for abstract art, Ehrenburg who put himself in the centre of attention with his memoirs People, Years, Life.(22) Khrushchev spoke unkindly of Ehrenburg, although not of course with the same unembarrassed use of language that Margarita Aliger and Ernst Neizvestnii experienced. We can talk about him very courteously, but we should not forget his sins - was Khrushchev's approach.(23) In the end the party leadership adopted a positive view of Ehrenburg. To a large degree this was to please the West, where Ehrenburg had many friends. Khrushchev enunciated a policy of peace with the West and was, despite his escapades, not indifferent to the West's opinion of him. Ehrenburg is going through a posthumous metamorphosis. They research his work, they publish collections of his documents, and recollections about him. Ehrenburg is one of those who in the Brezhnev era was rehabiliated by the General Secretary himself.(24)

How did the intelligentsia react to the events in Hungary? On the whole, with restraint. Although the events were discussed almost openly in the corridors of the institutes and creative unions, there were few who dared condemn the bloody repression of the Hungarian revolution by Soviet tanks. Indeed, there were few to whom it occurred that it was a genuine revolution that had taken place in Hungary. According to Bukovskii the violence inflicted on Hungary made a strong impression on the young people involved,(25) but the older generations, blinded by habit and Soviet propaganda that communists were being killed and the West was sending arms and men, kept themselves aloof. For that part of the intelligentsia better equipped to analyse what was going on – I have in mind the social scientists – the fact that broad strata of the peasantry had not participated in the revolution strengthened their cautious attitude. For the authorities this was enough. The October 1956 war in the Middle East had given the Soviet government the opportunity to link the events there and those in Hungary and represent them as a single conspiracy of the imperialists. Although many of the intelligentsia could see the absurdity of this proposition, it was very convenient for them to use it as a cover for their own indifference or even support for the bloody violence in Budapest. Further, there was such a short period between the 20th Congress and the Hungarian events that many were still not psychologically prepared for an independent evaluation of the events – they still had not developed a feeling of individual responsibility, they all still thought as a group and were all still bound together by the chains of mutual self-interest. The situation was somewhat different as far as the professional interests of individual sections of the intelligentsia were concerned. Their own affairs interested them much more than did international events. For the humanities specialists, for example, and for the rather broad stratum of secondary school teachers great significance attached to the criticism in the press and discussions of the 'Short Course' of the history of the All-Union Communist Party (Bolsheviks), published in 1938 as the gospel of Soviet society. This criticism opened up new possibilities for the study of the past. After all there was in it literally not a single event the history of which had not been distorted. The history of collectivisation, industrialisation, the Civil War and the war against Germany, the history of Russian social thought, the revolutionary movement in Russia, Tsarist foreign policy and the nationalities' questions – all this required radical revision. Even the history of the state in ancient Russia, Russian feudalism, etc. required a more objective examination. The same tasks arose for the philosophers, while the economists had to face up to even more serious problems - problems of the stimulation of production, economic management, profitability and the situation in agriculture. Between the 20th and the 22nd Congresses Khrushchev implemented a number of reforms, primarily in agriculture. In 1962 he tried radically to change the management of industry and the control of agriculture by dividing the party apparatus into two parts, rural and urban. The period of reforms brought great benefits to the creative intelligentsia. It is not hard to see why. The reforms assumed a significant degree of freedom and the unleashing of individual initiative, the growth of a feeling of individual self-interest and personal responsibility. The moral problems of society are also closely linked with the reforms, and in this period they figuratively crawled to the surface. At the same time the reforms sharpened the internal contradictions of the society and increased the bitterness of the struggle between the proponents of reform and their adversaries. There was a polarisation of forces and the neutral ground became increasingly constricted. It should be remembered, however, that Khrushchev carried on his course for reform in a state in which no structural changes had occurred in comparison with Stalinist times. Thus Khrushchev's reforming crusade only once went beyond the boundaries defined by the unwritten rules of a totalitarian system of the Soviet type, when he decided to divide the party organisation along urban and rural lines. There were moments when Khrushchev could have broken down such boundaries, but he did not permit himself to go that far. Thus the reforms, like all other phenomena, past and present, in Soviet society, took on an incomplete, contradictory, mongrel character. And in the final analysis the reflection of the spirit of reform in the works of writers, artists, composers and other creative people was of the same character. L.F. Il'ichev, the chairman of the Ideological Commission of the Central Committee, on one occasion strongly warned the creative intelligentsia: 'We must make ourselves completely understood on the question of creative freedom ... We possess complete freedom to struggle for communism. We do not and cannot have freedom to fight against communism'.(26) Not long before his fall from power Khrushchev once again confirmed at a meeting with representatives of the creative intelligentsia, held on 8 March 1963, that all their work continues to be under the unwavering control and direction of the party: 'The press and radio, literature, art, music, the cinema and the theatre are among the sharpest weapons at the disposal of the party. The party will always ensure that its weapon is ready for battle, to strike accurately at the enemy. The party will not allow anyone to blunt its weapon, to weaken its operational strength! Soviet literature and art are developing under the direct leadership of the Communist Party and its Central Committee'.(27)

Of course, such appeals and concealed threats had an obvious effect on the men of art and literature, but such was the influence of Khrushchev's reforms that these warnings and threats were unable to halt the progressive development of literature and art. During Khrushchev's time only a few abstract artists openly revolted, but in the 70s this unofficial trend in art established itself, and the authorities were forced to permit the organisation of exhibitions of non-orthodox artists, that is, to recognise their right to work. During the Khrushchev reform years Samizdat was conceived, that phenomenon unique in the social thought of the Soviet Union. Thanks to Samizdat a whole new movement was established in Soviet literature. It also created the conditions for the international solidarity of Soviet intellectuals with their brothers abroad. This was preceded by the widening of contacts with foreign countries which occurred during the reform period. This enriched the knowledge of Soviet intellectuals of the outside world while their colleagues abroad began to receive a clearer picture of life in the Soviet Union. But all this came later. It is curious to note that it was only the ideological opponents of the reforms who occupied relatively clear and consistent positions: Kochetov, Sofronov, Gribachev, Sobolev; among the artists, Vuchetich and Serov. Socially they belonged to the stratum of the higher party bureaucracy, and politically with the Stalinists. But they defended, and this was their undoubted strength, also the interests of the faceless masses of members of the creative unions, for whom any appearance of talent was a threat to their more or less secure existence.

In 1964, during the trial in Leningrad of Iosif Brodsky, the poet accused of parasitism, the judge, in giving his verdict, based his argument on the fact that Brodsky was not a member of the Union of Writers, but he showed very little interest in the question of Brodsky the poet.(28) Being a writer means being a member of the Union of Soviet Writers; being a composer means being a member of the Union of Soviet Composers; and an artist, a member of the Union of Soviet Artists. Outside these Unions and their close relations, the so-called group committees, neither writers, nor composers, nor artists exist, as far as the Soviet authorities are concerned. If you are not a member of the Union, you are a loafer, a parasite, or, for some reason, a homosexual (which is severely punished under the Criminal Code in the Soviet Union).

A significant group among the intelligentsia sympathising with Khrushchev's reforms were people with what one might call a false bottom to their intellectual baggage. Somewhere deep inside them was the fear to express a fresh and seditious thought, but at the same time they had developed the need for self-expression beyond the limits of the censorship. And yet they were still limited by their own self-censorship and by the necessity to find a balance in their creative work between self-expression and conformism. The poet Yevgenii Yevtushenko was such a person. With his lyrics and such works as 'Babyi Yar'(29) and 'Stalin's Heirs'(30) and his polemic with Khrushchev at his meeting with the creative intelligentsia, Yevtushenko was for a long time the hero of the youth, but then paid his tribute to the party with his terrible poems excoriating capitalism. Ilya Ehrenburg was another. Even in his memoirs published after the death of Stalin he sought a justification for Stalin's crimes and for those who with their pens had helped spread the Stalin legend, thus strengthening the Stalinist regime.

The five years between the 20th and 22nd Party Congresses were the years of the full blooming of Khrushchev's reformism, the growth of the expansionist element of Soviet foreign policy and of major internal and external political defeats. In the internal sphere this could be seen very clearly in the failure of agricultural policy; and in foreign affairs, in the worsening of relations with China and the Cuban missile crisis.

The fruits of reform were particularly noticeable and tangible in literature and art. The critical events of this period were Doctor Zhivago and 'the Pasternak affair' of 1958 and One Day in the Life of Ivan Denisovich, by A.I. Solzhenitsyn, in 1962. The history of the Pasternak affair is well known. Here we need only to emphasise the new element that this affair brought to the political situation and to the definition of the position of the intelligentsia. For the first time in many years there appeared on the surface the question of attitudes to the revolution. It was the apparent beginning of a public dispute that continues even today, sometimes quietening down and then flaring up again with new strength. This is the argument about the October Revolution, about how to evaluate it, about its legality, about revolutions in general, and about the fate of the intelligentsia in the revolution. The party bureaucracy, of course, at the instigation of 'advisors' from the Union of Writers, immediately seized upon this aspect of Pasternak's work, leaving aside the most important question when judging any work of literature - its artistic value. Pasternak probably understood well enough what he was doing. This is evident in his letter of surrender published in Pravda on

5 November 1958. There he wrote: '... In fact, if one looks at the conclusions flowing from the critical analysis of the novel, one must come to the conclusion that in the novel I hold the following incorrect positions. It is as if I consider that any revolution is an historically illegal phenomenon, that the October Revolution is an example of such an illegal act, that it brought misfortune to Russia and led to the destruction of the Russian hereditary intelligentsia'.(31)

Probably, more than one reader of these lines pondered over them. Within quite a short time another writer, too, Aleksandr Solzhenitsyn, would talk about the same thing in his epic of the Revolution. The beginning of this epic was his novel August 1914. For instance, in his speech at the meeting of Soviet leaders with writers and artists on 8 March 1963, Khrushchev mentioned One Day in the Life of Ivan Denisovich amongst creative works in which Soviet reality in the Stalin period was illuminated 'trustworthily, from a party position'.(32)

Why did Khrushchev allow the publication of One Day in the Life of Ivan Denisovich, indeed not only allowing its publication, but several times favourably commenting on it in public and did not even oppose raising the question of awarding its author the Lenin Prize for literature? The usual answer is that Khrushchev did not understand the real depth of the book, that to him Ivan Denisovich was an expression of the spirit of Russian (Soviet) man, who no matter what the circumstances loves to work and concern himself with the good of the cause. To this is added the persistence of Tvardovskii, the efforts of Khrushchev's assistant, Lebedev, and the fact that the time was right, coming when Khrushchev was trying to deal the final, fatal blow to the Stalinists at the 22nd Party Congress. One must further add, of course, that One Day in the Life of Ivan Denisovich was seen by his assistants and probably by Khrushchev himself, as a weapon in the struggle with the Maoists and as aid to the West European communist parties in their struggle for the support of the intellectuals of the West.

It has long been the habit of Soviet ideologists to claim as the property of Marxism any sensible thought expressed by non-communists that is not clearly anti-communist. The method of 'creative Marxism' is precisely this, the adaptation of foreign ideas to the vital tasks of communism. A sharp struggle raged round One Day in the Life of Ivan Denisovich virtually to the day of Khrushchev's fall. About four to six weeks previously Novy mir had published an article by a talented young party publicist named Iurii Kariakin. The article, entitled 'An Episode From Today's Struggle of Ideas',

was first published in September 1964, in the central
theoretical organ of the international communist movement
Problems of Peace and Socialism(33) (No. 9, 1964), and was
reprinted in the same month in Novy mir (No. 9, 1964.(34) In
it he described in detail the moral significance of
Solzhenitsyn's story and linked it to the Leninist ideas of
morality, contrasting them to such 'virtues' of cult
consciousness as 'taking someone else's word for it, doing
deals with your conscience, covering up all difficulties, and
quavering every time you have to choose between a struggle
charged with risk and accommodation'.(35)

Kariakin said very bluntly that One Day in the Life of
Ivan Denisovich and its publication were another significant
victory on the course set at the 20th Congress and a defeat
for the opponents of this course. He wrote: 'Marxist
criticism uncompromisingly opposes all those who believe that
this is an anti-Soviet, anti-communist, anti-party work'.(36)
One could suggest that Kariakin was putting forward in his
article the same arguments that convinced Khrushchev to agree
to the publication of One Day in the Life of Ivan Denisovich.
We must not forget the 22nd Party Congress, at which all the
fire was directed against the Stalinists. And it was at this
Congress that the conspiracy against Khrushchev, which was to
achieve its goal in October 1964, was first formed.

Life is full of contradictions. In December 1962, while
the organisation of the conspiracy was in full swing, the
All-Union Conference of Historians was meeting. Thanks to
this conference the anti-Stalinist historians were able to
hold out for a few more years against the onslaught of
conformism on their science. And this applied undoubtedly to
the intelligentsia as a whole. The significance of the
conference was that there, for the first time in many years,
an attempt was made to analyse the situation in the historical
and other social sciences under Stalin. The key-note address
was given by Academician B.N. Ponomarev, secretary of the
party's Central Committee and head of the International
Department. One might have assumed that at such an important
conference the address would have been read by the chief
ideologist in the Central Committee, Mikhail Suslov, a member
of the Politburo. But he probably deliberately stayed away.
The role he was to play, as organiser of the conspiracy
against Khrushchev, explains his non-participation in the
conference. Ponomarev noted three major points among the
negative consequences of the cult of personality for the
historical sciences: 'first, the diminution of the role of
Lenin and the role of the masses and the party in the history
of our country and the unjustified exaggeration of the role of
Stalin'; secondly, the propagation of an un-Marxist approach
to the study of the historical process, subjectivism and

arbitrariness in the evaluation of historical events and actors; and third, there was a situation of administrative interference, of dishonest criticism and the pinning of various labels on persons.(37) These basic points were then developed by other speakers and participants at the conference. The conclusion was clear - no matter what aspect of historical knowledge you take, you will find only falsification, lies, or, at the very best, alterations and strained interpretations. But the same things recurred at the conference itself. The doyen of Soviet historians, Academician E.M. Zhukov, declared in his speech that such an unsatisfactory situation had reigned in the historical sciences for the last 20 years.(38) In fact it had existed for 40 years. This was not a simple error of arithmetic, but a deliberate distortion, and at the same time an official instruction to the historians of when things had turned bad and up to which time things were, if not entirely good, at least bearable. Most of those speaking at the conference supported one way or another the effort to continue the struggle against the consequences of the cult of personality, although voices were heard expressing displeasure with this policy, for example that of the director of the Institute of Archeology of the USSR Academy of Sciences, B.A. Rybakov.(39) The former Central Committee secretary and director of the Institute of Marxism-Leninism, P.N. Pospelov, in answering a question about the Central Committee's decree of 9 March 1957 condemning Burdzhalov's article in <u>Voprosy istorii</u>, confirmed the decree.(40) It followed from this that the Central Committee was not intending to re-examine its decisions taken since 1956, even though some of them definitely contradicted the spirit of the decisions of the 20th and 22nd Party Congresses. The proceedings of the conference were published only after an interval of almost two years, in a limited and shortened version. Conservative elements in the social sciences simply ignored the findings of the conference, knowing that they could rely on the support of influential party leaders. But since none could give a formal directive that the findings of the conference were to be ignored, publishing houses continued to publish books and research which three or four years later were to be formally classified as 'slanderous'.

In the period between the Congresses a gradual process of liberation from self-censorship began. It touched an extremely small number of intellectuals. The average intellectual continued to be wary and uncertain as to the stability of the new situation. Typical was the remark of one capable historian, who was later to become a corresponding member of the Academy of Sciences. The remark was made not long after the historian heard Khrushchev's secret speech at the 20th Party Congress. 'Well', he said, 'it would be better not to publish anything for the next ten years'. But conversely, the range of problems agitating the intelligentsia significantly widened. The 'father' of the Soviet hydrogen bomb, Andrei Sakharov, made his first appeal to Khrushchev for a moratorium on testing of the hydrogen bomb in 1959.(41) He was to make the same request a number of times. Sakharov's appeal marked a qualitative leap in the intelligentsia's understanding not only of the situation in the Soviet Union, but in the world as a whole. Sakharov wrote later that he did it under the influence of the ideas of the Nobel Prize winner Linus Pauling. Here began the path which gradually and not without difficulty tore Sakharov away from the conformism of Soviet society, the path which eventually brought him into the ranks of the active fighters for human rights, brought him international recognition, and ... exile. A characteristic feature of this period was the appearance of people ready for an active struggle - Bukovskii, Galanskov, Ginzburg, Grigorenko. Groups and organisations were born, distributing pamphlets and typewritten journals and discussing programmes for the transformation of Soviet society. And among the intelligentsia there occurred a change in attitude towards religion.

But as before, the intelligentsia was still far removed from other social strata. In the 1962 worker uprising in Novocherkassk only students participated and then only to a limited extent.

Among the intelligentsia there developed a sympathy for the small nations being persecuted by authority - the Crimean Tatars, Meskhi and others. The national question again became the centre of attention in the Ukraine, the Caucasus and Central Asia. It attracted the attention of the Moscow and Leningrad intelligentsia. General Grigorenko openly defended the small nations, as had the writer A. Kosterin before him. Thus gradually developed the ill-sorted amalgam which would later be known as the dissident movement. It was born in the years of Khrushchev's reforms and lives on to this day.

The influence of the ideas and events of that decade of reform turned out to be so great that the new leadership replacing Khrushchev needed a year and a half to strike the first serious blow at the non-conformists (the Sinyavskii-Daniel trial of February 1966) and 15 years to deal with the dissident movement. And they still have not managed it completely. Stalin once said to the investigator Mironov, who could find no way of extracting an admission of guilt to charges of treason, espionage and anti-Soviet activity from the important party and state leader Lev Kamenev: 'Do you know how much our State weighs with all the factories, machines, the army, with all the armaments and the navy?'

Feeling somewhat confused the investigator answered: 'Nobody can know that Iosif Vissarionovich. It is in a realm of astronomical figures'. 'Well, and can one man withstand that pressure? Don't come to report to me until you have in this briefcase the confession of Kamenev!'(42) Since then the might of the Soviet state has grown immeasurably. But it is still unable to finally break the resistance of the non-conformists, among whom the leading role continues to be played by intellectuals. The state has been forced officially to recognise the existence of the dissidents. Through the efforts of the Soviet dissidents human rights have become an international problem which the Soviet regime cannot solve by the use of naked terror. This is the historical significance of Khrushchev's reforms and their influence on the Soviet intelligentsia. And as Zinoviev described so well in his comic verse 'The Intellectual's Prayer', the Soviet intellectual continues to dream about freedom:

> It's me talking to you, God
> So don't play deaf!
> Let all good things happen
> Except the bad.
> Give positions to those who aspire to them
> And pay them ten times more.
> Give victory to those who contend for it
> And all kinds of privileges to those who can
>   bribe their way.
> Festoon the streets with their mugs
> Give them all medals
> Let them grace television screens
> Let them reign
> But - not over us.(43)

NOTES

1. Andrei Amal'rik, 'Pis'mo A. Kuznetsovu', in Amal'rik, Stat'i i pis'ma. Amsterdam: The Alexander Herzen Foundation, 1971, pp. 17-18.

2. See, for example, Stephen F. Cohen, Bukharin and the Bolshevik Revolution: A Political Biography, 1888-1938. New York: Alfred A. Knopf, 1973.

3. Michael Heller and Alexander Nekrich, Geschichte der Sowjet Union, Vol. 1, 1914-1939. Konigstein: Athenium Verlag, 1981, p. 186.

4. Izvestiia, 7 March 1953.

5. Izvestiia, 4 April 1953.

6. <u>Novy mir</u>. No. 12 (December 1953), pp. 218-245.

7. Ilia Erenburg, 'Ottepel'', <u>Znamia</u>, No. 5 (May 1954), pp. 14-87.

8. Nazym Hikmet, 'A byl li Ivan Ivanovich?' <u>'Novy mir</u>, No. 4 (April 1956), pp. 18-58.

9. <u>Literaturnaia gazeta</u>, 30 January 1954.

10. <u>Pravda</u>, 25 May 1954.

11. <u>Khrushchev Remembers: The Last Testament.</u> Translated and edited by Strobe Talbott. Boston: Little, Brown and Company, 1974, p. 78.

12. L. Zorin, 'Gosti', <u>Teatr</u>, No. 2 (February 1954).

13. A. Likholat, <u>Pobeda Velikoi Oktiabr'skoi sotsialisticheskoi revoliutsii na Ukraine</u>. Moscow: Politizdat, 1955.

14. <u>XX s"ed Kommunisticheskoi partii Sovetskogo Soiuza 14-25 fevralia 1956 g.: Stenograficheskii otchet.</u> Moscow: Politizdat, 1956, Vol. I, p. 326.

15. <u>Khrushchev Remembers</u>. Edited and translated by Strobe Talbott. Boston: Little, Brown and Company, 1970, pp. 559-618.

16. A. Nekrich, <u>Otreshis' ot strakha</u>. London: Overseas Interchange Ltd, 1979, p. 142.

17. Khrushchev referred to this episode in his speech on 17 July 1960. See N.S. Khrushchev, <u>Vysokoe prizvanie literatury i iskusstva</u>. Moscow: Izdatel'stvo 'Pravda', 1963, p. 134.

18. Vladimir Dudintsev, 'Ne khlebom edinym', <u>Novy mir</u>, Nos 8,9,10 (August, September, October 1956).

19. <u>Literaturnaia gazeta</u>, 27 October 1956.

20. ibid. See also, Grigorii Svirskii, <u>A History of Post-War Soviet Writings: The Literature of Moral Opposition</u>. Ann Arbor, Michigan: Ardis, 1981, pp. 123-128.

21. N.S. Khrushchev, <u>Vysokoe prizvanie...</u>, op.cit., p. 39.

22. I. Erenburg, 'Liudi, gody, zhizn', <u>Novy mir</u>, Nos 5,6, (May, June 1962).

23. N.S. Khrushchev, Vysokoe prizvanie..., op.cit., p. 39.

24. L.I. Brezhnev, Aktual'nye voprosy ideologicheskoi raboty KPSS, Vol. I. Moscow: Politizdat, 1978, p. 24.

25. V. Bukovskii, I vozvrashchaetsia veter... New York: Khronika, 1978, pp. 97-98.

26. L.F. Ilichev, speech delivered on 17 December 1962, quoted in Priscilla Johnson, Khrushchev and the Arts Cambridge, Mass.: The MIT Press, 1965, p. 116.

27. N.S. Khrushchev, Vysokoe prizvanie..., op.cit., p. 221.

28. 'Zapis' sudebnogo razbiratel'stva po delu Iosifa Brodskogo, fevral'-mart 1964 goda', Arkhiv Samizdata. Munich: Radio Liberty, Vol. 4, No. 236, pp. 1-13.

29. Literaturnaia gazeta, 19 September 1961.

30. Pravda, 21 October 1962.

31. Pravda, 5 November 1958.

32. N.S. Khrushchev, Vysokoe prizvanie..., op.cit., p. 181.

33. Problemy mira i sotsializma, No. 9 (September 1964).

34. Novy mir, No. 9 (September 1964).

35. ibid., p. 239.

36. ibid.

37. Vsesoiuznoe soveshchanie istorikov, 18-21 dekabria 1962 g. Moscow: 'Nauka', 1964, p. 19.

38. ibid., pp. 55-56.

39. ibid., p. 105.

40. ibid., p. 299.

41. Khrushchev Remembers: The Last Testament, op.cit., pp. 68-71.

42. Alexander Orlov, The Secret History of Stalin's Crimes New York: Random House, 1953, pp. 117-118.

43. Aleksandr Zinoviev, Ziiaiushchie vysoty. Lausanne: L'Age d'Homme, 1976, p. 384.

Chapter Four

KHRUSHCHEV AND THE SOVIET ECONOMY:
MANAGEMENT BY RE-ORGANISATION

Robert F. Miller

> If 'too little, too late' can be catastrophic in
> war, too much, too soon can be equally disastrous
> for a nation.
> (Roy A. Medvedev and Zhores A. Medvedev,
> Khrushchev: The Years in Power, p.1.)

'Too much, too soon', is an eloquent, if somewhat misleading,
description of Khrushchevism in the management of the Soviet
economy during the hectic decade when Nikita Sergeevich held
sway. In a sense it is true that Khrushchev tried to do
perhaps too many things in too short a time to lift the Soviet
economy out of the slough of Stalinist brutality and
stagnation: too much, too soon for his own long-term
political survival, that is. Yet surely the improvements in
public welfare and economic progress which he sought for the
long suffering peoples of the Soviet Union were not premature.
Nor could it be said that what he was attempting to offer them
was really too much, considering the privations and sacrifices
they had had to undergo from the Stalinist model of 'socialist
construction'.

Whether the Khrushchev era was a net gain or loss for
Soviet society perhaps depends on the observer's point of
view. By most objective standards, the assessment must be
positive, it seems to me. The judgment of the brothers
Medvedev that its ultimate results represented a tragic waste
of golden opportunities, a betrayal of initially promising
expectations, undoubtedly merits attention.(1) But it largely
misses the point. For the weaknesses of Khrushchevism were to
a great extent the obverse side of its strengths. Had a
Molotov, a Malenkov (or a Brezhnev) taken power immediately
following Stalin's death, it is unlikely that even so much as
a sense of the possibilities of change opened up by Khrushchev
in the Soviet economy, society, and culture would have
emerged. Would the world then have become aware of the
Solzhenitsyns, Yevtushenkos, Sakharovs, Libermans - or
Medvedevs? Probably not.

Merely to speculate on these questions suggests how
difficult and analytically hazardous it is to treat the
concept of Khrushchevism in abstraction from the personality
of N.S. Khrushchev and the concrete policies and events

associated with his incumbency. Yet it is equally evident
that there are certain general characteristics overarching
this amalgam of stylistic, atmospheric, and situational
factors which make the study of Khrushchevism as a broader
phenomenon, or stage, of Soviet history worthy of special
consideration.

The complexity of this mixture of ingredients in
Khrushchevism is as noteworthy in the sphere of economic
policy and management as it is in the other areas discussed by
our authors. Indeed, in some respects it is even more central
to our understanding, since this was a problem area to which
Khrushchev himself obviously attributed crucial significance.
Before attempting to illustrate these propositions with
specific policy references, we might begin by introducing a
rough catalogue of the most salient elements of Khrushchevism
as a technique of policy-making and administration.

Turning first to the elusive psychological, or stylistic,
dimension of Khrushchevism, one notes from the outset Nikita
Sergeevich's talent for 'lateral thinking' - the ability to
conceive innovative or unconventional alternative solutions to
problems. Given the hide-bound, highly routinised nature of
the late Stalinist system of party and state organisation
within which Khrushchev rose to prominence - a system where
administrative structures commonly acquired a deep overlay of
ideological rationale which served to legitimise them and
given them an aura of systemic inevitability - this talent was
all the more remarkable. Stalin's rude condemnation in 1952
of Venzher and Sanina's proposal to dismantle the MTS as
allegedly an attack on the basic foundations of socialist
agriculture was a poignant illustration of this tendency
toward the 'ideologisation' of structure.(2) The Stalinist
penchant for regarding existing Soviet patterns of political
and administrative organisation as sacrosanct seems to have
enjoyed something of a revival in the Brezhnev era.

Whether Khrushchev's organisational innovations were
effective or not is quite another matter. The main thing is
that he was never afraid to abolish existing basic structures
and experiment with new ones, or to scrap these, in turn, if
they seemed unresponsive to the aims and influences he was
determined to foster. On the whole, this must be regarded as
a positive feature of his modus operandi. A much less
admirable feature was his impatience for quick results. In
contrast to Brezhnev's cautious experimentation and long-term
testing before undertaking major administrative changes,
Khrushchev was inclined to rush headlong into untested
patterns of administration and to demand their immediate
implementation on a nationwide scale. And he was just as
likely to order immediate modifications if the initial

solution proved defective. It is doubtful whether any administrative mechanism as complex as the Soviet economy could be effectively manipulated in this fashion. Soviet party and governmental officials certainly found such kaleidoscopic shifts in structure and policy uncomfortable in the extreme, and their disaffection was undoubtedly an important factor in Khrushchev's ultimate downfall.(3)

Indeed, it was precisely Khrushchev's awareness of the depth of bureaucratic opposition to fundamental change which impelled him to pursue such radical reorganisations and to demand their immediate and universal implementation. At times he seemed to be actively seeking to provoke bureaucratic opposition in order to smoke out his prinicpal conservative opponents in the party leadership. This lusty combattiveness in dealing with bureaucracy was another important, generally positive, element of Khrushchev's style. It became negative and self-defeating only after he had effectively defeated his major opponents, when, according to the Medvedevs, it turned into a bullying kind of arrogance of the classical Actonian variety.

Still within the framework of the idiosyncratic motivational dimension of Khrushchevism was the apparent contradiction between Khrushchev's vaunted practicality and his patent ideological activism. While, on the one hand, he persistently championed the principle of material incentives as the essential spur to collective and individual performance – for which the Chinese leaders roundly condemned him, as Woodward and Young demonstrate in their chapter; on the other hand, he retained a remarkably orthodox conception of proper socialist social relations. He was apparently genuinely convinced of the inherent superiority of socialist forms of social organisation and production. There was something noticeably 'Old Bolshevik' about his belief in the efficacy of proper organisation and indomitable human will for the attainment of great objectives. It was undoubtedly this optimism and missionary zeal which led him frankly to confront the obvious lag of Soviet science and technology in many areas and to encourage an opening of Soviet society to selective borrowing from the West. He obviously relished the prospect of international competition with the West for the proverbial 'hearts and minds' of the uncommitted peoples of the world, banking on what he considered the greater potential social and economic attractiveness of socialism.

Yet at the same time he was orthodox enough in his Marxism-Leninism to reject the consumerist corollaries of Western technological influence for his own society; and despite his commitment to material incentives, he actively sought to counter certain individualistic tendencies arising from conventional Soviet practices. Thus, for example, he stubbornly resisted pressures for an expansion of private automobile production and ownership. And in the latter half of his term of office he tried to encourage peasants to give up their private household plots, even though the consequences were bound to be disastrous for food supplies.(4) There were economic reasons for these policies, no doubt, but ideological considerations were obviously also very important.

Another striking characteristic of Khrushchev's idiosyncratic style was his tendency to involve himself in concrete details of production and management. Khrushchev fancied himself as an agricultural expert and did not hesitate to impose his views on agronomists and agricultural officials, for example on the 'square-nest' method of potato planting(5) and the universal cultivation of corn (hence his sobriquet 'Nikita kukuruznik' - 'Nikita the corn ball'). He was somewhat less inclined to interfere directly in scientific and industrial matters, but there, too, once he had listened to a particular groups of specialists who told him what he wanted to hear, he showed little reluctance to champion a particular technical position and brush aside the cautionary recommendations of responsible officials and opposing experts. Had he been successful, this tendency would have reinforced his popularity. The ultimate failure of many of his policies eventually made him an object of popular ridicule.

Underlying this tendency to meddle in concrete matters was a crude, if complex, type of anti-intellectualism which took the form of depreciating the importance of theoretical expertise divorced from direct production activity.(6) This prejudice was especially noticeable in areas where Khrushchev considered himself something of an expert - agriculture, for example. It was evident in his insistence on transferring specialists and administrators from central ministries and research organisations directly into the field and in his demand that agricultural research institutes carry on regular farming operations to 'show their worth'. Similar motives can probably be adduced for his policy of dispersing high-level ministerial officials to the provinces to staff the new sovnarkhozy in connection with the industrial reorganisation and de-centralisation of 1957. Also worth noting in this regard perhaps was his express favoritism for academicians like I.V. Kurchatov, the nuclear physicist, who were willing to lend their talents to concrete military applications, as against those like P.L. Kapitsa and, later, A.D. Sakharov, who were not.(7)

Despite his sporadic excursions into Marxist fundamentalism Khrushchev brought about a significant opening up of Soviet society to external ideas, particularly in the areas of technology and management techniques. Similarly, his rule witnessed the development of a measure of sensitivity to international public opinion and the external image of the Soviet Union. This sensitivity applied not only to manifestations of the cultural, social, and political legacy of Stalinism, but to economic 'survivals' as well. Khrushchev was particularly sensitive to the low level of 'culture' of Soviet management practices and the quality and finish of Soviet products, especially after his travels in the West. Not only was the Soviet bureaucracy manifestly cumbersome and 'nekul'turnaia', he concluded, but it wasn't even effective! In Khrushchev's eyes, these failings were giving the noble ideas of socialism and the reputation of the USSR a bad image.

One way of acting upon such a diagnosis might have been to adopt an incremental strategy by seeking the refinement and improvement of specific elements of the existing administrative machine. This is essentially the mode of administrative change developed under Brezhnev. The other way, the Khrushchevist mode, required the fundamental restructuring of entire industrial sectors. Viewed in this light, the two alternative modes suggest the dichotomy between 'mechanistic' and 'organic' models of administration elaborated by Burns and Stalker in their analysis of the innovative capacity of British research and development institutions.(8) Khrushchev seemed intuitively to have grasped what Burns and Stalker discovered: namely, that the more fluid, horizontally biassed organic system of organisation is more conducive to innovative behaviour and the exercise of initiative by individual administrators and specialists than is the structurally neater, hierarchically more coherent mechanistic model.

To be sure, the corespondence is far from perfect. A British R&D organisation is hardly a precise analog for the Soviet economy or even its individual sectors, such as heavy industry or agriculture. Nevertheless, some of the general propositions derived from the Burns and Stalker model do appear relevant to our quest for the essence of Khrushchevism, especially if certain analogies are assumed. In the conventional Soviet administrative paradigm there is a formal division of labour between the state administrative bureaucracy and the hierarchy of professional party officials, in which the latter are nominally charged with exercising political guidance and coordination of the activities of the former within a given territory or sphere. In actual practice the party officials in question are expected to intervene more or less directly in the conduct of administration to guarantee the attainment of specific policy objectives. This may be done by the application of political pressure on management, by circumventing formal supply channels to obtain deficit production inputs or labour supplies in emergency situations, and by close monitoring of the performance of responsible state officials and managers.(9) Under Stalin the role of the party had been gradually reduced to a largely auxiliary one, particularly in industrial management, where the primary chain of responsibility and managerial authority had accrued to the ministerial bureaucratic command structure, which was directly subordinated to Stalin's personal <u>apparat</u>. The security police apparatus was an especially important part of Stalin's personal control system, providing political 'stiffening' to the policy implementation process through its unique type of supervision of responsible personnel. This ministry-centred hierarchy of administration could be viewed as essentially a mechanistic system in the Burns and Stalker framework. The routinising tendencies of such a system were reinforced under Stalin by the fear of unnecessary risk and exposure imparted to administrators by the practices of party and secret police supervision. Routine and mutual cover-ups offered a degree of security. Innovation and risky personal initiative meant insecurity and possible disaster.

This was precisely the behavioural nexus that Khrushchev was determined to smash. But his preferred techniques for doing so involved a curiously anachronistic form of the 'organic' model. Essentially they consisted in elevating the role of the party by making party officials directly responsible for substantive production performance, especially at the intermediate levels of the system. In industry this meant primarily the provincial (or republican) level; in agriculture, the district (<u>raion</u>). This party-centred approach to administration was a direct throw-back to the early days of the industrialisation drive and forced collectivisation, when party 'plenipotentiaries' were sent out to the hinterlands to take charge of important industrial projects and organise the new collective farms and machine-tractor stations (MTS). Then, iron will and general organisational talent were viewed as counting for more than technical expertise. The available experts were often non-party people of allegedly dubious loyalty to the Soviet regime.

Khrushchevism meant a return to this earlier pattern of administration, despite the fact that by the time Khrushchev had come to power the overwhelming majority of administrators and managers were already both 'red' and 'expert'. (Party officials were also likely to have had a substantial degree of specialised training and experience, although generally not on a par with that of the professional specialists and administrators.) His focus on the party as the core of his administrative model reflected a combination of factors: among them an ideological belief in the party as the uniquely appropriate institution to manage the building of communism; a substantive judgment that it was relatively untainted, as an organisation, by the 'bureaupathic'(10) behavioural immobilisme and structural and procedural rigidity of the state administrative machine; and a cool political calculation that the party could be effectively refurbished as a personal power base for the protracted struggle with his ministerially-based rivals in the political leadership. Events were to prove him right, at least on the last point. His ultimate downfall, however, can largely be traced to his underestimation of the extent of 'bureaupathology' in the party machine itself and his consequent failure to make sure that the 'boys' were still 'on side' when difficulties arose in the early sixties.

To summarise, then, Khrushchevism in economic policy was characterised by an openness to experiment with both foreign and unconventional domestic techniques for the accelerated modernisation of the Soviet economy. At the same time, this eclecticism was persistently informed by a strong commitment to collectivist socialist values. In the area of economic administration it was distinguished by the concentration of a degree of power and responsibility in the hands of specific individuals unusual in Soviet practice, at least since the early thirties. The communist party apparatus was Khrushchev's preferred vehicle for the exercise of this enhanced personal responsibility and power. The essence of Khrushchev's administrative style was movement. If a given policy or structural pattern proved ineffective in achieving his declared objectives, his reaction was to reorganise swiftly and attack the problem from another angle. Increasingly, as his reign drew to a close and resources for his grandiose objectives became overcommitted and hence scarce, reorganisations became a surrogate for hard policy choice. He began to operate in the manner of a financial manipulator desperately trying to stave off bankruptcy.

His failure demonstrated that organisational reform, while important, has its limitations as an administrative technique. It is a valuable means of optimising the utilization of available resources, but it is not a substitute for resources themselves. His failure also demonstrated the importance of the human factor in administrative reorganisation - that the capacity of bureaucrats to adapt to change is not infinite, even in so highly disciplined an organisation as the communist party apparatus.

From this introductory overview of Khrushchevism it is clear that at least along the economic-administrative dimension the Khrushchev era was so greatly influenced by the idiosyncratic elements of Nikita Sergeevich's personality that

it is difficult to conceive of Khrushchevism as a more general
leadership phenomenon of Soviet-type systems. Difficult, but
not impossible. For certain positive characteristics
enumerated above - e.g., lateral thinking, openness to
experimentation in keeping with an organic structural
preference, and, perhaps, intelligent enthusiasm - could well
serve as a periodic functional alternative to the prevailing
mechanistic system at certain stages of Soviet development.

Before considering this possibility further we shall now
turn to an analysis of certain key examples of Khrushchevism
in action in the period of its original incarnation.

KHRUSHCHEV'S AGRICULTURAL POLICIES

Khrushchev's talent for lateral thinking and bold innovation
was already evident well before he became a principal
contender for power in the post-Stalin leadership. Summoned
to Moscow in late 1949 by Stalin to become the Politburo's
chief agricultural spokesman, he immediately undertook a major
reorganisation of the morbid kolkhoz system through the
amalgamation of small kolkhozy. Within one short year the
number of kolkhozy in the USSR was reduced through these
mergers by more than half, from 254,000 to 121,000.(11)
Naturally, this policy had had to obtain Stalin's personal
endorsement and was, thus, not entirely Khrushchev's own
initiative. Nevertheless, it bore the clear stamp of his
personal approach to agriculture and illustrated two of the
three fundamental pillars of his strategy: administrative
rationalisation and improved technical competence (the third
pillar being material incentives to stimulate individual and
collective performance). The purpose of the amalgamation
campaign was to facilitate central management of the small,
scattered production units and to maximise the effectiveness
of the specialised personnel and farm equipment resources
inadequately supplied to agriculture. It also helped to
strengthen party control in the village by concentrating the
efforts of the sparse party forces in the rural areas on a
smaller number of producing units.

In the course of the amalgamation campaign Khrushchev
also introduced his bold 'agro-city' (<u>agrogorod</u>) idea, a
grandiose program for resettlement of peasants from their
traditional small villages into large urban-type settlements
with a full range of modern commercial, service, and cultural
facilities. The scheme offered some interesting insights into
Khrushchev's thinking on the future of Soviet agriculture and
the ideological conceptions behind it. It also foreshadowed
the financial and technical recklessness of many of his later
policy initiatives. The express goal of the idea was to bring

closer the Marxian utopia of eliminating the difference between urban and rural life and labour. But the sheer magnitude of the project and its timing - 1950/51 - made it financially impractical, especially given Stalin's well-known preference for exploiting agriculture to finance industrial development. And it made Khrushchev vulnerable to attack by Malenkov, his main rival for Stalin's favour, at the Nineteenth Party Congress in 1952, when he was forced to beat a hasty retreat and confess that the idea had been a serious mistake.(12) His boldness had evidently earned him Stalin's wrath.

Fortunately for Khrushchev, Stalin died before irreparable damage had been done to his career. From then on he would be able to push his pet ideas more or less independently, as at least a ranking member of the leadership collective and ultimately as virtual dictator of Soviet agricultural policy. His reign as agricultural tsar began at the September (1953) Plenum of the party Central Committee, where he was formally designated as First Secretary of the CC, CPSU. In his Report to the Plenum he set forth what was to be the basic structural and attitudinal framework of Khrushchevism in agriculture. One of the most radical departures was his emphasis on material incentives, both to individual kolkhoz members and to the kolkhozy, as a principal means of raising agricultural output. The strategy was two-fold: to raise the below-cost producer prices to the kolkhozy for their obligatory deliveries to the State; and to reduce the volume of obligatory deliveries of livestock products from the peasants' private plots.(13)

Although the actual producer price increases were at first relatively modest, they were soon to become substantial; the change in policy from that of the Stalin era was striking. Khrushchev clearly regarded the policy as a major change and sought to justify it as a return to Leninist principles:

> Among the causes of shortcomings in agricultural leadership is first of all the violation in a number of agricultural branches of the principle of material incentive. The principle of material interest of the enterprise and each worker in particular in the results of work is one of the basic principles of socialist management. V.I. Lenin pointed out that a long period of years is needed for the transition to communism and in that period of transition the economy must be built 'not on enthusiasm directly, but with the aid of enthusiasm born of the great revolution, on personal interest, on personal incentive, on economic accounting'.(14)

This stress on material incentive through increased producer prices and a clearer relationship between payment and actual work done by the individual and the collective was a continuing feature of Khrushchevism and was especially prominent in the first half of Khrushchev's reign. During the second half, notably after the excellent harvest of 1958, when Khrushchev began to divert funds once again away from agriculture, support for the principle became more rhetorical than substantive, with greater emphasis on 'social consumption funds', rather than individual rewards, and on increased production of goods to absorb the enhanced purchasing power of the populace. There was obviously an element of ideological re-thinking of the implications of the earlier stress on individual reward in this change of emphasis, perhaps partly in response to Chinese criticism. In his concluding speech to the December (1963) Plenum of the Central Committee devoted to the rapid expansion of the chemical industry Khrushchev declared:

> What is essential is the correct combination of the two paths of material reward to people for their labour. Together with the regulation of individual pay for labour ... the role and significance of social funds, which even now plays a huge part in our country, also increases.

> But of course for the growth of individual pay and social funds one must work. Everyone understands this. We can't create illusions - once, say, good resolutions have been passed at a Plenum, everything will fall like manna from heaven. No, one has to work hard for the creation of material goods.(15)

The message was clear, and it was one which the Chinese comrades might well have understood - had they still been inclined to listen. The early reliance on material incentives and a high level of state investment in direct consumer welfare, urban and rural alike, had been effective; but it had created expectations which Khrushchev, with his multifarious schemes for development, had neither the patience nor the political and economic resources to satisfy. In any case, material incentives were far from the only arrow in his quiver.

The Virgin Lands program was one of the most radical of his alternative schemes for the rapid solution of the grain problem. Despairing of a quick increase in production from the traditional grain regions because of the long lead time that would be required to develop the necessary chemical fertilizer capacity and complete the projected land improvement programs, Khrushchev began in 1953 to encourage discussion of a major expansion of the sown area under grain in virgin and abandoned lands in Kazakhstan, Western Siberia, the Urals, and other sparsely populated regions. This idea was not entirely new. It had been tried in some of these areas with disappointing results during the critical 1928-1932 period and again, during the war, to provide a rapid supplement to the grain supply from land not already under cultivation.(16) Khrushchev's motivation in 1954, when he first publicly broached the subject, was similar. Originally he had envisaged it as a stop-gap measure until the increased yields from projects in the traditional areas could be brought on stream. But gradually, as he became politically identified with the success of the scheme, it took on a degree of permanency which allowed it to survive his own term of office. The main reason, of course, was its overall success; and it proved to be one of the few really durable agricultural achievements of his reign.

From the beginning Khrushchev ran into considerable opposition to the scheme from his Presidium rivals. Malenkov, Molotov, and Kaganovich consisently ridiculed it as an economically and financially unsound 'adventure'.(17) And indeed the first two years of its operation, when almost two-thirds of the eventual total during his reign of 41 million hectares of land had already been plowed up, were a decided disappointment. Then, in 1956, when Khrushchev was especially vulnerable because of the turmoil in Eastern Europe set off by his de-Stalinisation campaign, nature smiled upon him. Over 63 million tonnes of grain were produced in the Virgin Lands, approximately half the total grain production in the USSR that year, when the Ukraine and other traditional grain regions had suffered a severe drought.(18)

But the program had been extremely costly. Almost the entire addition to the national pool of tractors and combines produced between 1954 and 1958 was absorbed by the new farms (mainly sovkhozy) being established in the Virgin Lands - equipment that was desperately needed in the older regions. And the recruitment, transportation, and accommodation of the huge labour force required to farm the new lands were also a serious drain on agricultural funds. Nevertheless, Khrushchev would claim after 1956 that the grain produced in the Virgin Lands was significantly cheaper than grain from the older regions and that the State had made a handsome profit on the venture.(19)

Whether these claims were true or not, the Virgin Lands program had a revolutionising impact on Soviet agriculture, an impact which Khrushchev used to both positive and negative effect. On the positive side it made possible the diversion of considerable acreage in the traditional farming areas from less productive grain crops to more productive technical crops and livestock. It is worth noting in this connection that in his circular to the Central Committee in January 1954, when he first formally proposed the Virgin Lands scheme to his colleagues, he explicitly cited US and Canadian experience with corn growing as the key to high agricultural productivity.(20) Evidently the idea of regional crop specialisation was already in the back of his mind at the onset of the project.

The decision to concentrate on sovkhozy in the new lands and the apparently positive experience with this form of organisation convinced Khrushchev of the labour-saving and managerial advantages of the more heavily mechanised sovkhozy. In a sense, this was something of an ideological turning point for him, and it undoubtedly paved the way for his subsequent decision to sell off the MTS. The resulting mechanised kolkhozy could ultimately be converted to sovkhozy when the circumstances permitted. In the Soviet rural social context it could perhaps be argued that this, too, was basically a positive consequence of the Virgin Lands program.

More clearly on the negative side was Khrushchev's tendency to draw from the sporadic successes of the program certain dubious conclusions which reinforced his over-confidence and his propensity for unnecessary risk-taking. Thus, he interpreted the excellent results of the 1956 and 1958 harvests in the Virgin Lands as a stable, long-term achievement; as if, that is, the grain problem was effectively solved. He took obvious pleasure in twitting his opponents for their earlier skepticism when he boasted of the profitability of the scheme.(21) But his victory celebrations were, alas, premature. The large-scale shift of the traditional grain regions to corn and other crops associated with his grandiose livestock plans for overtaking the US in per capita meat, milk, and butter production by the early 1960s put unbearable pressure on the Virgin Lands (and on Khrushchev himself) to maintain grain supplies when the weather turned bad. This pressure led him to force the adoption of continuous-cropping and fallow-planting practices which quickly depleted the thin fertility reserves of the soil and led to massive problems of soil erosion and weed infestation. The disastrous harvest of 1963, especially in the Virgin Lands, compelled Khrushchev to import huge quantitites of grain from the West and accelerated his loss of prestige and popularity in the country. It was this failure which gave rise to deprecatory anecdotes about his agricultural wizardry.

'In what way is Khrushchev one of the greatest magicians in history'?'

'He can plant grain in Kazakhstan and harvest it in the USA and Canada.'

The liquidation of the MTS was undoubtedly one of the most revolutionary and far-reaching of his attempts at administration by reorganisation. In fact, his handling of the MTS illustrated the whole range of Khrushchev's administrative strategies and style of leadership. Apparently having accepted Stalin's decisive ideological re-affirmation of the role of the MTS in 1952, Khrushchev began his agricultural offensive a year later by fundamentally strengthening the MTS as the key governmental instrument for the management of collective farm agriculture.

'The main and decisive role in the further upsurge of agriculture belongs to the machine-tractor stations', he declared at the September Plenum of the Central Committee in 1953.(22) And to reinforce this 'main and decisive role' the MTS were assigned almost total responsibility for the economic and political leadership of the kolkhozy. The raion units of the agricultural administrative system (the so-called raizos) were abolished, and most of their supervisory, planning and managerial tasks were transferred to the MTS. By the mid-fifties the stations were given responsibility for agricultural procurements as well.(23)

To help fulfill these new tasks Khrushchev saw to it that the MTS were given massive infusions of skilled managerial, technical, and operating personnel. Tens of thousands of agricultural specialists were transferred from the agricultural bureaucracy 'closer to production' in the MTS, whence they were to exercise direct supervision of production operations in the surrounding kolkhozy - a perfect illustration of applied Khrushchevism. Finally, a total of one and a quarter million machinery operators and drivers, most of whom had formerly been kolkhozniks, were placed on the permanent MTS payroll to give the stations closer control over their productive activity and, incidentally, making them fully fledged members of the working class and hence subject to the rules of Soviet labour discipline.(24)

This concentration of managerial functions in the MTS fully encompassed the local party organs as well, in accordance with Khrushchev's commitment to strengthening party involvement in economic matters. The rural raikoms were reorganised and in effect decentralised by the permanent stationing in each MTS of a raikom secretary with a staff of instructors to supervise political and economic activity in each kolkhoz of the MTS zone. These so-called zonal secretaries and instructors' groups epitomised the Khrushchevist principle of bringing party work directly to bear on production. And their experiences illustrated the difficulties associated with the attempt. Their importance in his thinking was evident in Khrushchev's words at a Plenum of the Ukrainian Central Committee in mid-February 1955, when problems of suitable staffing for these party organs had begun to appear serious.

> Many raikom secretaries need to improve their knowledge, and some should be replaced. Insufficiently strong people have been selected for the instructors' groups as well.

> We should not begrudge sending the most worthy and best people in our party for work as raikom secretaries and instructors in the MTS zonal groups and especially as kolkhoz chairmen. These are people on whom the success of the enterprise depends; they are our eyes, our hands, our brain. Through these people we should also solve the task of obtaining an abundance of agricultural products, of raising agriculture as a whole. Everything depends on these people. If they are weak, we are wasting our time...(25)

Thus the MTS had been made the centrepiece of Khrushchev's initial campaign to raise agricultural production. But this enormous accretion of political and economic power made the MTS extremely vulnerable to criticism on pragmatic grounds. Nikita Sergeevich expected results, and the MTS soon proved incapable of providing them to his satisfaction. Most of all, he found fault with their persistently high production and administrative costs. At the 20th Party Congress in 1956 he revealed a decision to transfer them gradually from the state budget to a self-financing basis.(26)

Actually, he had raised this crucial question earlier, at a conference of federal and republican agricultural officials in November 1955, when he had released a trial balloon with seeming diffidence and willingness to experiment:

> ...Shouldn't we now, under the new conditions, begin the transfer of the MTS to cost accounting? I think that now, when our cadres have developed and the kolkhozy have grown strong, perhaps we ought to go that route, since the maintenance of the MTS on the state budget is not justifying itself. However we have tried to influence the MTS director, whatever we've said to him, we are not always able to reach him. Let's try material influence. Let's see what happens with this. It seems to me that material

influence is more effective. It will make the
director approach the organisation of MTS work in a
businesslike way. If his plan is incorrectly
formulated or it isn't fulfilled, then the MTS won't
make ends meet and the director will fall flat on
his face.(27)

In the event, Khrushchev evidently lacked either the
patience or the inclination to give the self-financing scheme
an adequate test. For in the meantime he had already begun to
reason that the kolkhozy, having benefitted from increased
producer prices and improved managerial and technical
leadership, were becoming strong enough to bail the State out
and take over the costly managerial and production services of
the MTS themselves.(28) At least that was Khrushchev's stated
opinion on the matter. The problem was to find a suitable
means for putting the question so as to overcome the
ideological barriers which Stalin had erected around the MTS
system and to disarm the bureaucratic and political forces
with a vested interest in its survival. The ideological side
of the problem probably involved a certain amount of
self-directed de-mystification for Khrushchev himself, for
there is no reason to believe that he was not genuinely
convinced that the 'main and decisive role' in the management
of kolkhoz agriculture must indeed belong to the MTS. The
conventional ideological image of the MTS-kolkhoz relationship
had depicted the kolkhoz as an inferior 'inconsistently
socialist enterprise', which required the state-owned,
'consistently socialist' MTS, with its monopoly of the main
mechanical means of agricultural production, to link it to the
overall socialist economic system. In essence, the kolkhoz
could not be trusted to own and operate these instruments of
production, in contrast to the consistently socialist sovkhoz,
for the kolkhoz was a cooperative based on group property
relations.(29)

Khrushchev's main tack in formally proposing the
liquidation of the MTS in February 1958 was to stress the
historical contingency of the above formulations. He now
argued that the growth of the kolkhozy and their 'indivisible
funds' in recent years had transformed them into what he
called 'developed socialist enterprises'.(30) Now, he argued,
there was little difference between the kolkhoz and the
sovkhoz as fully fledged socialist production units. Whatever
differences still existed could be eliminated by further
increasing the level of socialisation of kolkhoz property and
methods of work. The sale of MTS machinery to the kolkhozy
would facilitate this process. Khrushchev's subsequent
encouragement for the kolkhozniki to sell their private cows
to the kolkhozy and concentrate their efforts on the socialist
sector rather than on their private plots was a further

corollary of this formula and suggests that it was more than mere rationale for a pragmatic economic decision.

Perhaps the most striking thing about the decision to liquidate the MTS was the speed with which it was carried out. Despite Khrushchev's assurances that the process would be gradual, that poor or small kolkhozy could continue to rely on MTS services, and that at least one MTS would be retained in each district as a repair and technical service centre (RTS), by the end of 1958 only 345 of the almost 8000 MTS in the country at the end of 1957 were still in existence.(31) Indeed, within less than two years even the RTS had mostly disappeared, having been sold off to the kolkhozy or simply diverted to non-agricultural uses. This was another of Khrushchev's abrupt changes of heart.

How is one to explain this extraordinary haste in demolishing one of the main pillars of the Soviet agricultural system? Certainly Khrushchev's temperament played an important part. Having decided that the MTS were expendable, he saw them as an unnecessary burden, to be gotten rid of as quickly as possible. But there were deeper political reasons for haste as well. The opposition to the proposal was especially strong among the recently defeated, but still influential, conservatives of the 'anti-party group'. There was also evidently considerable resistance by officials in the agricultural bureaucracy who saw the MTS as an important instrument of control with a valuable resource of administrative posts. In order to prevent these two opposition streams from coalescing and using the issue to discredit Khrushchev at an opportune moment, while the bureaucracy used delaying tactics at the implementation stage, he decided to present them with a <u>fait accompli</u>. The fact that 1958 was such a good year in agriculture undoubtedly helped him and made his policies in general, and this one in particular, appear better than they actually turned out to be in the long run.

From the end of 1958 until his political demise Khrushchev's agricultural fortunes went steadily downhill. The method of disposition of the MTS was an important contributing factor. Part of his remaining period in office was occupied in trying to find some way to replace the functions of the MTS by the back door, as it were, and even more in trying to repair the financial damage to the kolkhozy caused by the hasty, enforced purchases of MTS equipment. Although the decision was probably correct in the long run for perhaps the majority of kolkhozy, the reckless way in which it was implemented nullified many, if not most, of its benefits. This was an all too characteristic feature of Khrushchev's record in economic policy.

Before turning to the last great reorganisation spasm of his career, chiefly concerned with agriculture, let us first consider briefly some of his experiences in industrial management.

KHRUSHCHEV'S INDUSTRIAL POLICIES

Although there were, of course, many common features in Khrushchev's approach to agriculture and industry, there were certain nuances of difference as well. · These can partly be attributed to his self-image as an agricultural expert, for whom the achievements of science bore no particular aura of mystery. They either contributed directly to the growth of production or they didn't. (His sponsorship of T.D. Lysenko's quackery suggests that this self-confidence in his own agricultural discrimination was hardly well placed.) He had an essentially similar attitude towards 'normal' industrial production as well, owing perhaps to his earlier experience as a worker and party industrial overseer. But in the areas of high technology and the natural sciences he was considerably more respectful of expertise.

This enthusiastic receptivity to scientific and technical innovation was, in fact, one of the more positive features of Khrushchevism. Khrushchev evidently relished being surrounded and pressured by the leading scientific talent of the country.(32) It is hardly accidental that the new 1961 Communist Party Program proposed by Khrushchev elevated science to the status of a 'direct productive force'; that is, part of the determinant economic base of the emergent communist social formation.(33) Nikita Sergeevich expressly contrasted his own openness to scientific and technological innovation to the conservatism and skepticism of his rivals.(34) And there is no reason to doubt that this was often the case.

Yet there was a darker side to his relationship with scientists. As noted earlier, Khrushchev had little tolerance for acknowledged scientific geniuses like P.L. Kapitsa and A.D. Sakharov, who refused to apply their talents to military and strategic uses, and he did not hesitate to impugn their motives and personal character for doing so.(35) As in all else, he viewed everything from the standpoint of utility for the building of communism, as he understood it. His personal opponents thus took on an 'anti-party' colouration in his eyes.

Thus, science, too, was expected to have a practical payoff, even if Khrushchev was willing to extend the time-frame for such a payoff for the more theoretical sciences. This pragmatic bias was evident in his much publicised and ill-conceived educational reforms of 1958. The basic thrust of the reforms - another major reorganisation of a traditional structure - was to give every secondary school pupil at least two years of practical training in an industrial skill even if that meant reducing the time available for theoretical training considered essential for tertiary education in science and engineering.(36) More important, in his view, than imparting manual skills and enlarging the pool of potential industrial labour was the objective of overcoming the scorn for manual labour by a growing stratum of Soviet youth. Like many of Khrushchev's ideologically inspired initiatives, this shift to a polytechnical educational system proved to be almost impossible to apply satisfactorily and it was eventually abandoned.

Nevertheless, despite his often misguided efforts, Khrushchev was clearly more conscious of the requirements of scientific and technological change for industrial progress than Stalin and his own conservative opponents showed themselves to be. He was particularly annoyed at resistance to innovation within the administrative bureaucracy, where the mechanistic structure itself seemed to breed psychological barriers to progress. His annoyance was particularly eloquently stated in his Central Committee Report to the 20th Party Congress:

> The Central Committee of the party has implemented important measures during the accounting period directed at the further improvement of industrial performance, first of all in the introduction of the latest achievements of science and technology into production. Why has the Central Committee concentrated the attention of the party and the people precisely on these questions?

> The fact is that the successes of our industry have turned the heads of some economic and party officials, engendered conceit and self-satisfaction in them, have led in a number of instances to an underestimation of the need for constant improvement of production, the introduction of the latest achievements of domestic and overseas science and technology. We still have quite a few such officials, 'men wrapped in cotton wool', who shun all that is new and progressive. This kind of callous official sits and thinks: 'Why should I get involved in this thing? A lot of trouble, and what's the use - it might make for unpleasantness. They talk about improvement of production! Is it

worth breaking your head over this! Let them think about it at the top, let the bosses think about it. When there's a directive - then we'll see'. And another, even after he has received a directive, devotes his energy mainly toward how to side-step or give only formal compliance to this vital matter.(37)

Khrushchev's approach to solving this problem of bureaucratic inertia was two-fold: first of all, to improve the efficiency and practical applicability of scientific and technical research work itself; and secondly, to smash the bureaucratic barriers to the rapid introduction of results of R&D work in industry. The opening salvo of the former campaign was his sponsorship of a party and governmental decree in May 1955, shortly after his victory over Malenkov, setting up a new State Committee - 'Gostekhnika' - to coordinate and oversee science policy, to encourage technical innovation, and to systematise the collation and dissemination of foreign and domestic technical information. Also under this decree each production ministry was to establish a high-level technical department to plan and introduce technological innovations. R&D establishments were specifically ordered to give up routine production-related activities in order to concentrate on innovative, 'state-of-the-art' projects.(38)

Dissatisfaction with the practical results of these arrangements, particularly the weaknesses of Gostekhnika, prompted Khrushchev to undertake a further reorganisation in 1961. This time the USSR Academy of Sciences was directly enlisted to assume important responsibilities for the identification and assignment of priorities to major areas of potential scientific and technical breakthrough. Gostekhnika was replaced by a more powerful operational body, the USSR State Committee for the Coordination of Scientific Research, which was charged with the planning and coordination of inter-departmental scientific and industrial R&D work, the supply of scientific equipment for priority projects, and the collation of foreign and domestic technical information. In this last function the Committee developed important links to the main civilian and military intelligence organisations.(39)

These were Khrushchev's main organisational changes in the field of science and technology. Except for a certain amount of structural tinkering in the last two years of his reign and later amendments by his successors, they have remained more or less intact to the present day. This continuity suggests that his initiatives were relatively successful and testifies to the unusual degree of circumspection and sobriety manifested by Nikita Sergeevich in this area. His initial impulses were good ones, and he obviously sought out good advice in the design and staffing of the agencies involved.

A less charitable judgment must unfortunately be made on the second part of his approach to fostering innovation, the industrial reorganisation of 1957. He had taken some preliminary steps toward the devolution of certain aspects of administration and finance of selected industries in 1954 and 1955, presumably with the full acquiescence of his Presidium colleagues. He gave further hints of what he had in mind in his Central Committee Report at the 20th Party Congress. We have already noted his strictures on bureaucratic inertia at that forum. But he also paid special attention to the question of regional economic development, especially with respect to energy and raw material sources in the eastern regions of the country.(40) And he devoted considerable time to his favorite theme of increasing the involvement of local party officials in production management in industry as well as agriculture, decrying the tendency to shun such direct involvement as a peculiar type of conceit:

> Unfortunately, even up to the present an absurd contrast between party-political and economic activity is permitted in many party organisations. One meets such, if you'll pardon the expression, party 'officials' who think that party work is one thing and economic and soviet work is quite another. One can even hear complaints from such 'officials' that they are being torn away from so-called 'pure party' work and made to study economics, technology, agronomy, to study production.

> Such a conception of the tasks of party work is fundamentally incorrect and harmful...

> That is why the party demands of party cadres that they not isolate party work from economics, that they direct the economy concretely, with a good knowledge of business.(41)

These three elements thus comprised the basic structural impulse behind the 1957 reorganisation: the destruction of the centralised industrial bureaucracy, a territorial focus for economic development and administration, and the elevation of the regional party apparatus to a key position in the industrial management system. The crucial political dimension of the reorganisation is treated in detail in T.H. Rigby's essay and will be mentioned here only in passing. Suffice it to note that Khrushchev regarded the reorganisation as an opportunity to destroy the political base of his main opponents, while the latter struggled mightily to block the entire scheme. Khrushchev gained powerful political support from the regional party secretaries, who were increasingly prominent as an organised factor in the Central Committee and who stood to gain so much from their enhanced status as territorial satraps under the reorganisation.

Nevertheless, it would be a mistake to interpret the decentralisation scheme solely in terms of the struggle for power. Khrushchev obviously placed great store in the expectation that new creative energies would be released by shattering the vertical management hierarchy and by applying direct party responsibility in the old Bolshevik manner.

The precise form of the reorganisation has been well described many times and requires only brief comment here. Some 140 central and republican ministries concerned with industrial production and construction were abolished and replaced by 105 regional economic councils (<u>sovnarkhozy</u>).   In most cases the territorial boundaries of the sovnarkhozy coincided with the existing provincial subdivisions (oblasts and krais, mainly);   in others, they encompassed the entire territory of the smaller republics. The sovnarkhozy thus came under the direct purview of the provincial and republican party first secretaries.(42) Personnel from the old ministries, including some of the ministers themselves, were sent out 'closer to production' to staff the new sovnarkhozy. The production enterprises of the former ministries, as well as a selected number under the jurisdiction of the few surviving central ministries (mainly defense-related) were transferred to the control of the respective sovnarkhozy on whose territory they were located.(43) Overall coordination of the sovnarkhozy was to reside in a strengthened USSR Gosplan and the USSR Council of Ministers, with a considerable share of secondary level coordination devolving upon the republican governments and gosplans.

The enterprises themselves gained virtually no additional autonomy from the reorganisation. In some ways the change from branch-ministerial to territorial overlords actually reduced their room for manoeuvre, and did so in a quite irrational manner. For, in place of the problem of 'departmental' barriers (<u>vedomstvennost'</u>) the 1957 arrangements quickly gave rise to the equally grave evil of 'localist' barriers ('<u>mestnichestvo</u>'). This problem might not have proven so serious had the Soviet economy already attained a sufficient level of development and had Khrushchev's demands for production performance been less insistent. As it was, the combination of regional underdevelopment and the heightened burden of personal responsibility on party and sovnarkhoz leaders made it inevitable that regional enterprises would be compelled to satisfy intra-regional requirements before fulfilling inter-regional obligations. The consequences for national economic coordination and development were disastrous.

Under different circumstances the arrangement would have been useful for the concentrated development of selected resource-rich areas, but as a universal scheme it was obviously deficient. The USSR Gosplan soon showed itself incapable of combatting the regional tendencies toward autarchy. Khrushchev's reaction was almost immediately to undertake the re-establishment of a more centralised command structure. The economic regions themselves were progressively amalgamated, and a number of USSR State Committees with operational powers rapidly proliferated to handle functions that were essentially the same as those of the former ministries. In short, the reorganisation had been a striking failure. Khrushchev never admitted as much publicly, but his subsequent reorganisational efforts were an eloquent enough confession of error. He undoubtedly lost much in overall authority from the exercise. Perhaps even more fatefully, he lost the confidence of his erstwhile supporters among the regional party secretaries, as the successive re-centralisatons reduced their status as local economic chieftains. Moreover, his thorough-going purge of their ranks during 1960 and 1961, ostensibly to weed out incompetents, demonstrated his unreliability as a patron. This virtual sacrifice of a vital support base reflected an amazing degree of political recklessness on Khrushchev's part. There were few among his erstwhile supporters who mourned his political passing in October 1964.

Nevertheless, it would be unfair to dismiss his industrial reorganisational efforts out of hand - as 'hare-brained schemes' - as Khrushchev's successors are wont to do. Given his strong commitment to reform and the modernisation of the Soviet economy and the nature of the structural and political opposition he faced, the 1957 reorganisation was really quite ingenious. It was premature at the existing level and areal distribution of development, but as a method of alleviating the central planning and administrative log-jam and stimulating local initiative it was not inherently irrational. Indeed, some of the most recent proposals for regional development - the so-called 'territorial-production complexes', with de-centralised Gosplan supervision - have adopted essentially the same approach.(44) The main fault was in the tempo and scope of the devolutionary program. Some of the dangers were easily foreseeable, but Khrushchev refused to consider them. His rambunctious temperament and his perception of the strengths and likely tactics of his opponents evidently prompted him, as in the case of the MTS liquidation and the corn-growing campaign, to conclude that he had no choice but to act summarily.

THE BIFURCATION OF PARTY LEADERSHIP, 1962-1964

The hiatus in party and governmental control over agriculture following the liquidation of the MTS was allowed to continue for more than two years. Khrushchev was adamant in his opposition to a return to the pre-1953 setup. Not only did he refuse to re-establish the raizos, but he even deprived the party raikoms of their separate agricultural departments. In place of the raizo he installed a corps of agricultural 'inspectors', attached directly to the raiispolkom (executive committee of the raion soviet) and funded by it. To emphasise the serious but strictly local responsibilities of these 'inspectorates', the chief inspector was made ex officio deputy chairman of the raiispolkom. The aim of the changes in the raikom was clearly to make the entire raikom apparatus, and not just its agricultural department, directly responsible for agriculture on a continuing basis.(45)

This arrangement illustrated Khrushchev's preference for organic structural patterns, with overlapping horizontal responsibilities and purposely vague lines of vertical authority. Under the conditions prevailing in the Soviet countryside in the post-MTS vacuum, it simply did not work. By early 1961 he was again under some pressure to restore the Ministry of Agriculture's chain of command, presumably by high-level persons supporting the Minister, V.V. Matskevich, with whom he had recently had a rather stormy relationship. Instead, Khrushchev staged a counter-coup of his own by summarily liquidating the USSR Ministry of Agriculture as an operational agency. Henceforth the central ministry became primarily a research and educational coordinating body, and most of its personnel were transferred to experimental stations and research institutions outside of Moscow.(46) At the same time the raion inspectorates were also abolished.

To replace the latter Khrushchev adopted a substantially new tack, using an idea he had been pushing for several years: namely, to involve the procurement organs more closely in production matters. A decree of 26 February 1961 accordingly established raion or inter-raion inspectorates for procurements, subordinated to the provincial procurement organs, with responsibilities for insuring that kolkhoz and sovkhoz production plans and operations corresponded to the output levels contracted for with the State.(47)

It soon turned out that this technique of relying on procurement agencies backed by the party raikom to direct agricultural production was lacking in punch. Nevertheless, its multi-functional essence was carried over to the next burst of reorganisation, carried out in two phases in 1962. The Khrushchevian syndrome of management by reorganisation was by this time reaching feverish intensity, as his lateral thinking became almost three-dimensional.

The heart of the first phase of the 1962 reorganisation, in March, was at the lowest level of administration, the raion. More precisely, it was now shifted to an inter-raion basis. The new 'Territorial Kolkhoz-Sovkhoz Production Administrations' (TPAs), each covering roughly 3.5 raions, were conceived as high-powered bodies of agricultural experts. Each 'inspector-organiser' within the TPA was assigned to a specific group of three to six farms (no distinction was made bewtween kolkhozy and sovkhozy), where he became responsible for the supervision of the full range of operational activities, from planning and bookkeeping to the application of modern agronomic and veterinary techniques. The chief of the TPA was formally subordinate on the vertical plane to a new hierarchy of combined production and procurement organs at the oblast and republican levels. A major feature of the reorganisation was its provision for party guidance. Each TPA contained a strong party committee, reminiscent of the old MTS politotdel, and headed by a 'Party Organiser' (on the nomenklatura of the obkom) who led a corps of 'inspector-party organisers' similarly assigned to oversee party work in a specific number of farms (usually five to seven). In essence, the TPA was, thus, an MTS without tractors: a production oriented administrative body with its own party supervisory component.

Inevitably such an organisation soon came into conflict with the raikom, especially on questions of jurisdiction over farm party organisations. In the second phase of the 1962 reorganisation, in November, Khrushchev cut the traditional structural Gordian Knot by simply abolishing the raikom! At this stage he introduced the most radical method of bringing party leadership 'closer to production' yet attempted by any Soviet leader before or since by splitting the party organisations at the regional level into functionally distinct and organisationally separate systems, one for agriculture and the other for industry. Residual functions, such as community services and transportation were to be divided up between them. The Medvedevs have described this radical bifurcation as essentially a 'two-party' system'.(48) And indeed, had Khrushchev remained in office and maintained this arrangement, two distinct party career channels would necessarily have developed. Presumably those relegated to the agricultural 'party' would have experienced considerable difficulties in eventually attaining general political leadership status.

The new setup clearly diminished the power and prestige of oblast party leadership. Jeremy Azrael has argued that this was Khrushchev's main intention - to undermine the position of the oblast secretaries upon whom he had become uncomfortably dependent for the maintenance of his power.(49) This was undoubtedly an important part of the story, at least as far as the ultimate effect was concerned. However, the interpretation of Zbigniew K. Brzezinski, that the reorganisation was designed primarily to guarantee the continuing relevance of Party leadership by strengthening its involvement in concrete production concerns seems to correspond somewhat better to our image of Khrushchev's style and administrative strategies.(50)

Whichever motivation predominated, it was clear that by the end of his reign the wily Soviet leader was acting out of desperation. Resources for his ambitious schemes in agriculture, industry, and defense were extremely tight, and he was frantically thrashing about in search of some quick and easy method of maximising the economic payoff from the limited funds available. For Khrushchev the characteristic answer was to reorganise. In fact, on the eve of his overthrow he was preparing yet another reorganisation of the agricultural administrative structure - this time, along crop specialty lines.(51)

KHRUSHCHEVISM IN RETROSPECT

A helpful starting point for evaluating the nature and consequences of Khrushchevism is to paraphrase the question which occasioned the great sovietological debate of a decade ago: 'Was Khrushchev really necessary?' The answer is perhaps no simpler than it was for the original variant involving Stalin. Different areas of policy will suggest different responses. Nevertheless, by making us consider possible alternative scenarios, the question does help us to focus more closely on what Khrushchevism was and what it accomplished.

Had Malenkov been able to maintain his position as <u>primus</u> in the collective of Stalin's heirs, the consumer goods orientation with which he was identified would necessarily have brought in its train a turn toward the nation's acute agricultural problems. Greater agricultural investment would undoubtedly have produced substantial growth, although probably at a somewhat slower pace than was attained by Khrushchev's radical policies. Indeed, it is arguable that slower agricultural growth, within the existing institutional and territorial framework, might have provided a surer basis for subsequent long-term development.

Furthermore, Malenkov's commitment to a relaxation of tensions with the West might well have produced a similar opening of the USSR to significant injections of Western scientific and technical innovation. However, the continued presence in the leadership collective of persons of Molotov's conservative ilk would certainly have attenuated moves in this direction. Similarly, the strict avoidance of an overt repudiation of Stalin by such a leadership would perhaps have postponed certain healthy movements toward greater autonomy in intra-Bloc relations - and made the rapprochement with Tito impossible. But it would most likely have delayed and moderated the abrupt and deep-seated conflict with Mao and hence decreased pressures on Moscow from that quarter, not least among them pressures to demonstrate the viability of new economic initiatives at home.

In short, a more balanced distribution between consumer goods and producer goods production and greater attention to agriculture would have occurred in any case, although at a considerably slower pace than under Khrushchev. Existing administrative structures and procedures would have been preserved, further dampening any impulses to radical change, as proved to be the case under Brezhnev. The question is whether such a pace and such institutional arrangements would have been sufficient to satisfy the rising expectations of the Soviet people, suddenly relieved of Stalin's looming presence to keep the lid on socio-economic pressures.

There is obviously little point in attempting to speculate much further on such matters. But from the scenario presented so far it is clear that the essence of Khrushchevism was leadership style and a high rate of change, rather than a different basic direction of change. For, as a neutral Soviet observer (if such could be found) would argue, the 'objective conditions' of the Soviet economy and society in 1953 indicated fairly clearly what needed to be done. Yet style and pace are obviously anything but secondary considerations. Khrushchevism represented a unique combination of utopianism in goals, radicalism in organisational strategies, and pragmatism in operational tactics. Its most striking characteristic was the second of these (although few of his colleagues possessed the other two in any marked degree either) - a kind of structural iconoclasm, informed by a belief in the salutary behavioural consequences of purposeful disruption and the substantive efficacy of proper organisation. Initially Khrushchev showed a definite preference for looser organic structural patterns with scope for the personal enthusiasm and meddlesome party guidance he favoured. Gradually this preference was modified by experience to give greater recognition to the need for specialised expertise and tighter central control. This change applied to party leadership as well as state administration. The creation of the TPAs and the bifurcation of the party into separate agricultural and industrial hierarchies was the culmination of this process of increasing specialisation and de facto re-centralisation.

The fact that Khrushchev pointedly included the party apparatus in this process of specialisation was particularly reckless politically. Ever since Lenin's day the party had prided itself on its generalist leadership competence - its mandate to give 'political guidance' to administrators and technical experts. Khrushchev evidently had little regard for this tradition and in fact saw it as a guarantee of the eventual obsolescence of the party in a modern economy. Perhaps he will be proven right in the long run. But the party apparatchiki themselves obviously did not think so at the time - or did not wish to consider the possibility. Nor did the failure of most of Khrushchev's policies using his more specialised approach provide much convincing evidence for his argument.

The judgment of the Medvedev brothers is perhaps a fitting epitaph for Khrushchev's organisational efforts:

> He did not succeed in making the Soviet variety of socialism 'free' in the sense of permitting the development of free economic initiatives, and his incessantly feverish reorganisation of persons, places, and things acted as a brake on national economic development rather than a stimulant.(52)

Yet Khrushchev was hardly a total failure. He opened up new possibilities for the Soviet economy by de-mystifying traditional structures and putting them to the test of practice. Unfortunately, at the same time he also demonstrated the limitations and perils of structural manipulation for the maintenance of central party control over society and the preservation of the leaders' credibility and authority. It is significant that in repudiating Khrushchev his successors did not return completely to the Stalinist institutional setup.

Radicalism of change in policy and structure is, potentially at least, a more enduring legacy of Khrushchevism as a method of political leadership in Soviet-type systems. It is conceivable that after prolonged periods of economic stagnation and moral decay, such as the present one, a new leader or leadership collective with a similarly iconoclastic attitude toward the traditional mechanistic patterns of policy-making and administration may arise. The experiences of Czechoslovakia in the spring of 1968 and Poland in 1980-81 illustrate different variants of this possibility. In the era of the 'scientific and technical revolution' such leaders will probably not exhibit the simplistic utopianism and overall panache of Nikita Sergeevich, but that would not necessarily be a bad thing.

NOTES

1. Roy Medvedev and Zhores A. Medvedev, Khrushchev: The Years in Power. Translated by Andrew R. Durkin. New York: Columbia University Press, 1976, p. ix.

2. J. Stalin, Economic Problems of Socialism in the USSR. Moscow: Foreign Languages Publishing House, 1952, pp. 93-94.

3. For a comprehensive sovietological treatment of Khrushchev's continuing struggle for power see Carl A. Linden, Khrushchev and the Soviet Leadership, 1957-1964. Baltimore: The Johns Hopkins Press, 1966.

4. See, for example, Khrushchev's account of his successful urging of the peasants in his home village of Kalinovka to sell off their private cows to the kolkhoz. In the same speech he predicts the disappearance of the private plot as a source of kolkhoz household income. The speech was delivered at the December (1958) Plenum of the CC, CPSU. N.S. Khrushchev, Stroitel'stvo kommunizma v SSSR i razvitie sel'skogo khoziaistva, Vol. 3. Moscow: Gos. izdat. polit. lit., 1962, pp. 404-405.

5. Khrushchev, speech at the September (1953) Plenum, in op. cit., Vol. 1, p. 36.

6. See, for example, Khrushchev's complaints about useless post-graduate theses, devoid of practical relevance, in Khrushchev, op.cit., Vol. 2, pp. 169-170.

7. Khrushchev Remembers: The Last Testament. Translated and edited by Strobe Talbott. Boston: Little, Brown and Company, 1974), Chapter 4.

8. Tom Burns and G.M. Stalker, The Management of Innovation. London: Tavistock Publications, 1959, esp. Chapter 6.

9. For a comprehensive account of party involvement in industrial management see Jerry F. Hough, The Soviet

Prefects: The Local Party Organs in Industrial Decision-making. Cambridge, Mass.: Harvard University Press, 1969), Chapters 9 and 10.

10. This term was coined by Victor A. Thompson in his excellent analysis of the psychological dimension of bureaucratic behaviour, *Modern Organization*. New York: Alfred A. Knopf, 1961.

11. Iu.V. Arutiunian and M.A. Vyltsan, *Istoricheskaia rol' MTS i ikh reorganizatsiia*. Moscow, 1958, p. 95.

12. Linden, op.cit., p. 25.

13. Khrushchev, op.cit., Vol. 1, pp. 23,31; and *KPSS v rezoliutsiiakh i resheniiakh s"ezdov, konferentsii, i plenumov TsK*. Moscow, 1954, Vol. III, pp. 616-624.

14. Khrushchev, op.cit., Vol. 1, p. 11.

15. Khrushchev, op.cit., Vol. 8, p. 363.

16. Frank A. Durgin, Jr., 'The Virgin Lands Programme 1954-1960', *Soviet Studies*, Vol. XIII, No. 3 (January 1962), pp. 255-256.

17. Khrushchev, op.cit., Vol. 3, p. 348.

18. Durgin, op.cit., p. 261.

19. Khrushchev, op.cit., Vol. 3, p. 419.

20. Khrushchev, op.cit., Vol. 1, pp. 99-100.

21. Khrushchev, op.cit., Vol. 3, p. 348.

22. Khrushchev, op.cit., Vol. 1, p. 51.

23. Robert F. Miller, *One Hundred Thousand Tractors: The MTS and the Development of Controls in Soviet Agriculture*. Cambridge, Mass.: Harvard University Press, 1970, p. 60.

24. Khrushchev, op.cit., Vol. 1, pp. 53, 229-230.

25. Khrushchev, op.cit., Vol. 2, p. 10.

26. ibid., p. 203.

27. ibid., p. 163.

28. A decree of the 6th of March 1956 gave the kolkhozy the right to amend their charters more easily. The tacit aim of this dispensation was to encourage them to increase their contributions to their so-called 'indivisible fund', thus expanding the supply of locally generated capital for investment in agriculture. Spravochnik partiinogo rabotnika, First edition. Moscow, 1957, pp. 158-159.

29. For a discussion of the ideological basis of the MTS system see Robert F. Miller, op.cit., Chapter 3.

30. Khrushchev, op.cit., Vol. 3, p. 63.

31. Miller, op.cit, p. 329.

32. Khrushchev Remembers: The Last Testament, esp. Chapters 3 and 4.

33. Jan F. Triska, ed., Soviet Communism: Programs and Rules. San Francisco: Chandler Publishing Company, 1962, p. 77.

34. Khrushchev Remembers: The Last Testament, p. 45.

35. ibid., pp. 64-65, where he dismisses Kapitsa's refusal as mere vanity and the product of an undue taste for publicity.

36. For an interesting analysis of the education reform debates see Joel J. Schwarz and William R. Keech, 'Group Influence on the Policy Process in the Soviet Union', American Political Science Review, Vol. LXIII, No. 3 (September 1968), pp. 840-851.

37. XX S"ezd Kommunisticheskoi partii Sovetskogo Soiuza, 14-25 fevralia 1956 goda: Stenograficheskii otchet. Moscow, 1956, Vol. I, pp. 45-46.

38. Decree of the CC CPSU and the Council of Ministers of the USSR of 28 May 1955, 'Ob uluchshenii dela izucheniia i vnedreniia v narodnoe khoziaistvo opyta i dostizhenii peredovoi otechestvennoi i zarubezhoi nauki i tekhniki', Direktivy KPSS i Sovetskogo pravitel'stva po khozias-tvennym voprosam. Moscow, 1958, Vol. 4, pp. 417-421.

39. John Barron, KGB: The Secret Work of Soviet Secret Agents. London: Hodder and Stoughton, 1974, p. 76. For organisation charts illustrating this relationship see Oleg Penkovsky, The Penkovsky Papers. Translated

by P. Deriabin. Garden City, N.Y. Doubleday, 1965, Appendix II.

40. XX S"ezd..., op.cit, Vol. I, pp. 52-53.

41. ibid., pp. 103-104.

42. Merle Fainsod, How Russia is Ruled. Revised edition enlarged. Cambridge, Mass.: Harvard University Press, 1963, p. 395.

43. Spravochnik partiinogo rabotnika, First edition, op.cit., pp. 227-233.

44. See, for example, Brezhnev's Central Committee Report to the 26th Congress of the CPSU, Izvestiia, 24 February 1981, p. 6.

45. Robert F. Miller, 'Continuity and Change in the Administration of Soviet Agriculture Since Stalin', in James R. Millar, ed., The Soviet Rural Community. Urbana, Ill.: University of Illinois Press, 1971, pp. 90-91.

46. Decree of the CC CPSU and the Council of Ministers of the USSR of 21 February 1961, 'O reorganizatsii Ministerstva sel'skogo khoziaistva SSSR', Spravochnik partiinogo rabotnika, Third edition, Moscow, 1961, pp. 342-352.

47. ibid., pp. 358-366.

48. Medvedev and Medvedev, op.cit., pp. 156-157.

49. Jeremy R. Azrael, Managerial Power and Soviet Politics. Cambridge, Mass.: Harvard University Press, 1966, pp. 145-147.

50. Zbigniew K. Brzezinski, 'The Soviet Political System: Transformation or Degeneration?', Problems of Communism, Vol. XV, No. 1 (January-February 1966), pp. 1-15.

51. Erich Strauss, Soviet Agriculture in Perspective: A Study of Its Successes and Failures. New York: Frederick A. Praeger Publishers, 1969, p. 221.

52. Medvedev and Medvedev, op.cit., p. 103.

PART II: KHRUSHCHEV IN THE 'SOCIALIST WORLD'

Chapter Five

KHRUSHCHEV AND MAO: A COMPARISON

Bill Brugger

Nikita Sergeevich Khrushchev strode brashly across the face of Soviet history engendering an odd mixture of hope, exasperation and ridicule. To some he appeared as a man of vision whilst to others he was the author of 'hare-brained schemes'. To some he was an intensely practical man whilst to others he seemed willing only to listen to information which confirmed his own prejudices. To some his genius for 'lateral thinking' revealed the mind of a creative dialectician whilst to others he was theoretically unsophisticated. To some he was a man attuned to the demands of modernisation who correctly realised that science was a 'productive force' in its own right whilst to others his faith in science prevented an adequate understanding of the social determination of technological choice. To some he was the promoter of a new and exciting approach to long-term planning whilst others felt that he all too readily mistook a single good harvest as the indicator of a fundamentally new trend.

    Much of the above has also been said about the man who was to become his arch rival - Mao Zedong. Biographers of Mao have found it just as difficult to make the real man stand up as have biographers of Khrushchev. This is because we are never sure of the extent to which the picture of the two leaders has been filtered by officialdom. But even when we know this not to have been the case, can we ever be sure when a loss of temper was a deliberate ploy or a lack of self control, when a personal initiative was the result of a committee decision, when considerations of power dictated policy or vice versa? Both men were 'natural Leninists' in the sense that they understood the value of organisation and discipline, but both understood even better than Lenin the dangers of bureaucratic routinisation. Both also were Marxist-Leninists, anxious to avoid the label of 'revisionist', yet recognising the need for the creative development of Marxist theory and never quite sure of the permissible limits. Both men were committed to much greater freedom than had existed under the Stalinist system but were shocked at the consequences of that greater freedom. Khrushchev, who encouraged criticism and deprecated the Stalinist terror, occasionally felt the urge to shoot artists and writers(1) though fortunately he stopped short of that course of action. Similarly Mao, the author of the policy to 'let a hundred flowers bloom and a hundred schools of thought

contend', was also convinced of the need to root out
'poisonous weeds'.(2) Both men felt the need for firm
leadership of the 'socialist camp', and each rejected the
other's claim to provide it. Both also saw the need for
socialist influence in the third world, and each felt the
other had distorted that influence. It may be, therefore,
that the personal enmity between the two men which grew out of
initial warmth was exacerbated by a similarity of temperament.
But it may also be the case that both Khrushchev and Mao,
having inherited similar things from Stalin and having to face
similar problems which resulted from the Stalinist system, saw
in each other the consequences of inadequate solutions. Their
division, moreover, may have been exacerbated by their
different 'national interests'.

LEADERSHIP STYLE

One thing that both Khrushchev and Mao inherited from Stalin
was a particular style of leadership. For Khrushchev the
development of this style was the sequel to his Stalinist
style of gaining power. In retrospect one can say that
Khrushchev showed remarkable skill in going against the tide
sufficiently to make his mark without incurring the
displeasure of Stalin and consequent elimination. But that
might be ex post facto rationalisation, since Khrushchev and
others might only have been saved by Stalin's timely death.
Whatever the truth about Khrushchev's tactics under Stalin,
there can be little doubt that Khrushchev was able to
eliminate opponents after March 1953 by Stalinist methods.
Malenkov was initially cut down to size by an appeal to more
Stalinist elements in the leadership. Then the Stalinist
'anti-Party' group was dealt with by an appeal to regional
interests. Khrushchev was as adept as Stalin in playing off
one faction against another. So indeed was Mao!

Mao's rise to power took place in a very different
environment. The exigencies of civil war involved methods
more ruthless even than those of Stalin. Nevertheless after a
bloody incident in 1930,(3) the inner-party struggles in China
were much less savage. By the end of the war with Japan Mao
was secure in his position of leadership, and it was not until
1953 that anything like a challenge occurred. The Gao Gang
case at that time is still too obscure for us to reach any
definitive conclusion as to what went on.(4) But what does
seem clear is that Liu Shaoqi rallied behind Mao, and in the
aftermath of the incident Lin Biao and Deng Xiaoping were
introduced into positions of considerable power. Lin was
later to replace Defence Minister Peng Dehuai who was branded
as a 'right opportunist' and was eventually in a position
almost to take over the 'revisionist' Liu Shaoqi's position as

state chairman. At that point Mao turned against Lin and propelled policies in a more conservative direction, which involved the rehabilitation of Deng Xiaoping who had fallen along with Liu Shaoqi. Then once again in the final years of his life, Mao sought out (or came under the influence of) people such as the 'Gang of Four' who wished to move against those who had benefitted by the conservative switch in the early 1970s.

The above 'Stalinist' features of Mao are, however, more in accord with the tactics of Khrushchev than those of the master. After 1930, Mao did not seek the physical elimination of opponents by the public security apparatus. This is not to deny that many of his opponents were persecuted by Red Guards during the Cultural Revolution (1966-69) though this, I doubt, was Mao's intention. Despite recent claims that Liu Shaoqi was hounded to death in 1969, we must note the circumstantial evidence that Mao might have protected Liu when Red Guards moved to storm Zhongnanhai in 1967.(5) Peng Dehuai, for his part, remained a nominal member of the Central Committee until the Cultural Revolution and, even then, survived to die a natural death in 1974. Gao Gang committed suicide, and Lin Biao died in a plane crash en route for the Soviet Union, and one may only speculate as to what their fates might have been at Mao's hands. Suffice it to note that Mao's official treatment of enemies was Khrushchevian rather than Stalinist, as Deng Xiaoping must note to his satisfaction.

A further similarity between Khrushchev and Mao is apparent in the way each leader mobilised supporters to push through policies and silence opponents. Unlike Stalin, both Khrushchev and Mao made use of full meetings of the party Central Committee when they did not have a majority in the Politburo/Praesidium. In China the Lushan Plenum in 1959, which ousted Peng Dehuai, and the Eleventh Plenum of the Eighth Central Committee in August 1966 stand out. The use of these plenary sessions was clearly not dictated by any considerations of correct procedure. They were sometimes 'enlarged' (stacked), and when a deadlock in the leadership offered no signs of immediate resolution, the Central Committee just did not meet (e.g. between 1962 and 1966). Under such circumstances, major issues of policy were discussed by central work conferences in which Mao's influence fluctuated.(6)

Khrushchev's ability to mobilise a wide audience behind his policies were a consequence of the 'something extra' in his style which Harry Rigby has noted.(7) That 'something extra' was two-edged. Khrushchev's common touch and down-to-earth folksiness could generate mass support but could also degenerate into what was seen as boorishness and crudity.

Such a folksy appeal was, it seems, open to Mao in the 1940s.
In Yan'an, Mao often presented a very earthy image.(8) The
unedited versions of his speeches from the 1950s, which came
to us via Red Guard sources, reveal a mixture of Marxist
theoretician, poet and student of literature, heavily
supplemented with an admixture of down to earth horse sense,
suitably laced with popular obscenities. Yet Mao did not
choose to capitalise on this characteristic. His officially
edited <u>Selected Works</u> read like the product of an editorial
committee. From the early 1950s he rarely addressed a mass
audience, and most Chinese had never heard a recording of his
voice. I remember in 1965 the gasps of a Chinese student
audience at hearing one of the few recordings of his voice
simply uttering a couple of sentences at the opening of the
Eighth Party Congress. Somehow ordinary Chinese people were
not prepared for the Chairman's rich local (Hunan) accent.
Throughout, Mao was portrayed as an Olympian figure, and his
appearances in the late 1950s doing manual labour and urging
people to use his favoured plough were never presented in
Khrushchevian style. Surely this was the product of a
propaganda apparatus which wished to capitalise on the Chinese
tradition of the leader, the Soviet equivalent of which had
long been dispensed with. It was not until 1981 that a mass
Chinese audience was greeted by a Chairman of the party making
an animated histrionic speech.(9)

KHRUSHCHEV AND MAO AS THEORISTS

Mao's Olympian style was reflected in the difference between
his cult and the cults of Stalin and Khrushchev. Stalin was
portrayed as the all-wise father figure who may have been
capricious and demonic but was <u>our</u> father, determined to
preserve our family at a time of crisis. This image was
reinforced by a nationalist appeal fostered carefully during
the Second World War and continued afterwards in the
Russification of newly acquired territories and Zhdanov's
attacks on 'rootless cosmopolitanism'. That nationalism could
be reconciled with Stalin's original theoretical innovation of
'socialism in one country', though one might argue that it
raised serious problems with regard to Stalin's claim to be
the heir of Lenin. Stalin could obscure much theoretical
inconsistency precisely because of that nationalist appeal and
the constant invocation of external threat. By recourse to
that external threat he could get away with the nonsensical
contradiction between his justification of the 1936
Constitution (which prefigured Khrushchev's 'state and party
of the whole people') and the call for continued vanguard
leadership. By invoking the idea of foreign subversion he
could gloss over the contradiction between his theoretical
liquidation of the proletariat in 1936 and the affirmation of

a coercive dictatorship in the name of the proletariat. So long as anti-Soviet forces were daily growing stronger it did not matter very much whether one could reconcile a remnant notion of class struggle with the doctrine of its intensification.(10)

But Khrushchev could not so easily get away with inconsistencies. This was not only because he was less secure and not only because his opportunistic style belied the cult image of the man who had charted the course of transition from socialism to communism. It was also surely because he found it difficult to appeal to nationalism and convincingly to invoke the idea of external threat. Though the Chinese were to find Khrushchev's 'proletarian internationalism' wanting, he was much more of a Marxist internationalist than Stalin ever was. He was clearly embarrassed by Stalin's concessions to nationalism during the 'great patriotic war' as is evidenced in his attempts to reverse the Stalinist policy on religion. If Khrushchev was a nationalist it could not have been in the sense of a 'Great Russian chauvinist'; indeed in Stalin's day he had been suspected by his colleagues of not pursuing the Russification of the Ukraine with sufficient conviction.(11) The idea of an external threat, moreover, could not convincingly be maintained so long as Khrushchev remained committed to 'peaceful co-existence' and 'peaceful competition' with the West. It might have been possible to explain the need for intervention in Hungary in terms of external subversion but the same argument was difficult to apply to Poland, much less the Soviet Union.

Without the theoretical smoke screen provided by the idea of an external threat, it became extremely difficult to gloss over the inconsistencies between what appear to be the two elements necessary for the legitimation of the leader of a communist party - the claim to theoretical innovation and the defence of orthodoxy (in this case Leninist party norms subverted by Stalin). It did not need a Chinese commentator to spell out the problems for Leninist theory posed by the idea of a 'party of the whole people'. Nor could anyone with the vaguest idea about Marxist theory have been content with the 1961 formula whereby, as a result of technological change, communism would arrive 'in one country' by 1980 with the state still in existence, having been 'perfected' rather than transcended' or 'abolished' and with the armed forces stronger than ever before.(12) One might indeed sympathise with Khrushchev's aim to promote voluntary organisations rather than those rigidly controlled by the state, but one cannot admire his theoretical crudity. His cult image as a Marxist theorist was unconvincing. And when Sir Alex Douglas Home proclaimed his preference for 'goulash communists' rather than the original 'lean and hungry' variety, the Soviet leader was open to ridicule.(13)

Mao Zedong's attempt to combine orthodoxy with innovation as a legitimising formula initially took the form of a desire to 'sinify Marxism'. In this process he could invoke nationalist symbols and project the Chinese Communist Party as the only effective force fighting China's equivalent of the 'great patriotic war'. Mao's efforts here took place within the united front formula laid down by the Comintern. Accordingly, the Chinese Communist Party supported a 'four class bloc' (workers, peasants, petty bourgeoisie and national capitalists) in the struggle against the 'comprador bourgeoisie'.(14) There was nothing particularly novel in Mao's formula for the 'new democratic' (a kind of bourgeois democratic) revolution, the roots of which could be traced back to Lenin's theses on the national and colonial question. What was new in Mao's approach was not so much the overall theory but specific policy prescriptions such as 'rectification', 'the mass line', 'cadre leadership' etc., which were more suited to a united front situtaion and a decentralised network of liberated areas than the Stalinist system of administration. Mao's claim to innovation at that time rested on his approach to party leadership of which Liu Shaoqi was also a pre-eminent exponent.(15) Eventually, however, Mao was to be become much more famous for his views on 'people's war' which in 1965 were to be elevated by Lin Biao into something like a world view ('the world's countryside surrounding the world's cities').(16) Within the theory of 'people's war' there was very clearly an emphasis on the progressive nature of nationalism in the third world, far greater than that of Lenin. It was Mao who was celebrated as the major exponent of the doctrine of rallying all forces which could be mobilised to oppose imperialism. By that time, Soviet commentators had reinterpreted the Yan'an tradition in terms of Mao's 'bourgeois chauvinism'.(17)

But did this nationalist appeal serve as a smokescreen to hide theoretical inconsistencies? I do not think so. Of course, there were to be inconsistencies in Mao's position, but they did not have much bearing on the nationalist appeal. In the late 1950s the formula of orthodoxy plus innovation took the form of a defence of some Stalinist norms whilst advancing the idea of the continuation of the class struggle under socialism. On the face of it, Mao's statements on class struggle looked very much like Stalin's ideas about the intensification of class struggle, and the party press was not slow to portray the similarity. In fact, Mao's ideas contained elements which were much more unorthodox and much more subversive. As early as 1957 Mao put forward his own version of the 'secret speech' entitled 'On the Correct

Handling of Contradictions Among the People'. Though very different from Khrushchev's speech in that it dealt with the structural generation of contradictions rather than the personality of the leader, it constituted much the same kind of bombshell as Khrushchev's effort one year before. It was read to select audiences and never published (nor, as far as we know, leaked to the West). Its unorthodox nature was soon to produce a reaction in the party, and an official and toned-down version was published to signal the end of the movement to 'let a hundred flowers bloom' which the first version had done so much to promote.(18) Yet the flavour of the original seems to have been retained in the argument that 'non-antagonistic contradictions', handled inappropriately, could become 'antagonistic'. This was a different formulation from that of Stalin in 1952, who was only prepared to see the exacerbation of social contradictions in terms of the ageing relations of production. Stalin's view was the product of a technologically determinist conception of socialism. This 'socialism', according to Stalin, had 'basically' been achieved in the Soviet Union in 1936(19), and from that position Khrushchev never deviated. Such also was the position which informed China's Eighth Party Congress in 1956 in which the major contradiction in society was described as that between 'the advanced socialist system' and the 'backward productive forces'.(20) By 1957, Mao was beginning to move away from that technological determinist view and was soon to revise the Eighth Congress Line(21) in a way in which Khrushchev, with his much greater confidence in the social neutrality of science and technology, could never do. Nevertheless, it was not clear in 1957 just how radical Mao's position would become, and it was possible to read the speech 'On the Correct Handling...', at least in its revised form, in terms of the orthodox remnant view of class struggle. This was probably how <u>Pravda</u> interpreted Mao's revised speech when it declared it to contain points of significance for Marxist-Leninist theory.(22)

Mao's backtracking on the position maintained in the original speech 'On the Correct Handling...' was reminiscent of Khrushchev's partial rehabilitation of Stalin under pressure from his more orthodox colleagues. The Soviet leader was, however, finally to legitimise the original position on Stalin at the Twenty Second Party Congress, when he made his bid for recognition as a theorist. At that time, when Khrushchev clearly revealed his technological determinist orientation, Mao was in eclipse after the Great Leap Forward. Nevertheless this period proved for Mao to be theoretically very productive, and he began to develop a very un-technological-determinist position.(23) This was more unorthodox even than Khrushchev's views on the transition to communism. Mao was toying with the idea that new classes might be generated in the course of socialist construction and that those classes would be represented in the vanguard party itself; no longer was class struggle seen merely as a remnant of the past or the result of external pressure.(24) Implicit in this view was a rejection of Stalin's 1936 portrayal of socialism as a _model_ which might be attained and consolidated. Socialism was now seen as a _process_ of transition which was reversible. Yet once again Mao's views on the continued existence of class struggle under socialism could be dressed up in Stalinist garb. To establish effectively his credentials as the developer of an innovative view of class struggle Mao would have had to criticise Stalin openly as he did privately. He was never willing to do this, not merely because of the Chinese commitment to Stalin's international role, but also because of the un-Leninist implications of Mao's generative view. Having accused Khrushchev of violating Leninism, Mao could hardly be seen doing the same thing. This in my view was a great pity. It resulted in the Cultural Revolution of 1966-69, exploding in all directions without any clear sense of purpose, and in a convincing reaction in the name of Leninist orthodoxy. By that time Khrushchev's 'phoney communism' was dead and buried, and the way was prepared in the Soviet Union for Brezhnev's claim to theoretical pre-eminence - the unedifying rationalisation of technocracy known as 'mature socialism'.(25)

ECONOMIC POLICY

Though Khrushchev and Mao were to arrive at very different formulations about socialist transition, they both saw the need to combine orthodoxy with personal innovation. In economic policy, where the views of an international audience seemed less important, they were both to be much less cautious. Yet despite their different views on technology their innovations were remarkably similar. After all, they had both inherited problems caused by the Stalinist system, and the range of options was limited. Of course, Khrushchev inherited much more than Mao. Stalinist forms of economic administration, though pioneered in North East China since 1948,(26) were only extended to the rest of the country in 1953, just in time for the death of Stalin to lead to their being questioned. Mao approached those problems with a certain degree of ignorance, whilst Khrushchev, the product of the Stalinist system, was surely more aware of the situation.

Perhaps the most important problem stemming from the Stalinist system was the neglect of agriculture. This called for much 'lateral thinking', and even whilst Stalin was alive, Khrushchev was able to bring about the rationalisation of _kolkhozy_ in the interest of better technical management.(27)

But there was much more to it than that. Khrushchev strove actively to close the gap between rural and urban standards of living. Mao's moves in this direction were not to occur until much later, since China's acceleration of collectivisation did not begin until mid-1955. Nevertheless, both men realised that the investment crisis produced by an excessive concentration on heavy industry required fundamental agricultural reorganisation. Thus, Mao was actively to promote the amalgamation of co-operatives not long after their formation and the eventual creation of communes in which the explicit goal was progressively to eliminate the 'three major differences' (between town and country, worker and peasant, mental and manual labour). Mao's aim was to get industry into the countryside and even to make the cities a little more like the rural areas.(28) Over a decade after Khrushchev's agrogorod proposals, Mao was to hail similar ideas under the rubric of learning from the Daqing Oilfield.(29)

Khrushchev's original agrogorod proposals were to be shelved at the Nineteenth Party Congress in 1952, when the initiative passed to Malenkov. After Stalin's death Malenkov proposed to give priority in reform not to agricultural reorganisation but to solving another legacy of Stalinism – the lack of consumer goods. For Khrushchev this was always secondary to the reform of agriculture, but it was an issue which he did address after the demotion of Malenkov. At the same time Mao Zedong began to tackle the same problem, though likewise it remained subordinate to agricultural reorganisation, and, as in the Soviet Union, the results were not spectacular.

Having been informed by official Chinese publications in recent years about the high accumulation targets during the Great Leap Forward (1957-60),(30) we now tend to forget that attempts were made in 1955 to improve the urban-rural terms of trade to allow peasants to buy more consumer items. This point was stressed by Mao in his famous 1956 speech 'On the Ten Major Relationships'.(31) The parallel with Khrushchev is quite striking and is not, in my view, mitigated by the subsequent Chinese attack on Khrushchev's policy of 'material incentives'.(32) Though no-one may doubt that moral incentives became much more important in China after 1957, the real switch in the mid-1950s was not so much from material to moral incentives but from the individual to the collective dimensions of both. Such a view is Khrushchevian rather than Stalinist and is revealed in Khrushchev's removal of the huge bonuses paid to industrial officials.

One might argue that it is not very fruitful to compare Soviet agriculture suffering from profound neglect twenty years after collectivisation and Chinese agriculture recovering from the devastation of war and just going through the process of collectivisation. Yet the same problem was foremost in both countries. Could agricultural production be increased to pay for increased industrial growth, and could the legitimacy of the regime be enhanced by greater supplies of food? In both countries the initial step was to bring virgin lands under cultivation, on the one hand in Kazakhstan and Western Siberia and on the other in Xinjiang and North East China. In both cases youth and technical personnel were transferred to work in state farms, and in both cases objections were subsequently raised. Recent Chinese press accounts of the 'dustbowl effect' and other ecological damage(33) are reminiscent of the attacks made upon Khrushchev, though China is still committed to enlarging the cultivated area. But despite the stress on reclaiming land, the fact that the total cultivated area in China shrank from 107 million hectares in the 1950s to some 100 million by the late 1970s(34) would suggest that the Chinese program of reclamation was much more modest than the Soviet.

Nevertheless, the key to raising food production lay ultimately in the achievement of higher productivity in existing cultivated areas. It was for this reason that Khrushchev continued to listen to Lysenko and became renowned for his promotion of maize. Mao was never to give overwhelming emphasis to a single crop, though he echoed Khrushchev in his personal endorsement of certain types of (often dubious) agricultural machinery.(35) In recent years Mao has (indirectly) been accused of insisting on local self-sufficiency in food staples before attention was given to industrial and other crops which might have been better suited to certain areas.(36) This was indeed one consequence of the Chinese stress on local self-reliance in the late 1950s, but one should note that at the height of Mao's influence on agriculture (1958) the area sown in food staples was actually reduced in the mistaken belief that the good harvest of that year revealed that the food problems had been solved once and for all.(37) Mao did not share Khrushchev's faith in an instant scientific breakthrough, but he was quite capable of responding in a Khrushchevian fashion to a good harvest.

Though Khrushchev differed from Mao in his enthusiasm for Western technology (despite Lysenko) and was not noted for any policy of combining the traditional and the modern ('walking on two legs'), he did share with Mao the belief that more innovations in agriculture would be forthcoming if agricultural research institutes were decentralised and located in the countryside. He believed also that machinery could be better utilised if <u>kolkhoz</u> members felt a sense of responsibility over its use. Considerations of this kind together with the high cost of machinery supplied by machine tractor stations led in 1958 to the amalgamation of those stations with the kolkhozy. This anticipated by a few months the Chinese program of rationalising the distribution of machinery within commune administration. Again the problems were similar. It proved very difficult for communes to raise the funds to purchase new equipment and to incorporate personnel who had been employed as regular blue collar workers (as opposed to collective or later commune members).

The above was but one manifestation of the problem of constructing communes simultaneously as organs of administration, agricultural and industrial production, education and defence. Within months the grandiose plans for the communes were scaled down, and Khrushchev became vocal in his opposition to them.(38) Yet for all that, they represented much that had been apparent in Khrushchev's own vision. Was his opposition directed to the premature nature of their formation, the extravagant claims about their being the 'sprouts of communism'(39) or the fact that they were simply Chinese? But one thing is sure, however premature they may be felt to have been, they were probably less premature than Khrushchev's own plans for agrogoroda in 1950.

Though I still maintain a certain enthusiasm for some of the developments during China's Great Leap Forward (precisely because of its promotion of what Burns and Stalker called 'organic solutions')(40) it cannot be denied that the years 1958-60 did see a collapse in China's industrial planning machinery. What happened in China, I suspect, confirmed the view of many of Khrushchev's critics that this might be the direction in which the Soviet Union was heading. After all both leaders had started with a similar view on the need for administrative decentralisation. In both the Soviet Union and China, the Stalinist system had clearly been over-centralised. Elongated chains of command prevented effective horizontal communication at an official level and had given rise to unofficial deals to ensure a minimum of efficiency. Blat networks operated in much the same way as quanxi connections, and the functional equivalent of the tolkachi(41) operated in certain Shanghai teashops.(42) In both countries the verticalisation of administration had resulted in party secretaries appearing more and more as simple 'staff' adjuncts to the line structure of state administration.(43) To be sure, the Chinese system was never as sclerotic as that of the Soviet Union, since it was much younger, less pervasive and staffed by people who remembered a very different system. Nevertheless, in both countries decentralisation was seen as imperative.

As both Khrushchev and Mao saw it, the model of decentralisation current in Yugoslavia was clearly not on the agenda, despite the rapprochement of 1955. The Yugoslav policy was to hand considerable decision making power down to the level of units of production in the state system. Such measures, it was felt, would result in a degree of market integration which might undermine the presumed socialist character of the regime. Despite subsequent Chinese accusations, Khrushchev was not a Libermanist any more than Mao was a follower of Xue Muqiao or Sun Yefang.(44) The 'Khrushchevist' reforms in a Libermanist direction were not to take place until 1965 when Khrushchev had departed from the scene, and at the time of writing are as defunct in the Soviet Union as they are flourishing in China.

The type of decentralisation favoured by both Khrushchev and Mao was the handing over of more power to local areas.(45) Pioneered by Khrushchev in 1955, the process was intensified in May 1957 and followed by Mao in November of that year. This decentralisation was predicated on a vastly enhanced role for local party committees in economic administration. It was the local party branch which was to provide the horizontal linkage so lacking in the Stalinist system. But was the party apparatus sufficiently competent to provide that linkage? Khrushchev evidently had doubts and supplemented local party leadership with various economic co-ordinating agencies. These, however, proved to be effective insofar as they were integrated into new vertical structures which operated in much the same way as the old Stalinist ministries. The problem was compounded by the fact that now that party control over economic administration was prescribed, the party structure began to separate along lines dictated by the structure of the economy. The eventual result was to be Khrushchev's proposal for the creation of separate industrial and agricultural wings of the party. Though I will not go so far as the Medvedev brothers in seeing this an an embryonic two party system,(46) it was clear that the vista of the party embodying different interests in its two wings was further than the Soviet leadership was prepared to go.

Mao, for his part, had greater confidence in the existing party apparatus to perform the necessary linkage role, though many party secretaries had to be removed in the process.(47) Fewer efforts were made in China to set up economic coordination agencies with the result that provincial party committees remained unchecked in their handling of economic problems and the transmission of data. The subsequent problems of 'localism', falsification of statistics and collapse of planning are too well known to warrant repetition here. But clearly, despite Mao's affirmation of 'creative imbalance',(48) this was far from his intentions.

There is still much debate on the various causes which brought China's Great Leap to an end. Though climatic conditions were paramount, there were many people both within China and without who laid the blame firmly on Mao's overall strategy. Although Khrushchev never endorsed any notion of 'creative imbalance', there is something of a Soviet parallel. The fiasco in Riazan oblast in 1960 in which animals were wantonly slaughtered to give the impression of a continued increase in meat supplies caused Khrushchev considerable embarrassment.(49) Similarly, the transformation of the Soviet Ministry of Agriculture into a research unit located in the countryside led to the resignation and disillusionment of ministry staff. The attempt, moreover, to integrate part of the education system with productive activity in agriculture and industry lowered the morale of many educators, and the Soviet equivalent of xiafang(50) was not greeted with universal enthusiasm. All the above could be endured until bad harvests (particularly in 1963) raised the question as to the relative contributions of climate and human error to the sad predicament.

But here the responses of Khrushchev and Mao differ. As the economic crisis in China deepened in 1960, Mao retired from the 'front line' of decision making and allowed a partial return to a more privatised market-oriented strategy.(51) Khrushchev on the other hand, faced with crisis, intensified his drive to reform the economy and party. In the process he antagonised the agricultural sector further by pressing for the reduction in the area of fallow land, demanding a reduction in the freedom granted to kolkhoz members to farm their private plots and keep animals and insisting on greatly increased fertiliser production at a time when transport and application facilities could not ensure its effective use. At the same time, Khrushchev antagonised the army by reducing military expenditure and the party apparat by the demand that one-third of all party committes retire at each election. Mao was in no position to do any of these things in the crisis of 1960-62, and he could only endorse the efforts of others to maintain a minimum level of production.

Khrushchev was finally brought down as he strove once again to promote a radical reorganisation of agriculture. At that time Mao could only call for the unfolding of a Socialist Education Movement to wipe out corruption in the countryside.(52) It was to be some time before Mao was in a position to unleash a movement which was aimed at reforming the party and removing from office those who had retreated too far from the ideals of the late 1950s. In the meantime Mao's focus of attention had shifted to overall strategy for socialist transition rather than the tactics of transforming agriculture and other sectors of the economy.

THE FOREIGN POLICY DISPUTE

Though there were marked similarities between the economic orientations of Khrushchev and Mao, one cannot deny that what increasingly divided the two men was their attitude towards the 'neutrality' of technology. In the early 1950s a large amount of technology was imported from the Soviet Union. This was at first welcomed by Mao, and the summit of Sino-Soviet cordiality was to be achieved in 1954 when Khrushchev visited China and promised even greater supplies in the future.(53) Initial criticisms of that policy focussed on the poor quality of the imported items, though by the late 1950s it became clear that the provision of complete plants was very difficult to reconcile with the policy of 'self reliant' development and the policy of 'walking on two legs'. Eventually some Chinese leaders (notably those subsequently known as the 'Gang of Four') came to oppose the indiscriminate importation of technology.(54) This time the main source was Western capitalist countries, and it was felt that complete plants embodied patterns of domination and subordination which reflected the relations of production in their place of origin. We cannot be sure as to Mao's precise attitude toward the large scale importation of complete plants from the West in the early 1970s, though, in the light of his earlier statements on 'self reliance' and his apparent endorsement of the 'Gang of Four's' attack on Deng Xiaoping in 1976, one doubts whether he would have disagreed with the 'Gang's diagnosis'. Much of the argument against Khrushchev's 'peaceful competition' with the West in which the rules of the game were felt to be set by a capitalist conception of technological progress would also support that conclusion.(55)

Similarly one of the major arguments against Khrushchev's conception of 'peaceful coexistence' with the United States rested on Khrushchev's view that nuclear weapons (technology) had changed the nature of imperialism. The United States could no longer afford to engage in major acts of aggression. Mao, in contrast, preferred the more orthodox Leninist focus on what was felt to be the inherent nature of capitalist monopolies to vie for power on the world stage. This lay at the heart of Mao's insistence on the inevitability of war. Khrushchev's response to that position was, of course, to see the Chinese attitude towards nuclear war as cavalier(56), though there was little evidence for such a claim. Despite Mao's view that the atom bomb was a 'paper tiger'(57), it is difficult to argue that the Chinese took nuclear weapons lightly. The internal military journals which became available in the West after their capture in Tibet reveals that the Chinese were fully aware of the devastating nature of nuclear war.(58) They were aware, too, of the value of a nuclear deterrent, and it is significant that the new stress on the value of Mao's doctrine of 'people's war' put forward by Lin Biao after his appointment as Minister of Defence in 1959 was accompanied by strong measures to develop nuclear weapons - the first test of which coincided with Khrushchev's political demise. Ironically it seems that the Chinese doctrine of military preparedness echoed that of Khrushchev in his earlier opposition to Marshal Zhukov's alleged stress on developing conventional military superiority.

Nor is there much evidence concerning Khrushchev's claim that the Chinese were military adventurists. The cases usually cited are the two Taiwan crises (1954 and 1958) which were unfinished business left over from the Chinese Civil War, and the war with India in 1962, as Neville Maxwell has so eloquently demonstrated was a response to an Indian 'forward policy'.(59) In the latter case the Chinese were incensed at the continued supply of Soviet arms to India during the fighting, which was most provocative. There was nothing in Chinese policy remotely comparable to the various Berlin crises or indeed the Cuban crisis which coincided with the Indian War. One remembers the Chinese criticism of Khrushchev for backing down under American threat but not the Chinese criticism of adventurism in the first place. Indeed it is probably fair to conclude that the Chinese attitude to world war was bold in words but cautious in actions. With Khrushchev a case could be made for the opposite, though no-one in retrospect could consider the attitudes of either leader as particularly bellicose.

What incensed Mao and the Chinese leadership above all was Khrushchev's practical diplomacy. His failure to consult the leaders of the 'socialist camp' on occasions such as Camp David and his crude attempts to bring members into line (particularly Albania and China) in the last few years of his rule contrasted markedly with the rather full consultation and negotiations which had attended the various crises in camp relations in the mid-1950s. After Khrushchev was confirmed in power, he apparently adopted a high-handed and hectoring tone which Mao never adopted. But then Mao never had a socialist camp to lead. One wonders, however, whether Mao objected to the high-handed actions in themselves or the fact that they were practised by a leader who had lost prestige.

Perhaps it is futile to compare Khrushchev and Mao in terms of foreign policy in that the former was determined to cut a figure in that field whilst the latter was not. Mao's contribution to the Sino-Soviet polemics of the early 1960s was at the level of theory and the diagnosis of 'revisionism'. That a 'revisionist' leadership should seek a reconciliation with the United States was fully explicable. That China should do so whilst Mao was still alive was less so. By then

it could be argued that the decline in United States power   in
Asia   in   the   wake   of Vietnam had made the Soviet Union (now
described   as   'hegemonist')   by   far   the   most   dangerous
adversary.(60) Recalling Mao's negotiations at Chongqing after
the war with Japan, China's leaders attempted to describe   the
change in policy in terms of driving a wedge between hegemonic
super-powers.(61) Yet even before Mao died, this took the form
of   supporting any group which opposed the Soviet Union in any
part of the globe (with a few exceptions such as   Timor),   and
the   recourse   was no longer to Marxist-Leninist theory but to
rather old fashioned 'balance of   power'   thinking.   How   Mao
contemplated   the switch from Marxist categories to discussion
in terms of global balance it is impossible to say.   Suffice
it   to   note   that   since   Yalta   the   Soviet   Union   had been
consistent   on   its   adherence   to   the   'balance   of   power'
paradigm, and from that position Khrushchev hardly budged.

The above would suggest that Mao   will   not   go   down   in
history   as   an   innovator   in   foreign   policy.   In official
Chinese publications, however,   he   has   been   hailed   as   the
originator   of   the 'theory of the three worlds'.(62) The idea
here is that somehow an undifferentiated third world is to   be
supported   in   the   desire   to   drive   a   wedge   between   the
super-powers.   This is not just 'balance   of   power'   thinking
but   bad   balance   of   power thinking which ignores the diverse
interests of the very different regimes   found   in   the   third
world.   It has been castigated as such by Albania, that rather
strange bastion of orthodoxy.   The Albanians have decided that
Mao   Zedong was never a Marxist-Leninist but just a 'bourgeois
nationalist' whom Enver Hoxha tried   to   point   in   the   right
direction(63) - a strange epitaph from what used to be China's
most consistent ally.   But how much of the rethink in   Chinese
foreign   policy was due to Mao?   Throughout his years in power
Khrushchev thundered across   the   world   stage,   and   one   had
little   doubt   about where he stood on most major issues.   But
for Mao in the 1970s we can only guess.

CONCLUSION

In the Eighteenth Brumaire of Louis Bonaparte, Marx   commented
on the fetters imposed by history.

Men make their own history, but they do not make   it
just   as   they   please;   they   do not make it under
circumstances   chosen   by   themselves,   but   under
circumstances   directly   encountered,   given   and
transmitted from the past.   The tradition of all the
dead   generations   weighs   like   a   nightmare on the
brain   of   the   living.   And   just   when   they   seem
engaged in revolutionising themselves and things, in

creating something that has never existed, precisely
in such period of revolutionary crisis they
anxiously conjure up the spirit of the past to their
service and borrow from them names, battle cries and
costumes in order to present the new scene in world
history in this time honoured disguise and borrowed
language.(64)

Commenting on the English bourgeois revolution, Marx noted
that it took quite a long time before Locke supplanted
Habbakuk and revolutionaries extricated themselves from the
Old Testament.(65) A similar situation has also been true of
much of recent Marxism-Leninism. In using the word
'revisionist', Mao evoked the image of Bernstein and Kautsky
with whom Khrushchev bore little resemblance. Khrushchev, for
his part, painted Mao as another Trotsky, which, in the
context of Mao's ideas about the progressive role of
nationalism, was even more ridiculous.(66) Conversely,
Khrushchev restored a Leninism which violated some of the key
elements of Lenin's position, and Mao produced a Stalinist
orthodoxy which was even less like the ideas of Stalin than
the position of Khrushchev. Both Khrushchev and Mao were
prisoners of the past; they both strove to become a Locke and
could not escape from Habbakuk.

The above problem stemmed from the tension in the
requirement that the leader of a communist party appear both
as defender of orthodoxy and as innovator. That tension
always makes their speeches difficult to read, and one has to
be a skilled practitioner in hermeneutics to sort out the
interrelated strands in their thought. The problem is
compounded also by the use of analogy which clouds any attempt
to relate discussions to specific social structure. This has
been a consistent feature of both the Chinese and the Marxist
traditions. Some people have traced the Marxist use of
analogy back to the very book of Marx from which the above
quote is taken. We cannot be sure as to the extent that
Marx's description of France in 1848-51 was really a comment
on Germany.(67) We can be sure, however, that some of the
Chinese discussion of Yugoslavia was a comment on the Soviet
Union. What was ignored were the fundamental differences
between the two countries and the different structural
configurations within which policies were formulated. It is
somewhat tragic that Mao, for all his emphasis on structure,
was to fall into the analogical trap. At a different level,
when one considers personal orientation, it is plainly
erroneous to see Khrushchev as an exponent of market
socialism. On the other side, the Soviet discussions of
Albania were often really meant to be discussions of
China,(68) yet again it is plainly wrong to see the Stalinist
rule of Enver Hoxha in the Chinese reality.

When we enter the world of Habbakuk and the arguments by analogy, we tend to ignore the fundamental similarities between what Khrushchev and Mao actually did. Yet once again, if we concentrate on the level of policy, we will ignore what remains as the fundamental difference between the two leaders – Khrushchev's faith in the determining role of what Marx called the forces of production and Mao's concentration on the transformation of the relations of production. On this, the source of the most fundamental divergencies in Marxism, Khrushchev and Mao finished up on different sides with Khrushchev, ironically, more on the side of the man he so bitterly denounced – Josef Stalin.

NOTES

1. E. Crankshaw, <u>Khrushchev</u>, London: Collins, 1966, pp. 252-3.

2. Mao Zedong, 'On the Correct Handling of Contradictions among the People', 1957, <u>Selected Works</u>, Vol. V, Peking: Foreign Languages Press, 1977, pp. 408-14. It is said that Mao's six criteria for distinguishing between 'fragrant flowers' and 'poisonous weeds' were absent in the original version of the speech and were inserted in the revised version published at the beginning of the Anti-rightist Movement.

3. This was the Futian Incident. See S. Schram, <u>Mao Tse-tung</u>, Harmondsworth: Penguin, 1967, pp. 151-3.

4. Perhaps the most interesting discussion of the Gao Gang case is F. Teiwes, <u>Politics and Purges in China: Rectification and the Decline in Party Norms: 1950-1965</u>, White Plains, NY: M.E. Sharp Inc., 1979, pp. 166-210.

5. W. Hinton, <u>Hundred Day War: The Cultural Revolution at Tsinghua University</u>, New York: Monthly Review Press, 1972, pp. 118-22.

6. P. Chang, 'Research Notes on the Changing Loci of Decision in the Chinese Communist Party', <u>The China Quarterly</u> 44, October-December 1970, pp. 169-94.

7. See p. 53.

8. See e.g. E. Snow, <u>Red Star Over China</u>, New York: Grove Press, 1961, p. 79.

9. Chairman Hu Yaobang on his assumption of office.

10. J. Stalin, 'On the Draft Constitution of the U.S.S.R.', 25 November 1936, in J. Stalin, Problems of Leninism, Moscow: Foreign Languages Publishing House, 1947, pp. 540-68. See also my discussion; B. Brugger, 'Soviet and Chinese Views on Revolution and Socialism – Some Thoughts on the Problem of Diachrony and Synchrony', Journal of Contemporary Asia, September 1981.

11. Crankshaw 1966, op.cit., p. 158.

12. Communist Party of the Soviet Union, Programme, 31 October 1961, London: Soviet Booklet 83, 1961.

13. The Polemic on the General Line of the International Communist Movement, Peking: Foreign Languages Press, 1965, p. 466.

14. Mao Zedong, 'On New Democracy', January 1940, Selected Works, Vol. III, 1965, pp. 339-84.

15. Liu Shaoqi, How to Be a Good Communist, Peking: Foreign Languages Press, 1965.

16. Lin Biao 'Long Live the Victory of People's War', Peking Review 36, 3 September 1965, pp. 9-30.

17. See A Critique of Mao Tse-Tung's Theoretical Conceptions, Moscow: Progress Publishers, 1972, pp. 69-72.

18. Mao Zedong, 1957, loc.cit.

19. Stalin, 1936, loc.cit.

20. Communist Party of China, 'Resolution on the Political Report of the Central Committee', 27 September 1956, in Peking: Foreign Languages Press, Eighth National Congress of the Communist Party of China, 1956, vol. I, p. 116.

21. Mao Zedong, 'Talk at the Third Plenum of the Eighth Central Committee', 7 October 1957, In Miscellany of Mao Tse-tung Thought, Springfield Va.: Joint Publications Research Service, 1974, p. 75.

22. Discussed in G. Clark, In Fear of China, Melbourne: Landsdowne Press, 1967, p. 98.

23. See Mao Zedong, A Critique of Soviet Economics, New York: Monthly Review Press, 1977 and R. Levy, 'New Light on Mao: His Views on the Soviet Union's "Political

Economy"', <u>The China Quarterly</u> 61, March 1975, pp. 95-117.

24. Discussed in B. Brugger, <u>China: Liberation and Transformation: 1942-1962</u>, London: Croom Helm, 1981, pp. 248-53.

25. This is sometimes translated as 'advanced' or 'developed' socialism. For a discussion of the concept see A. Evans, 'Developed Socialism in Soviet Ideology', <u>Soviet Studies</u>, vol. XXIX, no. 3, July 1977, pp. 409-20 and M. Lavigne, 'Advanced Socialist Society', <u>Economy and Society</u> vol. VII, no. 4, November 1978, pp. 367-94.

26. See W. Brugger, <u>Democracy and Organisation in the Chinese Industrial Enterprise: 1948-53</u>, Cambridge: Cambridge University Press, 1976.

27. See p. 115.

28. See J. Salaff, 'The Urban Communes and Anti-City Experiment in Communist China', <u>The China Quarterly</u> 29, January-March 1967, pp. 82-110.

29. Mao promoted the integration of oil field operations with agricultural production. See K. Broadbent, 'The Transformation of Chinese Agriculture and its Effects on the Environment', <u>International Relations</u>, vol. IV, no. 1, 1972, pp. 38-51.

30. Liu Guiguang and Wang Xiangming 'Dui Woguo Guomin Jingji Fazhan Sudu he Bili Guanxi Wenti de Tantao', <u>Zongquo Shehui Kexue</u> 4, July 1980, pp. 8-9.

31. Mao Zedong, 'On the Ten Major Relationships', 25 April 1956, <u>Selected Works</u>, vol. V, p. 286.

32. See pp. 175-176.

33. <u>Renmin Ribao</u>, 28 February 1979, p. 1; Peking Radio, 16 April 1979, BBC, <u>Summary of World Broadcasts, Part III, The Far East</u>, FE/6096/B11/1.

34. Communist Party of China, <u>Zhongfa</u> 4 (1979), <u>Issues and Studies</u>, vol. XV, no. 7, July 1979, pp. 105 and 109. Note: the translation is in error.

35. In the Great Leap, Mao was portrayed as the promoter of a particular kind of plough.

36. Officially this has been attributed to 'Lin Biao and the Gang of Four', Renmin Ribao, 28 February 1979, p. 1.

37. K. Walker, 'Organisation of Agricultural Production', in A. Eckstein, W. Galenson and Liu Ta-chung (eds), Economic Trends in Communist China, Edinburgh: Edinburgh University Press, 1968, pp. 444-5.

38. D. Zagoria, The Sino-Soviet Conflict 1956-61, New York: Atheneum, 1966, p. 134.

39. See Xu Liqun, in R. Bowie and J. Fairbank (eds) Communist China, 1955-59:   Policy   Documents   with Analysis, Cambridge Mass.:   Harvard   University   Press,   1965, pp. 479-83.

40. See p. 112.

41. Blat - a   Russian   term   covering   corruption   and favouritism; quanxi - a Chinese term denoting personal relations; tolkachi - a Russian term denoting a 'fixer' who can cut through red tape.

42. A. Donnithorne, China's Economic System, London, George Allen and Unwin, 1967, pp. 290-1.

43. Discussed in Brugger, 1976, op.cit.

44. Sun Yefang was attacked in the Cultural Revolution as 'China's Liberman'. Since his rehabilitation he has become most influential as an economic theorist. Xue Muqiao who criticised aspects of the Great Leap Forward is now also seen as a major economic thinker. In his book, China's Socialist Economy (Peking: Foreign Languages Press 1981). Xue takes pains to show the identity between his views and those of Mao. The references to Mao, however, are selected to give a somewhat one-sided picture.

45. Schurmann calls this 'decentralisation II' as opposed to 'decentralisation   I'   (to   units   of   production); H.F. Schurmann, Ideology and Organisation in Communist China, Berkeley: University of California Press, 1966, pp. 175-8.

46. R. and Z. Medvedev, Khrushchev: The Years in Power, Oxford: Oxford University Press, 1977, pp. 156-7.

47. Teiwes 1979, op.cit., pp. 349-66.

48. Mao Zedong, 19 February 1958, from untitled Red Guard pamphlet, p. 33, translated in Current Background 892, 21 October 1969, p. 7.

49. Medvedev, op.cit., pp. 94-101.

50. Downward transfer of personnel. For a discussion of xiafang in China in the mid-1950s see R. Lee 'The Hsia Fang System: Marxism and Modernisation', The China Quarterly 28, October-December 1966, pp. 40-62. On the Soviet parallel, see Medvedev op.cit., pp. 113-6.

51. According to Teiwes (op.cit., pp. 441-92) it was not until 1962 that Mao felt that this process had gone too far.

52. The best account of this is R. Baum, Prelude to Revolution: Mao, the Party and the Peasant Question, 1962-66, New York: Columbia University Press, 1975.

53. See F. Schurmann and O. Schell, China Readings 3: Communist China, Harmondsworth: Penguin, 1968, pp. 258-60.

54. Chinese Communist Party, Zhongfa (1977) 37, 23 September, 1977, Issues and Studies, vol. XV, no. 5, May 1979, pp. 92-3. Discussed in B. Brugger, China: Radicalism to Revisionism, 1962-1979, London: Croom Helm, 1981, pp. 155-6 and 185.

55. A useful compendium of Chinese contributions to the debate is Peking: Foreign Languages Press, The Polemic..., op.cit. A good survey is J. Gittings, Survey of the Sino-Soviet Dispute: A Commentary and Extracts from the Recent Polemics, 1963-1967, Oxford: Oxford University Press, 1968.

56. E. Crankshaw, The New Cold War: Moscow v. Peking, Harmondsworth: Penguin, 1965, pp. 107-9.

57. Mao Zedong, 'Talk with the American Correspondent Anna Louise Strong', August 1946, Selected Works, vol. IV, 1961, p. 100.

58. See J. Cheng (ed.) The Politics of the Chinese Red Army: A Translation of the Bulletin of Activities of the People's Liberation Army, Stanford: Hoover Institution, 1966.

59. N. Maxwell, India's China War, Harmondsworth: Penguin, 1972.

60. Discussed in G. O'Leary, The Shaping of Chinese Foreign Policy, London: Croom Helm, 1980.

61. The original Chongqing speech, 17 October 1945, is in Selected Works, vol. IV, pp. 53-63. Certain direct quotes from this were made in a much publicised essay discussing Mao's 'On Policy' (1940), written not long after the visit of Henry Kissinger to China in 1971. See Peking Review 35, 27 August 1971, pp. 10-13 and Hongqi 9, 2 August 1971, pp. 10-17.

62. In fact the classic statement of this thesis was made by Deng Xiaoping in his speech to the United Nations, 9 April 1974, Peking Review, Supplement to No. 14, 12 April 1974. In this speech Deng placed both the United States and the Soviet Union in the first world, the developed capitalist and socialist states in the second and the remainder in the third. He thus revealed a concentration on power rather than social structure.

63. E. Hoxha, Imperialism and the Revolution, Tirana: The 8 Nentori Publishing House, 1979, pp. 384-453.

64. K. Marx, The Eighteenth Brumaire of Louis Bonaparte, New York: International Publishers, 1963, p. 15.

65. ibid., p. 17.

66. Zagoria, op.cit., pp. 281-4.

67. This view is discussed in M. Rose, 'The Holy Cloak of Criticism: Structuralism and Marx's Eighteenth Brumaire', Thesis Eleven 2, 1981, pp. 79-97.

68. See p. 200.

Chapter Six

KHRUSHCHEVISM IN CHINESE PERSPECTIVE

Graham Young and Dennis Woodward

When the Sino-Soviet dispute reached the stage of open polemics, the Chinese leaders usually traced its origins back to 1956. Certainly, many of the issues which were to be foci of the dispute emerged in 1956, and events after that time exacerbated disagreements. This was so particularly with respect to foreign policies and activities in the international communist movement. But it would be mistaken to interpret Sino-Soviet relations by projecting later antagonism backwards, or to accept the antagonists' claims about their own earlier positions. Indeed, contemporary evidence indicated that relations remained relatively harmonious during the late 1950s, and the emergent differences were subsumed within a general framework of cooperation. In particular, there was no evidence to support later Chinese assertions of consistent opposition to Khrushchev's domestic policies. In fact, the Chinese did not even identify Khrushchevism as a discrete trend in the Soviet Union. That identification was made only in the next decade, when the Chinese began to perceive Khrushchevism, or 'Khrushchev revisionism', as a systematic betrayal of socialist revolution.

One area of Chinese disquiet after 1956, and later of direct attacks, was Khrushchev's denunciation of Stalin beginning with the 'secret speech' at the 20th CPSU Congress. Chinese leaders came to pose as the chief defenders of Stalin. But this does not support the charge that the Chinese were advocates of maintaining Stalinism and its attendant evils. During the second half of the 1950s the Chinese, like the Soviets under Khrushchev, were moving away from the Stalinist model. It is ironical that, while defending Stalin, the Chinese leadership was adopting a series of policies which repudiated many of the most central aspects of the Stalinist model more thoroughly than did Khrushchev's reforms in the Soviet Union. Far from automatically rejecting Soviet reforms, the Chinese considered that Khrushchev had failed to deal adequately with legacies of the Stalinist model and to eliminate its undesirable consequences.

Chinese leaders also warned, however, that there might be overreaction to Stalinism, leading to trends inimical to socialism. They began to express greater concern at the growth of 'revisionism' in socialist countries. While arguing that each country should adopt its own socialist path, appropriate to its specific conditions, they also considered that major elements of Soviet practice, which were inevitably directly associated with Stalin, constituted indispensable principles applicable to all socialist countries. There was a risk of revising or abandoning such fundamental principles under the guise of repudiating Stalinist mistakes. For example, Stalin's argument that class struggle intensified under socialism had brought harm to the socialist cause and had to be rejected. But in doing so it was necessary to avoid the opposite, 'revisionist', mistake of denying class struggle under socialism.(1) At this stage, Chinese accusations of revisionism were directed primarily at Tito and the Yugoslav leadership. They did perceive a danger of revisionist trends in the Soviet Union, as in China itself, but did not consider that these had become dominant. Criticisms of Khrushchev, mostly implicit, were that his attempts to deal with the Stalinist model were not effective or thorough enough. It was only later that Chinese leaders began to adopt the far more severe assessment that Khrushchev's policies were revisionist.

In fact, the Chinese continued well after 1956 to see the Soviet Union as a socialist model. This was now interpreted differently from the early 1950s, when the Chinese First Five-Year Plan had been solidly based on the Stalinist model and under direct Soviet guidance. The CCP had then enthusiastically advocated following the Soviet model, although it had been resisted by Party members at lower levels and implementation was far from universal. After 1956, the Party's attitude was much more circumspect. The emphasis was on learning the good points of the Soviet Union, not following blindly, making proper analysis of Soviet experience, and making sure it was suitable for China's situation.(2) Although more qualified, however, the overall positive assessment of the Soviet Union remained. And the new recognition that the Soviet Union also exemplified mistakes to be avoided was not linked to Khrushchev and his policies but to the Stalinist model itself.

The later accusations of Khrushchev revisionism were to be associated with a reconsideration by Chinese leaders of the whole conception of socialist revolution. In the 1950s, however, underlying Chinese acceptance of a Soviet model was a shared conception of the nature of socialist revolution. This viewed socialism as a distinct system established by seizing state power and transforming ownership of the means of production. Having thus joined the ranks of the 'socialist camp', the socialist system had to be consolidated and the productive forces developed in order to achieve the ultimate goal of building communism. While this view was shared by the Chinese and the Soviets, there was still considerable scope for differences concerning the appropriate methods for bringing about further development and progress of the socialist system. This became the focus of Chinese repudiation of large parts of the Stalinist model. While recognising that both they and the Soviets were moving away from that model, and arguing that each country's policy should be appropriate to its own specific situation, the Chinese attitude towards Khrushchev's policies was very much conditioned by their own emerging analysis of how socialist construction should be effected.

REASSESSMENT OF THE STALINIST MODEL

The first signs of Chinese reassessment of the Stalinist model, on which their First Five-Year Plan had been based, became evident in 1956-57, culminating in the more complete formulation of an alternative strategy during the Great Leap Forward. At the core of the new course in China was the emergent analysis of the nature of socialist society and the manner in which its progress could be achieved. This was reflected first in the discussions of the continued existence of 'contradictions' in socialist society. Rather than emphasising harmony and correspondence, the Chinese asserted that there remained contradictions between the relations of production and the forces of production, and between the superstructure and the economic base. Such were general instances of a whole range of social contradictions pervading all aspects of socialist society. Contradictions would 'find expression in defects in certain links of the economic and political systems' and required timely adjustments. Not only were contradictions inevitable, but their appearance and resolution were beneficial. They provided the motive force for socialist development. In particular, Mao argued that progress would be achieved not through the struggle against enemy forces as in the past, but through the operation of 'non-antagonistic contradictions' among the 'people'.(3)

Mao and the other Chinese leaders were clearly influenced by events in Eastern Europe, particularly the rebellion in Hungary. The latter was explained, in part, as the product of incorrect handling of contradictions among the people which caused them to become 'antagonistic' and enabled domestic reactionaries and foreign imperialists to take advantage of them to create disorder. Similar disturbances within China were admitted, and attributed to economic and political mistakes.(4) Recognising the continued existence of contradictions in socialist society was but the first step in avoiding such mistakes. Rather than suppressing contradictions, they were to be given scope for expression and correct resolution. The Chinese reaction to contemporary events in Eastern Europe, therefore, was not just the identification of specific defects giving rise to problems. In the first place, they saw that defects were caused by uncritically copying the Stalinist model, and they argued that a proper method had to be adopted in learning from Soviet experience. But they also went beyond that to suggest that problems were not merely a consequence of failing to adapt to specific conditions, that they were inherent in the model itself.

The emergent Chinese conception of socialist progress was reinforced by other notions repudiating the Stalinist model as it had been applied in China. In particular, it began to challenge the linear, incremental view of socialist development, in which the prime focus was on growth of the 'productive forces'. Chinese leaders began to argue that socialist development was 'wave-like', with 'ups and downs'. That is, periods of intense social change, or 'leaps', alternated with periods of consolidation.(5) This constituted a direct challenge to the type of planning involved in the Stalinist model. Progress would be best stimulated by creative imbalance. Socialist construction should not proceed according to fixed blueprints, but in a more fluid manner relying on the dynamic force of social contradictions. It should not be circumscribed by excessively prescriptive planning - in Mao's metaphor, socialism was like Hunanese straw sandals, which took their shape only as they were being knitted.(6) Such thinking was also associated with rejection of concentrating on growth of the productive forces, a position which the CCP had officially reaffirmed as late as 1956. According to this new conception, socialist progress was not motivated, nor was it measured, by economic growth alone. It required transformation in all areas of society, on the political, ideological and cultural 'fronts' as well as the economic, and such transformation did not automatically follow economic change but occurred through the operation of contradictions in all areas of social activity.

Chinese leaders linked these arguments to public and, more often, private criticisms of Stalin. They objected to Khrushchev's method of denouncing Stalin without first consulting other parties and considering the ramifications of his attack. But they certainly agreed with many of the specific criticisms of Stalin and added more of their own. Stalin was guilty of metaphysics, subjectivism and lack of understanding of dialectics, and was divorced from reality and the masses. He failed to recognise the continued existence and role of contradictions in socialist society. This led to confusion of 'people' and 'enemy' and to injustices in the suppression of counter-revolutionaries. He behaved arbitrarily, violating the principles of democratic-centralism, imposing his own personal dominance and failing to

implement the 'mass line'. He also had an excessively
mechanistic view of socialism, as indicated by slogans such as
'cadres decide everything' and 'technology decides
everything', while ignoring the superstructure, politics and
the role of the masses.(7) Despite the large number of faults
they attributed to Stalin, however, the Chinese resisted
Khrushchev's concentration on Stalin personally. They argued
that the point at issue was not merely evaluation of Stalin
himself, but the far more important project of summing up the
historical experience of proletarian dictatorship and the
international communist movement. Khrushchev's method
obscured these more fundamental issues. By reducing all
problems to Stalin's individual aberrations, he failed to
recognise their systemic nature. Thus, the Chinese began to
imply that Khrushchev, despite his virulent attacks on Stalin
and his claim to be rectifying his errors, had neither
perceived nor transcended the source of those errors.

The Chinese reassessment of the Stalinist model was
evident in economic policies after 1956. The First Five-Year
Plan had achieved significant growth in the Chinese economy,
especially in heavy industry, but by 1956 the Chinese
leadership was becoming increasingly concerned with the
economic difficulties generated by this strategy. In April of
that year Mao addressed some of the main problems the Chinese
economy was experiencing.(8) He argued that excessive
concentration on the development of heavy industry,
overcentralisation and excessive accumulation policies were
retarding economic growth. Such arguments soon became more
frequent in Chinese discussions and influential in policy
making. They implied minor modifications to the First
Five-Year Plan strategy rather than a drastic break. The
mildness of disagreement with Soviet economic policies was
illustrated in Mao's claim that it would take three five-year
plans to assimilate their basic experience.(9) But learning
had to be more selective, recognising both the good and bad
lessons.

By 1958, however, Chinese economic strategy reached a
decisive break with the Stalinist model in the Great Leap
Forward program. The earlier stress on proportionate
development and opposition to setting 'too rapid a pace' was
now removed. Instead, as Liu Shaoqi announced, the goal
became that of achieving 'greater, faster, better and more
economical results' by mobilising all positive factors.(10)
This involved simultaneous development of the heavy
industrial, light industrial and agricultural sectors. In
contrast to the earlier emphasis on large-scale modern
enterprises directly controlled by the centre, locally
controlled small and medium-sized enterprises, often based on
indigenous or intermediate technology, were to be encouraged.

Other distinctive aspects of the new program were the fostering of local self-reliance, greater emphasis on labour-intensive rather than capital-intensive projects, and the use of mass campaigns to reach economic targets. Such policies were intended to overcome the problems generated in the First Five-Year Plan and constituted an attempt to formulate a novel strategy specifically designed for Chinese conditions.

The political and social implications of the Chinese reassessment of the Stalinist model were just as significant as the economic. As noted above, many of the Chinese criticisms of Stalin focussed on his violation of democratic-centralism in both party and state and on his estrangement from the masses. And relations between leaders and led were seen as one of the major contradictions in socialist society. The Stalinist model itself refused to acknowledge that particular contradiction and, more generally, stifled the expression and resolution of social contradictions. It was characterised by centralised control through bureaucratic hierarchies and the state's intrusive imposition upon social forces. According to the emergent view of how socialist society would advance, too great dominance by the state was anti-progressive. It led to problems such as 'bureaucratism', alienation of leaders from the masses, and inflexibility in decision-making at all levels.

Such problems were the principal focus in the early Chinese reassessment of the Stalinist model. Indeed, a major thrust in Mao's discussion of 'contradictions among the people' was that they must not be handled by administrative or coercive means. Rather, there had to be greater promotion of 'democracy' among the 'people'. This was interpreted as requiring greater scope for the expression of diverse opinions and was reflected in the 'Hundred Flowers' policy. Unfettering the political process would facilitate greater mass inputs. The party assumed renewed importance as the means of expediting this process. The party's role, in contrast to that of the state, was defined largely in terms of its relationship to the masses. The progressive impetus of social contradictions could be realised only if the party maintained close ties with the masses, remaining sensitive to mass opinion and receptive to criticism. Although some of the critics who took advantage of the Hundred Flowers policy were later suppressed, the emphasis on mass inputs became more pronounced during the Great Leap Forward. In fact, the whole strategy relied upon the stimulus of mass initiative and creativity. The ambitious programs of economic and social change were to be implemented not through government action but through party-led mass mobilisation.

The general attacks on bureaucratic ossification and rigidity, which the Chinese saw as consequences of the Stalinist model, culminated in the administrative reforms associated with the Great Leap Forward. The effects of bureaucratic centralisation were countered by administrative decentralisation and a new emphasis on local coordination in which the role of the party was again crucial. This was complemented by the policy of <u>xiafang</u>, the downward transfer of cadres, which was intended to streamline the bureaucracy and strengthen links between cadres and masses. Other related reforms included worker participation in management and cadre participation in manual labour. The Chinese leaders saw that many of the 'rules and regulations' inherited with the Stalinist model were 'hindrances to progressively raising mass activism and developing the productive forces'. It was, therefore, necessary to revise or abolish them and to encourage mass initiative in doing so.(11)

Hence, the Chinese moved from reassessment of the Stalinist model to formulation of a distinctively new developmental strategy. They did not maintain that other socialist countries should follow their example in the manner in which the Stalinist model had been exported from the Soviet Union.(12) Despite this, along with the recognition of the increasing irrelevance of Soviet experience to the present Chinese direction, there was also some muted suggestion of a Chinese model challenging the Soviet Union's exemplary role.(13) Although the Chinese did not explicitly say so, they hinted that Khrushchev and the Soviets had failed to break decisively with the Stalinist model. They did not acknowledge the existence of contradictions in socialist society and, therefore, did not have channels for the expression of diverse opinions such as the 'democratic parties' in China. And despite the reforms he had introduced, Khrushchev was explicitly criticised for being 'too cautious'. He still could not 'walk with both legs' - that is, those of industry and agriculture. And Soviet heavy industry remained too centralised and locked into a bureaucratic administration, disregarding smaller-scale enterprises, local initiative and the role of the masses.(14)

While embarking on a new course, however, Chinese leaders warned that certain indispensable socialist principles should not be forsaken. They perceived this to be a principal danger of indiscriminate attacks upon Stalin. Hence, while promoting greater democracy and the breaking down of bureaucratic rigidity and centralism, they also insisted upon the inviolability of party leadership and the need for suppressing counter- revolutionaries. Greater democracy did not imply the abandonment of 'dictatorship', nor of the process of socialist transformation and construction. Although condemning continued uncritical adherence to the Stalinist model as 'dogmatism', the Chinese argued that revisionism, as a manifestation of bourgeois ideology, was 'even more dangerous than dogmatism'. The revisionists, by following the opposite course of negating fundamental principles, were the 'right-hand men' of those opposing socialism.(15) At this stage, such accusations were not directed at Khrushchev but at the Yugoslavs who, under the pretext of criticising Stalin, had denied the need for proletarian dictatorship over class enemies and had undermined the socialist economy.

As the Great Leap Forward ran into difficulties and certain members of the CCP leadership expressed opposition to it, emphasis on the dangers of revisionism increased. In 1959 Mao labelled such opponents, with Peng Dehuai the chief spokesman, as 'Right opportunist', a term which was equated with 'revisionist'.(16) Most significantly, one of the charges directed at Peng was his alleged illegitimate relations with foreign countries, and specifically his collusion with Khrushchev. Chinese leaders strongly resented Khrushchev's ridiculing of the Great Leap Forward, as became clear in their later analyses of the exacerbation of Sino-Soviet differences. The linking of Khrushchev with a revisionist trend within China set the stage for the identification and condemnation of revisionism within the Soviet Union.

KHRUSHCHEV REVISIONISM

During the early 1960s, Chinese leaders not only began to disagree with the Soviets over a wider range of issues and to state these disagreements publicly, but also went beyond regarding the dispute as concerning specific or isolated issues in which reconciliation was still possible. They claimed that 'the errors of the CPSU leadership were not just accidental, individual and minor errors, but rather a whole series of errors of principle, which endanger the interests of the entire socialist camp and the international communist movement'.(17) They identified Khrushchevism, or 'Khrushchev revisionism', as a coherent and systematic position, incompatible with and antagonistic to Marxism-Leninism.

According to Chinese analyses, Khrushchev's errors had become the principal manifestations of 'modern revisionism'. In this usage, 'revisionism' was a very powerful term of condemnation. Many Chinese publications explicitly established the links between the modern and the older form of revisionism associated with Bernstein and Kautsky.(18) Historical continuity was provided by the argument that the international communist movement always progressed through Marxist-Leninist resistance to revisionist trends. Given the

orthodox interpretation of Lenin's battles with the older form
of revisionism, however, the most important implication of
labelling Khrushchev and the Soviet leadership as
'revisionist' was that they were traitors to the proletarian
revolutionary cause. In that case, those who wished to
persist in the cause had to repudiate Khrushchev completely.
Although many of the Chinese polemics dealt with the proper
interpretation of canonical texts, they were concerned with
more than the adulteration of theoretical positions. Rather,
as an 'ism', revisionism was a complete system of theory and
practice. It was not a deviation from Marxism-Leninism, but a
distinct entity comparable to, and wholly inconsistent with,
Marxism-Leninism. Just as Marxism-Leninism was identified
with the theory and practice of the revolutionary movement, so
revisionism was identified with the theory and practice of
counter-revolution. Such basic antagonism was reinforced by
the assertion of continued class struggle in socialist
society. Marxism-Leninism guided the proletarian
revolutionary movement, while revisionism was the means of
counter-attack by the bourgeoisie.

Use of the term 'modern revisionism' served to classify
and condemn Khrushchev's errors, but also meant that the
Chinese leaders did not wish their attacks to be seen as
directed at Khrushchev individually. Certainly, some of the
Chinese bitterness in polemics can be attributed to distaste
for Khrushchev himself. They saw him as a 'buffoon', as
'ridiculous'.(19) This attitude was reflected in Chinese
rejection of Soviet ideological authority. They were
particularly offended that someone whom they saw as lacking
any prestige in the international communist movement should
adopt a 'patriarchal' stance to fraternal parties, and were
angry that such a person should attempt to manipulate the
symbols of Leninism, the Bolshevik Party, and the USSR as the
homeland of socialism. As their polemics pointed out, Chinese
leaders had countered Stalin's meddling in their revolutionary
movement and, whatever criticism they had of Stalin, they
clearly saw him as a figure of much greater stature than
Khrushchev. Despite this, they considered that revisionism in
the Soviet Union was not simply a manifestation of
Khrushchev's individual aberrations. It was, rather, the
latest and most dangerous development of the revisionist
current which had infested the communist movement since the
1940s. Khrushchev was deemed to have inherited the erroneous
trends associated with Browder, Togliatti, and especially
Tito. By the 1960s, Khrushchev had become the arch culprit,
the 'chief representative' of modern revisionism, and he was
clearly more dangerous than his predecessors because he had
perverted the CPSU and the Soviet Union. And Khrushchev's own
personal culpability was so great that this latest development
deserved to be labelled 'Khrushchev revisionism'.

Nevertheless, Khrushchev was merely the expression of a more fundamental and durable underlying current, which could not be destroyed simply by removing Khrushchev himself. Thus, in 1965 Chinese articles claimed that the new leaders of the CPSU were pursuing 'Khrushchev revisionism without Khrushchev'.(20)

At first, Chinese attacks on Khrushchev revisionism concentrated almost exclusively on Soviet foreign policy and activities within the international communist movement, but there were several factors leading inexorably to a greater focus on Soviet domestic matters. For one thing, the Chinese were unwilling to view Soviet foreign policy as an autonomous sphere separable from origins within Soviet society. One reason for revisionist foreign policy was, of course, yielding to the threats and blandishments of imperialism, an explanation which had been used with respect to Yugoslavia.(21) The Chinese did not accept that this could be the whole explanation, however, since they saw the need to identify domestic social forces susceptible to such imperialist initiatives. This type of reasoning did not apply so long as the Chinese saw Soviet foreign policy as simply committing tactical mistakes. But as soon as they perceived that 'mistakes' were part of a systematic pattern, and labelled that pattern 'revisionism', then they were compelled to seek its roots within Soviet society. Another factor was that Chinese party leaders were concerned with the international communist movement not just as a form of inter-state or even inter-party relations but as the expression of the world revolutionary movement. They maintained that their own revolutionary victory had been a result of their own efforts and upheld the principle of not interfering in the affairs of another state or party. Nevertheless, they also considered that their own revolution, and all others as well, were intrinsic parts of the world revolutionary movement and direct descendants of the October Revolution. In that case, the direction in domestic policy of any socialist country (and especially of the Soviet Union, which had until recently been recognised as the head of the 'socialist camp') was a matter of direct relevance to other socialist countries. Domestic revisionism was such a serious matter because it undermined the world revolutionary movement, which transcended any specific country, and of which China was a part.

Following from this, just as events in the Soviet Union and Eastern Europe had reinforced the Chinese leaders' reassessment of the Stalinist model in the 1950s, so the more recent events led them to reconsider the whole notion of socialist revolution. The perception of revolutionary retrogression shattered the comfortable optimism on the inevitability of socialist triumph which had generally prevailed in China in the previous decade. This was especially pertinent when revisionism was seen as dominant in the Soviet Union, formerly the example for China's own socialist revolution and construction. Thus, Chinese leaders were forced to reexamine their earlier assumptions and began to study the Soviet experience in reformulating the conception of socialist revolution. That this was not merely a polemical means of discrediting the Soviet Union was demonstrated by the manner in which the analysis was related to the situation in China. The attacks on Khrushchev became increasingly linked to the need for drawing lessons applicable to China itself. The Soviet Union was still seen as a model, but now a negative one.(22) It was useful in indicating Chinese analogues of the Soviet experience and identifying possible sources of similar revolutionary retrogression in China.

The first signs of Khrushchev revisionism, the Chinese now argued, had emerged at the CPSU 20th Congress. After that time it had developed and grown, and was made systematic at the 22nd Congress, which formulated a revisionist 'general line'. That line had five principal components: 'peaceful coexistence', 'peaceful competition', 'peaceful transition', 'state of the whole people' and 'party of the whole people'. The first three of these points concerned Soviet foreign policy, especially relations with imperialism and foreign revolutionary movements, while the other two concerned Soviet domestic policy. The Chinese asserted that there was a basic continuity between these foreign and domestic aspects of the revisionist general line. They rested on the underlying foundation of repudiation of revolution and class struggle.(23) Thus, the Soviet leaders capitulated to the needs of imperialism and sabotaged revolutionary movements in non-socialist countries by advocating peaceful coexistence and competition and rejecting violent revolution against capitalism and imperialism. In the same manner, by adopting 'whole people' categories with respect to the Soviet party and state, they repudiated class struggle and the need for continued revolution in the Soviet Union, abandoning the dictatorship of the proletarian vanguard. Thus, all these points were parts of the same syndrome, constituent elements in a systematic revisionist line. As well as condemning betrayal of the international communist movement, the Chinese ridiculed Soviet claims to be preparing for the establishment of communism.(24) On the contrary, they argued, Khrushchev revisionism was undermining the progress of socialist revolution and leading to the restoration of capitalism in the Soviet Union.

DIMENSIONS OF KHRUSHCHEV REVISIONISM

The Chinese polemics charged that after seizing party and
state leadership Khrushchev had 'pushed through a whole series
of revisionist policies which have greatly hastened the growth
of the forces of capitalism' and that, as a result of the
abandonment of the dictatorship of the proletariat and 'the
execution of a whole series of erroneous domestic and foreign
policies, the capitalist forces in Soviet society have become
a deluge sweeping over all fields of life in the USSR,
including the political, economic, cultural and ideological
fields'.(25) While indicating mistakes in all these fields,
however, the accusations directed at Khrushchev usually
involved broad assertions with little elaboration or
substantiation. Attacks on Khrushchev's domestic policies
were far less specific than those on his foreign policies and
activities within the international communist movement, and
also less specific than the similar attacks on Yugoslav
policies.

In fact, one of the most striking features of Chinese
criticisms was the inaccuracy of their claims concerning the
Soviet situation. They attributed to Khrushchev policies
which were inconsistent with, and even the opposite of, those
he was pursuing and saw aspects of Soviet society which
Khrushchev actually was attempting to overcome as intended
consequences of Khrushchev revisionism. The tactics adopted
in the polemics prefigured those soon to dominate Chinese
domestic political struggles during the Cultural Revolution.
They included divorcing statements or events from context,
distorting and exaggerating their meaning and significance.
Isolated proposals appearing in any Soviet source were
interpreted as generalised tendencies and linked directly to
Khrushchev, even if he had resisted them. Most important was
guilt by association, particularly in connection with
Khrushchev's rapprochement with the Yugoslavs. Chinese
criticisms of the Yugoslavs were simply transferred to
Khrushchev, with little regard for their applicability.
Indeed, for the purposes of polemics, the accuracy of various
charges directed at Khrushchev seems to have been basically
irrelevant. The Chinese were preoccupied with what they
perceived to be the fundamentally mistaken 'line' or general
orientation adopted by Khrushchev, illustrated by
pronouncements such as 'state of the whole people' and his
willingness to embrace the Yugoslavs. Given the view that
revisionism was a complete system of theory and practice, the
Chinese sought to locate within the Soviet Union corresponding
mistaken policies, but their overriding concern was with the
'general line'.

It was in this sense that the Soviet Union was used as a negative model. Broad evaluative statements concerning socialist revolution, which were clearly influenced by the criticisms of Khrushchev's alleged line, could be linked to concrete policy implications in the Chinese context. At the same time, however, lack of specificity in criticisms of Khrushchev revisionism was associated with ambiguity and even confusion in the Chinese leadership during the early 1960s. It served to conceal the still implicit differences among Chinese leaders with respect to interpretation of the origins and character of Khrushchev revisionism and its implications for China - differences which later became more explicit and politically very significant in the Cultural Revolution. In this section we summarise the broad criticisms of Khrushchev's policies, while in the next we turn to analysis of differing interpretations within the Chinese leadership.

If we follow the Chinese division of Khrushchev's policies into political, economic and cultural-ideological fields, it appears that the political was the most important. The two principal characteristics attributed to Khrushchev revisionism domestically were the abandonment of the dictatorship of the proletariat and the party's role as the vanguard of the proletariat. But Chinese analyses usually saw the former in terms of failing to pursue tasks which the dictatorship of the proletariat had to accomplish in order to protect and promote the socialist revolution, and the latter in terms of the party's failure to adopt and implement policies for accomplishing those tasks. Thus, while degeneration of the political system was the crucial element in the growth of Khrushchev revisionism, the signs of this were not found specifically in political structures and processes but in all areas of party policy and state activity. In fact, there was little concrete criticism of Soviet political structures and processes under Khrushchev. The Chinese argued that abandoning the dictatorship of the proletariat under the rubric of 'state of the whole people' necessarily entailed instituting bourgeois dictatorship. Since the existence of a state was itself a sign of class division, as all state forms were means of class domination, then the dictatorship of the proletariat could not be replaced by a 'state of the whole people' but only by the dictatorship of another class, the bourgeoisie. A similar argument applied with respect to the necessary class character of political parties. These general arguments were accompanied by claims that Khrushchev was strengthening the state apparatus and intensifying popular repression, that like Stalin he was despotic, acting arbitrarily and dictatorially, and that he had violated the standards of inner-party democratic-centralism and of relations with the masses. Khrushchev was also accused of carrying out extensive purges in the Party and other leadership positions from central to local levels, dismissing cadres he did not trust and replacing them with his own proteges. And the division of the CPSU into 'industrial' and 'agricultural' wings contravened Marxist-Leninist principles of party organisation.(26) Chinese leaders also stated more forcefully their opposition to the denigration of Stalin and began to attribute more sinister motives to Khrushchev. As well as being guilty of the same improper political behaviour as Stalin, Khrushchev attempted to shift all blame, ignoring his own former support for Stalin and responsibility for mistakes. Most important was the assertion that Stalin, despite his manifold mistakes, had nonetheless maintained and protected proletarian dictatorship. Khrushchev's denigration of Stalin was not merely ill-considered and unwise, but was a deliberate tactic designed to disguise his attacks on Marxism-Leninism and a pretext for propagating his revisionist line.(27)

With respect to economic policy, apart from the charge that Khrushchev's vacillation and wastefulness had thrown the Soviet economy into chaos, Chinese criticism focussed on the undermining of the socialist economy's characteristics of state planning and state and collective forms of ownership. These had been replaced by reliance on profit criteria, market forces and free competition. Such were the main features of Khrushchev's revisionist economic policies, and they were directly responsible for renewed class polarisation in Soviet society. The Chinese quoted examples intended to illustrate the collapse of the socialist economy. These included functionaries in state enterprises engaging in illegal production of goods from which they amassed huge personal fortunes, embezzlement and bribery among enterprise managers, government officials and collective-farm functionaries, growth of private enterprise in production, contractor teams and services, commercial speculation, operations of brokers and middle-men, and so on. Despite the fact that examples were drawn from Soviet press articles of condemnation, the Chinese saw such activities as a consequence of Khrushchev's policies of weakening state planning and state and collective ownership and replacing them with profits, market forces, and competition. Thus, not only did Khrushchev fail to eliminate such activities, but his policies actively fostered them.(28)

Chinese criticisms also dealt with questions of incentive and management. They objected particularly to Khrushchev's promotion of 'material incentives', which they saw as replacing the socialist principle of distribution according to labour and as leading to a widening income gap between a small minority and the masses.(29) Khrushchev's retreat from state planning was also associated with encouraging greater autonomy of enterprise management and a corresponding division between workers and managers. This is a point which had been more fully developed in the attacks on 'workers' self-management' in Yugoslav enterprises. In this case the Chinese had claimed that the relations between workers and managers had become those between employees and employers, exploited and exploiters. They later charged that, under the new system of management introduced by Khrushchev's successors, Soviet managers had the right to hire and fire workers, fix the levels of wages and bonuses and dispose of large amounts of enterprise funds, thus becoming 'the virtual masters of the enterprises'. They argued that this was an important question concerning relations of production and that such provisions reflected degeneration of the system of state ownership. And they saw the introduction of the new system of management as a confirmation of the experiments begun under Khrushchev.(30) Thus, the dismantling of the socialist economy was not just a function of illegal or semi-legal activities (which were themselves fostered by Khrushchev's policies), but also of legal activities instituted by new revisionist policies.

In the ideological and cultural fields the attacks on Khrushchev were among the most strident, since accusations of revisionism necessarily dealt with perversions of Marxist-Leninist ideology. Chinese sources claimed that Khrushchev tolerated and encouraged the propagation of bourgeois ideology in art and literature, philosophy and all other areas of intellectual endeavour. In general, they saw pervasive ideological manifestations of revisionism in the Soviet Union. These included replacement of the Marxist-Leninist theory of class struggle with notions of 'supra-class' human nature, rejection of dialectical materialism in favour of bourgeois pragmatism, and fostering of bourgeois 'humanism'. The Soviets had abandoned scientific communism, trying to reconcile and merge Marxist materialism with all kinds of bourgeois idealism and even Christianity. As an example of ideological deterioration, the Soviets were said to have become increasingly receptive to the fashions of bourgeois economic theory.(31)

Apart from these ideological lapses, however, the Chinese charges adopted a tone of supreme moral repugnance at Khrushchev's policies. This was a period of accelerating campaigns of revolutionary virtue in China, with the propagation of several models of moral rectitude and service to the revolutionary cause. In this environment, Khrushchev was found to be severly wanting. He had changed all human relations into money relations, had encouraged individualism and selfishness. Manual labour was again considered sordid rather than glorious and necessary for rekindling revolutionary vigour, while selfish hedonism was considered favourably. In short, Khrushchev was seen as promoting attitudes and behaviour most inimical to revolutionary virtue and dangerous to the revolutionary cause. These cultural and ideological forms corresponded to and reinforced the restoration of capitalism. Even Khrushchev's portrayal of communism was morally base - it was goulash communism, the communism of the American way of life. That is, it was based on the selfish desire for narrow material self-interest and was completely antithetical to the moral values and commitment required for moving towards communism.(32)

ORIGINS OF KHRUSHCHEV REVISIONISM

The criticism of Khrushchev revisionism was developed in the most authoritative Chinese sources. Apart from CCP Central Committee letters addressed to the CPSU Central Committee, the most systematic and comprehensive attacks were published under the name of the editorial departments of the party's official organs, the journal Red Flag and the newspaper People's Daily. They clearly expressed the official party attitude to events in the Soviet Union, and there is considerable evidence that top party leaders were directly involved in their formulation.

Despite this, it is tempting to speculate, with Cultural Revolution hindsight, that there may have been major disagreements among the party leaders, or even a pro-Soviet faction. According to the 'two-line struggle' explanation of party history advanced in the Cultural Revolution, a number of party leaders in the early 1960s had been 'capitalist-roaders', a label obviously linked to the accusations directed at Khrushchev. In particular, Liu Shaoqi was designated as 'China's Khrushchev', and one of his supposed crimes was to advocate capitulation to Soviet revisionism.(33) The 'two-line struggle' notion, however, was a deliberate contrivance designed for political purposes during the Cultural Revolution itself, and there is little basis for accepting that it provides a valid interpretation of party history in general or specifically of different attitudes towards Khrushchev revisionism in the 1960s.(34) Certainly there was no evidence at the time that pro-Soviet attitudes prevailed among certain Chinese leaders. Major targets of the Cultural Revolution, including Liu, had been prominent in criticising Khrushchev revisionism.(35) And the Red Guard attempts to demonstrate identity of Liu's and Khrushchev's views, and even collusion between them in opposing Mao, are singularly clumsy and unpersuasive.

This is not to suggest that there were not differences within the Chinese leadership, but such differences cannot be explained in terms of a crude 'two-line struggle' notion, nor can they be linked to positions adopted by some Chinese leaders in opposition to others. Rather, there was a far more confused and fluid situation, whereby, within the framework of an official condemnation formulated at a high level of generality, there were major ambiguities in the analysis of the origin and nature of Khrushchev revisionism. This situation was hardly surprising, given the novelty and sensitivity of the issues which Chinese leaders confronted. The notion of reversal of socialist revolution had not been a major feature of the conception of socialism with which the Chinese had operated in the 1950s. The perception of such reversal, therefore, confronted them with a new problem which their former analytical framework was not equipped to handle. Thus, it was unlikely that any single leader, let alone a group of leaders, could immediately formulate a coherent explanation of what presented itself as a new, and formerly unimagined, phenomenon. And the issues involved were of the utmost importance, since they concerned not only the nature of the former homeland of socialism and leader of the socialist camp, but also raised fundamental questions relating to every revolutionary movement. They had direct implications for China, bearing upon the character of Chinese society, the legitimacy of political institutions, and the means of furthering revolutionary progress.

Hence, despite the assertive language in which they were framed, the early Chinese reactions to Khrushchev revisionism were rather tentative and exploratory. Beneath the official formulations lurked inconsistencies in interpretation of such questions as class struggle and restoration of capitalism. These inconsistencies persisted through the Cultural Revolution and beyond. While acknowledging the inherent oversimplification in attempting to abstract from a complex situation, it is possible to identify three major types of analysis of socialist revolution and the difficulties it faced as these were demonstrated in the interpretation of Khrushchev revisionism.

The first type of analysis was that most consistent with the view of socialist revolution which had prevailed in Chinese discussions during the 1950s. Its fundamental premise was that the institution of state and collective ownership and of state economic planning established a socialist system, defined as a socialist economic base. There were, however, remnants of the overthrown exploiting classes, who survived long after the economic foundation of their class positions had been eliminated. Such remnants often were not reconciled to the socialist system, and could attempt to resist or sabotage it. Spontaneous tendencies towards capitalism among peasants also threatened the socialist system. Most important, however, was the continuing ideological and political 'influence' of the overthrown exploiting classes. A bourgeois superstructure continued to exist despite the establishment of a socialist economic base, since superstructural change would take far longer and be much more difficult than changes in the economic system. Thus, the socialist system would long be threatened by backward ideas, traditions, habits and prejudices inherited from the former society. It was sometimes suggested that these superstructural forms were deliberately used by remnant forces in their resistance to socialism. But the danger was still great without this association, since vestigial superstructural forms were borne by peasants and workers in a socialist society. This view of insidious and pervasive influence of the bourgeoisie and other class forces in socialist society reached a height in the Cultural Revolution, whereby any tendency to be condemned could be attributed to nefarious activities of internal and external enemies or residual superstructural forces. A revisionist leader such as Khrushchev could be seen as a 'representative' of enemy classes, although it was never made clear what representation implied or how it was produced. It was merely asserted that the bourgeoisie's most cunning and sinister tactic was to cultivate agents within the proletarian ranks, and the most conspicuous examples of this were the revisionists. In less conspiratorial vein, Khrushchev could be seen as succumbing to the all-pervasive anti-proletarian influence and failing to counter it in the way Stalin had done. The growth and penetration of such influence posed the danger of undermining the socialist economic base and eventually leading to capitalist restoration.

A second type of analysis rested on a very different notion of socialist revolution. Rather than accepting that economic changes produced a distinct social system identified as socialism, it focussed on socialist revolution as a protracted process of transition from capitalism to communism. The capitalist mode of production persisted as an intrinsic part of socialist society, as Marx had indicated in his discussions of socialist society being stamped with the birthmarks of the capitalist society from the womb of which it had emerged. Ownership questions were important, since socialist revolution involved not only the abolition of private ownership but also the as yet unfulfilled task of eliminating differences between the two forms of 'socialist' ownership by moving from collective ownership to the higher form of 'ownership by the whole people'. But socialist revolution could not be reduced to ownership changes. It also required a far more inclusive transformation of relations of production. In particular, this type of analysis referred to the 'three major differences' between mental and manual labour, city and countryside, workers and peasants, systems of management, and 'bourgeois right' especially with respect to distribution.(36)   Socialist   revolution   and   capitalist restoration were defined as opposite directions of   change   in all   these   areas.   The latter did not mean sudden or dramatic overthrow of an established socialist system, but   rather   the reproduction and strengthening of capitalist forms inherent in socialism as a   transitional   society.   Its   signs   could   be observed   even   within the state-owned sector, which the first type of analysis considered   the   hallmark   of   the   socialist system.   And   class   struggle   was   not   merely a function of remnant forces, since there remained a material basis for   the regeneration   of classes, especially 'new bourgeois elements'. The tasks of the   dictatorship   of   the   proletariat   included continuing   socialist   revolution through progressive negation of the capitalist mode of production and   thereby   eliminating the   basis   for   reemergence of classes.   Khrushchev, however, had abandoned the dictatorship of the   proletariat, with   the result that capitalism was being restored in the Soviet Union. This did not mean   that   the   material   basis   for   capitalist restoration   had   arisen   since   1956.   It   had   been present before,   but   was   now   being   reinforced   and   expanded   by Khrushchev's   policies.   Under   Stalin new bourgeois elements had been subjected to restriction and suppression,   but   under Khrushchev   their numbers had grown, and they had risen to the ruling positions in   Soviet   society.   Khrushchev's   policies served   their   interests,   and they had come to form the social basis of the Khrushchev clique.

The third type of analysis also dealt with the growth   of new   classes   within   socialist   society, but it was concerned principally with the effects of privilege, especially as   this was associated with political power. 'New bourgeois elements' could arise   through   individual   degeneration   or   corruption among   those   in   official   positions.   Sometimes   this was a result of succumbing to blandishments of remnant classes,   but it   could be simply a case of cadres yielding to opportunities for privilege afforded by their   positions.   At   its   crudest this   type   of   analysis   saw capitalist restoration occurring because of the machinations of individuals who had usurped and then   perverted   the   dictatorship of the proletariat.   In the Soviet Union capitalist restoration could be   dated   precisely to   Khrushchev's   'coup'   in   which   he seized party and state power, and was a consequence of Khrushchev's evil   intentions. Thus,   socialist   revolution   and   capitalist restoration were seen in terms of a Manichaean   power   struggle   among   central leaders.   Such   an interpretation became prominent during the Cultural   Revolution,   when   the   equation   of   the   Chinese revolution   with   Mao   personally   was   complemented   by   the personification of   counter-revolution   in   the   attacks   upon Liu.(37)   There   was, however, also a less individualistic and more systemic interpretation of capitalist restoration.   This was   linked   not   to   persistence   of   the   capitalist mode of production but to inequality and privilege established by the socialist system itself. Party functionaries, government officials, enterprise managers, and so on, exercised control over the means of production to the exclusion of direct producers. They maintained their privileges by living off the fruits of others' labour. At times this explanation approached a view of bureaucracy as a class. It was most pronounced in criticism of Yugoslavia, which stressed the bureaucratic character of the new bourgeoisie. In the Soviet Union the 'bourgeois privileged stratum' included persons such as higher-level intellectuals, but the main components were those with political, administrative or managerial power. And in the Cultural Revolution this type of analysis was reflected in advocacy of completely restructuring political institutions using the Paris Commune model, and among those Red Guards who saw the target of attack not as a limited number of 'capitalist-roaders' and their revisionist policies but as the overwhelming majority of Chinese officials who constituted a new class.

Chinese criticisms, therefore, advanced several different explanations for the origins of Khrushchev revisionism and capitalist restoration in the Soviet Union. This is not to suggest, however, that any discrepancy was emphasised or even recognised in Chinese discussions. On the contrary, the explanations were advanced as complementary and mutually reinforcing rather than alternative or competing. Thus, the 'new bourgeois elements' or the 'bourgeois privileged stratum' were produced through persistence of capitalist forms, degeneration of individual officials, inequality and privilege within the political, administrative and managerial systems, influence of overthrown exploiting classes and vestigial superstructure. And they acted in collusion with remnant classes in opposing socialist revolution. All factors were combined in mounting as wide-ranging an attack as possible on Khrushchev revisionism.

The apparent complementarity of different types of analysis, however, disguised disagreement at the fundamental level of conception of socialist revolution. In the context of anti-Khrushchev polemics such disagreement was not important, largely because Chinese criticisms were essentially irresponsible. They could criticise Khrushchev's faults without having to bother about remedial measures. In attempting to apply the negative lessons of Soviet experience to the Chinese context during the Cultural Revolution, however, the potential for conflict between different types of analysis was realised. Was the movement to be directed against remnant class forces and superstructure, with the major activists being those of the best class background? Or were many of the latter themselves principal targets because they were becoming 'new bourgeois elements'?   Did   opposition to 'new bourgeois elements' imply destroying instances of privilege and even overthrowing the overwhelming   majority   of officials?   Or did it require fostering 'socialist new things' designed for progressively negating capitalist forms and leading the overwhelming majority of cadres to repudiate revisionist policies?   These and other questions resulted   not only in different emphases in the Cultural Revolution but also in often   sharp   antagonism   between   different   groups   whose interests were   directly affected.   The latent ambiguities in Chinese criticisms of Khrushchev revisionism led to severe division   and   political   antagonism   when   the   negative implications of Soviet experience for China itself became   the focus of attention during the Cultural Revolution.

CONCLUSION

The Chinese attitude to Khrushchevism was directly   associated with   use   of   the   Soviet   Union   as   a   model   for socialist development.   During the 1950s the Chinese regarded the Soviet Union   first as a model to be followed closely, then as one to be followed selectively and critically, and finally, with   the emergence   of their own distinctive developmental strategy, as one of little relevance and utility.   By the early 1960s there had   been   a   complete   <u>volte-face</u>.   The   relevance of Soviet experience was again acknowledged, but now as a negative model illustrating the danger of revolutionary reversal.   It was not until this last step was taken that the Chinese began to blame Khrushchev for   the   degeneration which they saw occurring in the Soviet Union, a process which   they   labelled   'Khrushchev revisionism'.   In   the   earlier period Chinese criticisms had been mild and covert and implied that, despite   his   measures for   reform, Khrushchev had failed to overcome problems of the Stalinist model.   The   later   public   attacks   on   Khrushchev claimed   that   he   had   gone too far by discarding essential socialist principles which Stalin had maintained, leading   to the   implementation of a systematic revisionist program in the Soviet Union.

Despite their virulent and sustained attacks, the Chinese polemicists rarely advanced specific evidence to support their broad assertions of Soviet domestic degeneration, in   contrast to   their   discussions   of   Soviet   foreign policy.   They also failed to provide a coherent analysis of the origin and nature of   Khrushchev revisionism.   In fact, the Chinese discussions suggested several distinct   types   of   analysis,   illustrating ambiguity   and   confusion among Chinese leaders on fundamental questions of socialist revolution.   If Khrushchev   revisionism was   recognised   as the principal negative model, it was still by no means clear what were its salient features, nor   how   it might be used to prevent capitalist restoration in the Chinese context. Khrushchev revisionism could play the role of universal scapegoat, incorporating any trend considered to be deviant and providing a symbolic target for political mobilisation. But when the focus shifted to specific definition of deviant trends and identification of dangers to socialist revolution in China, the failure to confront inconsistencies within the generalised analysis of Khrushchev revisionism rebounded with the growth of mutually antagonistic political positions.

However ill-defined, Khrushchev revisionism maintained its force as the principal source of negative instruction during the Cultural Revolution, because, according to Chinese analyses, it survived Khrushchev himself. An early Chinese reaction to Khrushchev's downfall was that his removal by the CPSU and the Soviet people was a victory for Marxism-Leninism and a discrediting of his revisionist line.(38) But that tone soon changed markedly. Later statements argued that Khrushchev revisionism was not an accidental phenomenon produced by a few individuals, but had 'deep social roots', especially in the 'bourgeois privileged stratum'. This stratum, rather than the CPSU and Soviet people, had removed Khrushchev, not because he was revisionist but because he was 'too stupid and disreputable', he had fostered mass resentment, and his bungling led to crises. His ineptitude was a threat to the dominant position of the privileged stratum. In that case, Khrushchev himself was an obstacle to Khrushchev revisonism. While it was necessary to replace Khrushchev, his revisionist line persisted. It was maintained by his successors, the only difference being that they were more cunning, more hypocritical, and more dangerous.(39) Khrushchev retained his position as chief representative of modern revisionism for several years, until the Chinese began to claim an even greater apostasy as his successors led the Soviet Union into 'social imperialism'.

NOTES

1. Wang Chia-hsiang, 'In Refutation of Modern Revisionism's Reactionary Theory of the State', in <u>In Refutation of Modern Revisionism</u>, Peking: Foreign Languages Press, 1958, p. 68.

2. Editorial Department of <u>People's Daily</u>, 'More on the Historical Experience of the Dictatorship of the Proletariat' in <u>Documents of Chinese Communist Party Central Committee Sept. 1956 - Apr. 1969</u> (2 vols., Hong Kong: Union Research Institute, 1974), Vol. 2, p. 1026 - hereafter cited as <u>Documents</u>; Mao in <u>Mao Zedong Sixiang</u>

Wansui (Long Live Mao Zedong Thought), no place, no publisher, 1969, pp. 39,66 - hereafter cited Wansui 1969.

3.   Editorial Department of People's Daily, 'On the Historical Experience of the Dictatorship of the Proletariat' and 'More on the Historical Experience of the Dictatorship of the Proletariat', both in Documents Vol. 2; Mao 'On the Correct Handling of Contradictions Among the People' (hereafter cited as 'Correct Handling') in Selected Works of Mao Tsetung Vol. V, Peking: Foreign Languages Press, 1977.

4.   "Correct Handling', p. 391; Wansui 1969, p. 87.

5.   Mao Zedong Sixiang Wansui (Long Live Mao Zedong Thought), no place, no publisher, 1967, pp. 51,125,150 - hereafter cited as Wansui 1967; Wansui 1969 p. 213;   Liu Shaoqi, 'Report on the Work of the Central Committee', in Second Session of the Eighth National Congress of the Communist Party of China, Peking: Foreign Languages Press, 1958, p. 39.

6.   In Stuart Schram (ed.) Mao Tse-tung Unrehearsed, Harmondsworth: Penguin, 1974, p. 94.

7.   'On the Historical Experience of the Dictatorship of the Proletariat', pp. 1000-1001; 'More on the Historical Experience of the Dictatorship of the Proletariat', pp. 1117-1020; Wansui 1969, pp. 77, 204-5,248-9. Mao also stated, however, that Stalin did have some understanding of dialectics, and that he recognised the role of contradictions before his death - Wansui, p. 205. Mao also suggested that criticisms of Stalin be restricted to within the Party - Wansui 1969, p. 40.

8.   'On Ten Major Relationships', Wansui 1969, pp. 40-59. An official version of this speech was not published until after Mao's death and is more explicitly critical of the Soviet Union: Selected Works of Mao Tsetung, Vol. V, pp. 284-307.

9.   Wansui 1969, p. 84.

10. 'Report on the Work of the Central Committee', loc.cit., p. 78.

11. Mao in an untitled collection of documents appended to Mao Zedong Sixiang Wansui (Long Live Mao Zedong Thought), no place, no publisher, April 1967), (a version separate from the pamphlet cited above as Wansui 1967), p. 33.

12. 'Correct Handling', p. 413.

13. <u>Wansui</u> 1969, p. 222.

14. <u>Wansui</u> 1969, pp. 105,255.

15. 'Correct Handling', pp. 411-412.

16. <u>Wansui</u> 1967, p. 82; Chen Po-ta, 'The Struggle Between the Proletarian World Outlook and the Bourgeois World Outlook' in <u>The Case of Peng Teh-huai 1959-1968</u>, Hong Kong: Union Research Institute, 1968, p. 110.

17. <u>The Polemic on the General Line of the International Communist Movement</u>, Peking: Foreign Languages Press, 1965, p. 101. Hereafter cited as <u>Polemic</u>.

18. For example, <u>Leninism and Modern Revisionism</u>, Peking: Foreign Languages Press, 1963, and 'Hold High the Revolutionary Banner of Marxism-Leninism', editorial of <u>Renmin Ribao</u> (<u>People's Daily</u>), 24 September 1964, in <u>Peking Review</u>, No. 41, 1964, pp. 8-9. It is interesting to note in passing a peculiarly mechanical interpretation of the development of revisionism. In 1964 there arose a brief but fierce theoretical debate in China, revolving around whether dialectics concerned 'two combining into one' or 'one dividing into two'. The former position was rejected because it implied reconciliation, while the latter was officially approved because it indicated the need for struggle. The principle of 'one dividing into two' was used to argue that within any Marxist-Leninist movement, a revisionist trend was bound to emerge. See, for example, An Ziewen, 'Cultivating Revolutionary Successors is a Strategic Task of the Party', <u>Hongqi</u> (<u>Red Flag</u>) No. 17-18, 1964, p. 3; Zhou Yang, 'The Fighting Task Confronting Workers in Philosophy and the Social Sciences', <u>Peking Review</u>, No. 1, 1964, p. 12. Zhou's speech actually pre-dated the campaign concerning 'one dividing into two' by several months.

19. <u>Polemic</u>, p. 490.

20. 'Unite Under the Banner of the Great October Revolution', editorial of <u>Renmin Ribao</u>, 7 November 1964, in <u>Peking Review</u>, No. 46, 1964, p. 16; <u>Carry the Struggle Against Khrushchev Revisionism Through to the End</u>, Peking: Foreign Languages Press, 1965, p. 4.

21. See the discussion of the 'comprador' character of the 'Tito clique', <u>Polemic</u>, pp. 161-175.

22. Mao indicated the use of the Soviet Union as a negative model as early as January 1962: <u>Wansui</u> 1969, p. 418.

23. For example, 'Hold High the Revolutionary Banner of Marxism-Leninism', loc.cit., p. 9. Mao, commenting on the beneficial or harmful effects of a single word, claimed that Marx was one word linked to proletarian revolution and dictatorship, while Khrushchev was one word linked to not wanting class struggle and revolution; <u>Wansui</u> 1969, p. 442.

24. <u>Polemic</u>, pp. 459-467. Mao had earlier, before the beginning of Chinese attacks on Soviet revisionism, welcomed Khrushchev's claims concerning rapid establishment of communism: <u>Wansui</u> 1967, pp. 133-134.

25. <u>Polemic</u>, pp. 429,410.

26. <u>Polemic</u>, pp. 36-39,444-458,462,479,440-442,489. In 1964, Mao asserted: 'Today the Soviet Union is a dictatorship of the bourgeoisie, a dictatorship of the big bourgeoisie, a German Fascist dictatorship, a Hitler-style dictatorship'. <u>Wansui</u> 1969, p. 496. The Yugoslav regime was also seen as a 'brutal fascist dictatorship', <u>Polemic</u>, p. 173.

27. <u>Polemic</u>, pp. 117-138,40,61,429.

28. <u>Polemic</u>, pp. 430-435, passim. Mao suggested that Khrushchev still did not dare to dissolve collective farms, implying that he would if he dared: <u>Wansui</u> 1969, p. 425. The argument concerning abandoning state planning and state and collective ownership was more fully developed with respect to Yugoslavia, and the Chinese claimed that Khrushchev was following the Yugoslav example: <u>Polemic</u>, pp. 145ff; Shi Dongxiang, 'Degeneration of the Yugoslav Economy of Ownership by the Whole People', <u>Hongqi</u> (<u>Red Flag</u>) No. 10, 1964, pp. 1-19 and 'Yugoslav Agriculture Develops Along the Capitalist Road', <u>Hongqi</u> No. 11, 1964, pp. 6-22.

29. <u>Polemic</u>, p. 439; Zhou Yang, loc.cit., p. 21.

30. <u>Polemic</u>, p. 157; Editorial Departments of <u>Renmin Ribao</u> and <u>Hongqi</u>, <u>Refutation of the New Leaders of the CPSU on 'United Action'</u>, Peking: Foreign Languages Press, 1965, pp. 27-8.

31. These charges are catalogued in Zhou Yang, loc.cit., pp. 16-21. Zhou also provides one of the few Chinese discussions of the concept of alienation, arguing that

the Soviets had distorted it into conformity with a bourgeois theory of human nature.

32. Polemic, pp. 461-466. Malraux reported Mao's quoting Kosygin that 'Communism means the raising of living standards' and Mao's contemptuous retort: 'Of course! And swimming is a way of putting on a pair of trunks!' A. Malraux, Anti-Memoirs trans. T. Kilmartin, London: Hamish Hamilton, 1968, p. 392.

33. Schurmann argues that, for all his opposition to the Soviets, Liu ultimately could see no alternative to Sino-Soviet alliance and the socialist camp: Franz Schurmann, The Logic of World Power, New York: Pantheon, 1974, pp. 336-344. Schurmann is probably right in stressing Liu's orientation towards the need for a coherent body encompassing the world revolutionary movement. It would appear more likely, however, that Liu would favour the establishment of an alternative body, excluding the Soviet Union. His early writings on revolutionary organisation stressed that such organisation had to be based on ideological uniformity.

34. On 'two-line struggle', see Lowell Dittmer, '"Line Struggle" in Theory and Practice: The Origins of the Cultural Revolution Reconsidered', China Quarterly, No. 72, 1977. For an extended analysis countering the 'two-line struggle' interpretation of Chinese politics in the early 1960s, see Frederick C. Teiwes, Politics and Purges in China: Rectification and the Decline of Party Norms 1950-1965, White Plains: M.E. Sharp, 1979, chapter 11.

35. For example, Zhou Yang, loc.cit.; Peng Zhen in Hongqi No. 6, 1965, p. 11; Liu Shaoqi, 'Speech at the Nguyen Ai Quoc Party School' in Collected Works of Liu Zhao-ch'i: 1958-1967, Hong Kong: Union Research Institute, 1968, pp. 212-213. At times it appeared that Mao was the main force in opposing Soviet revisionism. There is no doubt some basis for this, in that Mao was said to have retired from much daily policy-making in order to consider more fully general questions of socialist revolution. But the personal identification of Mao with the Chinese criticisms can easily be over-emphasised. One reason for this is that the period was one of tremendous growth in the authority of Mao's Thought. This meant that all attacks upon Khrushchev revisionism referred to Mao's authority, and also that Mao himself was the only leader with sufficient personal authority to advance new criticisms more or less independently. Secondly, it is largely accidental that we have such a large number of

Mao's non-public criticisms of the Soviets because of the unofficial publication of many of his earlier writings and speeches during the Cultural Revolution. There is no comparable set of materials for any other leader.

36. Mao in 1960 had prefigured this focus on relations between individuals in the production process and distribution as well as ownership in his 'Reading Notes on the Soviet Union's "Political Economy"'. At that time, however, his discussion was not linked to any notion of regeneration of classes or restoration of capitalism. Wansui 1969, pp. 319-399.

37. Lin Biao was most prominent in the emphasis on power struggle - see his 'Address to Politburo' (18 May 1966) in Zhonggong Wenhua Da Geming Zhongyao Wenjian Huibian (Collection of Important Documents of the Chinese Communist Great Cultural Revolution), Taipei: Institute for the Study of Chinese Communist Problems, 1973, pp. 334-338.. But Mao also was quoted as implying that capitalist restoration was a function of the subjective intentions of certain leaders - for example, Wansui 1969, pp. 620-621.

38. 'Unite Under the Banner of the Great October Revolution', loc.cit., p. 16; Polemic, pp. 483-492.

39. Carry the Struggle Against Khrushchev Revisionism Through to the End, passim; Refutation of the New Leaders of the CPSU on 'United Action', pp. 5,29.

Chapter Seven

KHRUSHCHEV AND TITO

Robert F. Miller

I Will shake my little finger - and there will be no
more Tito. He will fall.

We have paid dearly for this 'shaking of the little
finger'. This statement reflected Stalin's mania
for greatness, but he acted just that way... But
this did not happen to Tito. No matter how much or
how little Stalin shook, not only his little finger
but everything else that he could shake, Tito did
not fall. Why? The reason was that, in the case of
disagreement with the Yugoslav comrades, Tito had
behind him a state and a people who had gone through
a severe school of fighting for liberty and
independence, a people which gave support to its
leaders.

(Khrushchev, in his secret speech at the
20th Congress of the CPSU).

Khrushchev's unusual tribute to Tito, a foreign communist, in
his famous 'Secret Speech' at the 20th Party Congress 1956,
reflected his grudging respect for Tito as a communist
elder-statesman who had challenged Stalin and gotten away with
it, and who certainly knew how to run his own country.(1) But
it also reflected the special role he had in mind for Tito in
his strategy for improving the basis of intra-Bloc relations,
especially in Eastern Europe. The story of Khrushchev's
persistent efforts to lure Tito back into the Bloc is one of
the most fascinating examples of Khrushchevism in foreign
policy and the complex fabric of stylistic, political and
structural elements which contributed to its makeup.

    For Khrushchev, rapprochement with Tito had symbolic as
well as substantive value. As a corollary of his belief in
the genuinely attractive force of socialism he nurtured a
grand scheme for reconstructing internal relations within the
Bloc to eliminate the coercive, terror-centred linkages of the
Stalinist system. Gaining Tito's acquiescence in the new
order would at once symbolise the break with the past and
provide, through Tito's own efforts and his personal example,
a useful instrument for encouraging and cementing the new
relationships. As an added bonus, it would give Soviet policy
an entry into important areas of the Third World, where Tito

had been establishing firm links even prior to the formation of the non-aligned movement.(2)

The Khrushchev-Tito relationship featured certain interesting psychological components. Both men were consummate politicians and shrewd, if not always infallible, judges of character. And they were a good match for each other. Both were inclined to be tempestuous and rash on occasion, but were equally able to play their reputations for temperamentalism to good advantage. Tito was clever enough to realise that many of Khrushchev's rude outbursts against him and Yugoslav policy were designed for domestic and internal Bloc effect, a sign that temporary weakness before his conservative opponents had forced him to adopt a harder line than he intended. Khrushchev, of course, understood Tito's tolerance and made good use of it. He also understood Tito's desire for international acclaim and, above all, his wish to be accorded vindication and privileged status in the international communist movement. But he invariably misjudged the price Tito was willing to pay for such tribute, and his bullying impatience was often counter-productive.

Tito fundamentally shared Khrushchev's vision of a new basis for relations among socialist states and communist parties, but he often misjudged how far the Soviet leader was willing to go to achieve it. Khrushchev wanted Soviet predominance in the Bloc, which he considered self-evident, to be accepted voluntarily; while Tito wanted the principle of dominance by any party to be abolished in its entirety. He had acquired too much prestige as an international figure to be willing to submit ever again to Bloc discipline, no matter how democratically a common policy was arrived at. Democratic centralism was acceptable within a given party - it had always been mandatory in the League of Communists of Yugoslavia under Tito - but it was not acceptable in relations between parties. Thus, there was a basic contradiction in procedural and organisational norms, rather than in substantive policies, between Khrushchev and Tito, and this is what ultimately made complete agreement impossible.

THE FIRST ATTEMPT AT RAPPROCHEMENT

The death of Stalin in March 1953 was viewed by Tito and some of his colleagues as a major turning point in Soviet foreign policy with special implications for Soviet-Yugoslav relations in particular.(3) Edvard Kardelj, already by then Tito's chief ideological amenuensis, noted in a speech the following June that 'a new phase in the development of international relations' had begun, one 'which demands also a new testing of political methods and forms'.(4) Thus, when in mid-June the

USSR proposed to normalise relations with Belgrade by elevating its representation once again to the ambassadorial level, the Yugoslavs quickly assented. Tito did not expect immediate miracles, but he publicly professed to believe 'that the leaders of the Soviet Union have a real desire to make some changes in the methods of their foreign policy...'.(5) He was ready to let the Soviets make amends.

For Tito the chance for rapprochement with Moscow came at a very opportune time. He had already begun to worry - most recently at a Central Committee Plenum at his retreat on the Brioni Islands in June - over the excesses of liberalism which had crept into party affairs since the 6th LCY Congress the previous November. Because much of the impetus for liberalisation had come from the desire to buttress support for Yugoslavia in the West against Soviet pressures, the alleviation of the latter following Stalin's death provided Tito with a welcome breathing space for internal stock-taking.(6)

Khrushchev seemed to sense Tito's predicament and undertook to convince his reluctant colleagues in the CPSU Presidium and the foreign communist parties that the first steps toward rapproachement would have to come from Moscow.(7) Foreign Minister V.M. Molotov did not make his task any easier by publicly placing a major share of the onus for past ill feelings on the Yugoslav leadership. Khrushchev wisely chose to overlook Tito's umbrage at Molotov's conspicuous heavy-handedness.(8) And he decided to lead the Soviet delegation to Canossa himself in the famous pilgrimage to Belgrade in late May 1955.

On his arrival, however, Khrushchev immediately demon-strated that he was no stranger to heavy-handedness himself, seriously underestimating Tito's sensitivity by attempting to attribute the blame for past enmities entirely to Beria and his henchmen. In his memoirs he admits to being surprised and disappointed at the coolness of Tito's reaction to this ploy. He evidently found it difficult to comprehend the Yugoslav leader's refusal to accept the offer of the mutual face-saving gesture of diverting blame from Stalin and the Stalinist system, with which neither he nor his colleagues were as yet ready to break completely.(9)

Thus, if Khrushchev had expected to be able to lure Tito quickly and painlessly back into close inter-party relations and bring Yugoslavia back into the Bloc, he was in for something of a shock. Tito was pressing for nothing less than a complete vindication of Yugoslav conduct during and since the 1948 quarrel with Stalin; in particular he sought a Soviet repudiation of the June 1948 resolution of the

Cominform expelling Yugoslavia and branding her leaders as revisionists.(10) This Khrushchev was not prepared to do in 1955, nor, indeed, have any Soviet leaders been willing to do so since. It would have meant denying the legitimacy of the basically Stalinist Soviet model itself and of its imposition, in the name of anti-Titoism, on the rest of the East European Bloc states.

But neither could Khrushchev afford to return from Belgrade empty handed, not without appearing ridiculous before his conservative opponents who had resisted overtures to Tito in the first place. So he settled for half a loaf: in this case the re-establishment of normal state relations. In the process he grudgingly accepted Tito's demand for Soviet endorsement of the principles of 'sovereignty, independence, territorial integrity, equality and mutual respect, and non-interference in internal affairs for any reason'.(11) Khrushchev's memoirs reflect his continuing ambivalence over the acceptance of these principles.

> At the end of our first visit to Yugoslavia, we released a joint communique. This declaration was only a point of departure. Tito insisted on our commitment to the principles of complete non-interference in the internal affairs of other countries and other Parties and the right of every country to assert its own will without pressure from the outside. We agreed to do this, believing sincerely as we did that relations must be built on mutual trust. The joint communique raised some questions that might better have been avoided, but most of the rough spots were smoothed over. This accord, of course, was only the beginning. After such a long period of hostility, there was more to restoring relations than just sitting down at a table and drinking a glass of wine together.(12)

To raise the inducement for closer relations and help Tito reduce his uncomfortable dependence on Western economic aid, Khrushchev, soon after returning home, announced agreement to Yugoslav requests for development credits, in particular for a major aluminium plant to be built with Soviet equipment.

During his conversations with Tito, Khrushchev had evidently convinced him that he, Khrushchev, represented the only hope for a genuine de-Stalinisation of Soviet domestic and foreign policy and that he required all the help he could muster in resisting conservative forces in the USSR and the Bloc. With the partial exception of the deterioration in relations following the Hungarian events of 1956 and their repercussions, Tito's acceptance of this proposition shaped his policies toward the USSR throughout the years of Khrushchev's reign. There was, of course, a measure of truth in this picture of Soviet politics, and Khrushchev exercised considerable shrewdness in gaining all the mileage he could from it, playing on Tito's personal experience in the international movement in the periods of ascendant and mature Stalinism.

Khrushchev apparently removed any lingering doubts about his intentions in Tito's mind by his secret speech at the 20th Party Congress. Not only had he named Stalin as the chief culprit for the split with Yugoslavia, but he had confronted the issue of Stalinism itself as directly as Tito considered possible under existing circumstances. Clearly the way had been cleared for a genuine and close rapprochement between the two leaders, their parties, and their governments. On the 14th of March 1956, on the eve of his departure for Moscow as Yugoslav Ambassador-designate, Veljko Mićunović, a former Deputy Foreign Minister and erstwhile secret police official, wrote in his published diaries:

> I am going to Moscow with Tito's best wishes to Khrushchev in respect to the further development of Yugoslav-Soviet relations. Could one expect anything bigger and better than this? It has turned out that I have the exceptional luck to be going to Moscow under such circumstances and could wish for nothing better.(13)

Mićunović's euphoria would not survive the first few months of his new assignment, but his comments here are a good reflection of the atmosphere in high Yugoslav government and party circles created by Khrushchev's speech and the prospects for improved relations with Moscow and the Bloc.

Tito's return visit to the USSR the following June was celebrated as something of a personal triumph, just as Khrushchev intended it to be. Tito was given unusual opportunities to address Soviet workers and was received with extravagant pomp and ceremony throughout his stay.(14)* In the final communiqué, the so-called Moscow Declaration, signed on June 20th near the end of Tito's sojourn, Khrushchev accepted the principle of diverse roads to socialism and endorsed Yugoslavia's legitimacy as a state engaged in socialist construction. Direct relations between the CPSU and the LCY

---

* At a dinner at the Yugoslav Ambassador's residence even Molotov was reported to have hailed the new Soviet-Yugoslav relationship.

were now fully and formally restored. In the course of their
conversations Tito, in turn, promised Khrushchev to recognise
East Germany at the earliest opportune moment.

From the outside it appeared as if the visits had given
Khrushchev virtually everything he had sought. Indeed,
Western diplomats in Moscow took Yugoslavia's return to full
participation in the Bloc for granted as only a matter of
time.(15) Actually, the process of reconciliation had been
substantially more complicated than they had realised. From
Micunovic's diary we now understand that for Khrushchev the
principles enunciated in the Belgrade and Moscow Declarations,
and even the question of Yugoslavia's economic ties with the
West, were relatively secondary matters. What he was really
after was Tito's basic agreement on common ideological
principles and his commitment to the Bloc under tacit Soviet
pre-eminence.(16) Khrushchev kept insisting on these
concessions and was willing to settle for a secret separate
document to record them, but Tito refused, even if this meant
the failure of the entire trip. Both he and Khrushchev put up
a bold front of agreement at a mass meeting in Dinamo Stadium
on the 19th of June. But in the end only the more modest
Moscow Declaration on inter-party relations was signed the
following day.

Immediately after Tito's departure Khrushchev summoned
the leaders of the Bloc parties to Moscow to report on his
conversations, to clarify his ideas on proper relations within
the Bloc, and to announce the founding of a new theoretical
journal, with its editorial offices in Prague, to set forth
the authoritative ideological line on Bloc positions. (To
please Tito the Cominform had officially been buried the
previous April.) Of Khrushchev's behaviour Mićunović recalls:

> At this meeting of Bloc chiefs no one even mentioned
> the Moscow Declaration, which had been published
> here only two days before the meeting! This
> ignoring of the Moscow Declaration only the day
> after its signing can only mean Soviet
> dissatisfaction with that document. In any case the
> Russians in this manner put the leaders of the Bloc
> countries on notice that what had been signed with
> Tito did not apply to the policy of the USSR toward
> the states and communist parties of the Bloc
> countries. No one had anything to ask, anything to
> say.(17)

Yet Khrushchev did not give up trying. As is well known,
he consulted Tito on the replacement of the latter's
bête-noire, Matyas Rakosi, as Hungarian party boss, albeit
with the only slightly less objectionable Ernö Gerö in July,

thus pointedly involving Tito in Bloc affairs. Unfortunately for Nikita Sergeevich, the basic contradiction in his policy toward Tito - on the one hand, to lure him back among the faithful by conceding the legitimacy of most of what had come to be called 'Titoism'; on the other, to attempt to quarantine Yugoslav practices from emulation by others in the Bloc - soon began to assert itself. By the summer of 1956 reformers in the two most volatile satellite states, Poland and Hungary, had begun pressing for the introduction of workers' councils and other Yugoslav-type innovations.(18)

Suddenly Khrushchev began to have second thoughts on rapprochement with Tito. Sometime in September the CPSU Central Committee sent a confidential circular to the other Bloc parties on the recent Soviet-Yugoslav negotiations with an implicit warning that the permissible scope for national deviation from the orthodox Soviet model was decidedly limited. In effect the circular represented a disavowal of the Moscow Declaration as merely a diplomatic gesture to Tito and of no general significance. It also attempted to categorise individual Yugoslav leaders as pro- or anti-Soviet.(19)

The fact that little effort was apparently made to keep the contents of the circular from 'leaking' to Tito could hardly have strengthened his confidence in Soviet bona fides. And indeed Khrushchev found it necessary to make a hasty 'private' visit to Yugoslavia in mid-September to try to limit the damage already done. Exceptionally fortuitous for his purposes at this time was the increasing gravity of the Middle Eastern situation following Nasser's nationalisation of the Suez Canal. Tito had already established close links with Nasser and found Soviet policies of support for Egypt against mounting Western pressures quite congenial. In fact, as a general rule the foreign policy views of the two communist statesmen were, with the notable exception of intra-Bloc relations and nuclear testing, usually extremely close, not to say identical. Their common ideological heritage was undoubtedly the decisive factor here, although Tito was, by necessity, always more flexible in dealing with the 'imperialists' and the Third World than Khrushchev was, or could afford to be. In the case of Suez the imperatives of 'solidarity against imperialism' doubtless helped to smooth the difficulties over the secret circular.

The brutal Soviet repression of the Hungarian rebellion initially led by Imre Nagy, whom Tito closely supported, naturally caused a souring of Yugoslav-Soviet relations. For a time it appeared as if the process of rapprochement must certainly be terminated. But even here Khrushchev had striven to involve Tito by scrupulously consulting him at a secret meeting on Brioni in November 2nd and 3rd, on the arguments for the pending Soviet intervention. In short, Yugoslavia was being treated as a fully fledged member of the Bloc.* Khrushchev obviously felt he had Tito just where he wanted him. With the Suez Crisis in full swing and Nagy losing control over the events in Hungary, Tito would have to take a stand. Indeed, Tito did finally give tacit assent to Soviet actions, although he expressed concern for the fate of Nagy and thought he had obtained the necessary assurances for his safety.(20)

That is why Tito's speech at Pula on November 11th, condemning the entire Soviet handling of the Hungarian situation, although accepting the second Soviet intervention as a necessary evil, evoked such an angry Soviet response.(21) For the next six months Yugoslav-Soviet relations were tense and charged with mutual recriminations. However, realising that Khrushchev was under great pressure from his conservative opponents at home, Tito refrained from taking a direct personal part in the exchange of invectives with Moscow, leaving it to others in his entourage to reply to Soviet charges. He confined himself to bland assurances that relations would eventually be smoothed out since it was in no one's interest that they remain tense.(22) Significantly, Yugoslav representatives in the United Nations were instructed not to join in the almost universal condemnation of Soviet actions in Hungary. Mićunović in Moscow received orders in December not to let relations deteriorate further.(23) This self-restraint in the face of harsh Soviet provocation, including threats to renege on the aluminium smelter project, undoubtedly made it easier for Khrushchev to resume his efforts toward accommodation with Tito once he had the domestic political situation under control again in mid-1957.

But in the meantime another factor had arisen to complicate the further development of Yugoslav-Soviet relations: China. Zhou Enlai, who was travelling in Eastern Europe early in 1957 to help straighten out the situation after Hungary, added to the pressure on Khrushchev to rehabilitate Stalin. Khrushchev, at the time extremely vulnerable over the recent events, had accepted Zhou's lead on

---

* Mićunović (ibid, pp. 159-163) asserts that Tito's advice was decisive in getting Khrushchev to accept Janos Kadar, rather than the old war horse, Ferenc Munnich, as the replacement for Imre Nagy. In my opinion this is highly unlikely. Khrushchev may have thought it wise to let Tito think his advice was crucial - as a kind of ego massage, but by this time Tito's opinions were not likely to have been considered altogether reliable or safe.

this question, although friction between the two communist superpowers was beginning to emerge.(24) Chinese pressure was thus added to Khrushchev's to force Yugoslav submission to Bloc solidarity. Curiously, at this time the expectation was that China was still somehow exerting a moderating influence in Bloc policy.

As Khrushchev consolidated his position at home once again, however, he began to improve the atmosphere for a resumption of normal relations with Yugoslavia. In May the vicious Soviet propaganda campaign against Yugoslav revisionism suddenly came to a halt. Khrushchev informed Ambassador Mićunović of his desire to arrange a private meeting with Tito and Polish leader Gomulka.(25) Yugoslav Defense Secretary Ivan Gošnjak was invited to visit the USSR by his Soviet counterpart, Marshal Zhukov, Khrushchev's main ally against the 'anti-Party Group'; and in July Tito's principal lieutenants, Edvard Kardelj and Aleksandar Ranković, journeyed to Moscow to confer with Soviet and Bloc leaders.

The stage was now set for a direct meeting between the two main actors themselves. Their secret conference in Bucharest on the 1st and 2nd of August was to mark the high point in their efforts to reach a personal understanding. Khrushchev, now supremely confident, applied a maximum of pressure, and Tito apparently conceded almost everything short of formal membership in the Bloc's military, political, and economic organisations. Mićunović suggests that Tito was so ready to yield because of his desire to support Khrushchev, whose position was seen as still not totally secure against Stalinist attacks despite his recent victory over the anti-Party Group.(26) Richard Lowenthal, the well known authority on communist affairs, was less charitable in his interpretation. In his view,

> [Tito] was willing to stake the future of Yugoslavia on the chance of influencing Khrushchev; and once again he overruled the voices of caution, of which there were many.(27)

In the weeks that followed it did indeed look as if Khrushchev had Tito well and truly 'in the bag'. Tito virtually turned his back on non-alignment and his carefully nurtured ties with the West. In September he signed an agreement with Gomulka containing the previously objectionable commitment to 'proletarian internationalism'. And in October he announced Yugoslavia's formal diplomatic recognition of East Germany in the full realisation that under the Hallstein Doctrine this would mean the severance of diplomatic relations by West Germany. By this time it increasingly appeared as if Tito was more interested in rapproachement than was

Khrushchev. In Mićunović's usually sound judgment at least, Khrushchev had less need of Tito's endorsement now than two years earlier.(28) The Bulgarian and Albanian party leaders were not at all enthusiastic over the new rapprochement, but, contrary to Yugoslav expectations, neither were the Chinese.(29) By late summer the latter were eagerly plumping for broad foreign communist party representation at the Moscow celebration of the 40th Anniversary of the Bolshevik Revolution, and they were strongly urging the Yugoslavs to attend. Evidently, Mao and Zhou's reasons for welcoming the international communist summit conference were not necessarily identical to Khrushchev's.

When it became obvious that the forthcoming meeting would entail the promulgation of a joint policy declaration obligatory for all, Tito decided simply not to attend. Rapprochement was suddenly again in crisis. Relations were further strained by Khrushchev's abrupt move to oust Marshal Zhukov in October, while the latter was on a state visit to Yugoslavia! Once again, it was not so much what Khrushchev had done, but the way he had done it, which so rankled Tito. Yugoslavia, he felt, had been used badly in the Zhukov affair.

At the Moscow meetings in November the Yugoslav delegation, led by Kardelj and Ranković in Tito's absence, was conspicuously snubbed by Khrushchev, who evidently felt that Tito had cheated him of his anticipated victory. Now that Khrushchev was more or less free of his rivals, he seemed to grow increasingly arrogant and self-willed. This was certainly Mićunović's impression from a dinner hosted by the Soviet leader on November 8th:

> The impression in our delegation is that the events here in recent months have influenced the Russians to be so harsh and to exert such strong pressure on us. There was talk also about the recent meeting in Bucharest. The Russians now interpret this in their own fashion - the way they choose - as if we are not fulfilling something we had promised there. This, too, confirms that with the Russians it is better not to sign anything that won't be published. Khrushchev was harsher than before, and it looks to us as if it was easier to talk with him while Molotov and Malenkov, or Marshal Zhukov were still in the Presidium.(30)

Throughout the celebrations Khrushchev kept up the pressure on the Yugoslav delegation. When he saw that his hard-line tactics to get them to sign were not working, he shifted to a 'soft-sell' approach - which did not work either. The Yugoslavs ultimately consented to sign only the 'Peace

Manifesto', the second of the two main conference documents and much less ideologically contentious.

One incident, for which thus far we have only Lowenthal's evidence, possibly helps to explain the extent and nature of Tito's disillusionment and his sense of betrayal. According to Lowenthal, Khrushchev, either during or shortly after the Bucharest meeting, had demanded to see the unfinished draft of the new LCY Program, work on which had been interrupted in mid-1957 when the chance for rapprochement had suddenly improved once again. Not even many high level Yugoslav party officials - for example Svetozar Vukmanović-Tempo, then a leading economic policy-maker - had yet seen the draft which Khrushchev was demanding.(31) At about the same time, still according to Lowenthal, Khrushchev, feeling that he had Tito firmly in hand, presented him with a draft of the declaration to be signed in Moscow in November:

> It was a harsh, uncompromising Cold War document, and clearly faced the Yugoslavs with the implicit choice of either unconditionally joining the Warsaw Pact, or being attacked as 'revisionists' and expelled from the Communist family.(32)

IN THE WILDERNESS ONCE AGAIN

As we have seen, Tito accepted the challenge and refused to attend the November gathering. Work was promptly resumed on the LCY Program. Its publication and subsequent adoption at the 7th Congress of the LCY in April 1958, which the Soviet and Bloc parties boycotted, signalled the beginning of a serious new rift, the 'Second Soviet-Yugoslav Split', as it has come to be called. This time the Soviet anti-Yugoslav campaign lasted for almost four years, during which Yugoslavia's and Tito's status was reduced to that of a symbolic straw man in the developing Soviet quarrel with the Chinese. 'Yugoslav revisionism' became the code phrase for Chinese criticism of the kinds of domestic reforms Khrushchev was trying to introduce in the USSR. Yet Khrushchev during these years had neither the courage nor the evident inclination to be much more gentle toward the Yugoslavs. He carried out his threat to cancel developmental credits and justified this and other hostile actions by the offensiveness of Yugoslav doctrines allegedly intended for export in the new LCY Program. As late as the 22nd Congress of the CPSU in 1961, Khrushchev, in spite of his renewal of the offensive against Stalinists in the USSR, would still find it appropriate to attack Yugoslav revisionism as a major enemy of international socialism.

The Yugoslav leaders responded to the 1957 Declaration of the fraternal parties, which resounded throughout the world as a charter of communist unity and solidarity, with a revisionist, anti-Leninist programme that all the Marxist-Leninist parties criticised decisively and justly.

Revisionist ideas pervade not only the theory but also the practice of the leadership of the LCY. The line they have adopted - that of development in isolation, apart from the world socialist community - is harmful and dangerous. It plays into the hands of imperialist reaction, foments nationalist tendencies and may in the long run lead to the loss of socialist gains in the country, which has broken away from the friendly and united family of builders of a new world.(33)

By this time, verbal condemnation of Yugoslav revisionism was practically the only thing Khrushchev had in common with Mao. It was becoming patently obvious, however, why the Chinese were so increasingly strident in condemning Tito's sins. Khrushchev had in effect been mortgaging his freedom of domestic and foreign manoeuvre to the effort to maintain a facade of unity in the Bloc. That he was tiring of the effort was evidenced by his counter-campaign of invective against 'Albanian dogmatism' - the symbolic code phrase for Maoist radicalism in the Sino-Soviet polemic. The collapse of Soviet-Albanian relations in June 1960 and the subsequent closure of Soviet submarine bases and other facilities on the Albanian littoral in May of the following year were a significant turning point in both Sino-Soviet and Soviet-Yugoslav relations. For if the maintenance of overall Bloc unity on terms which Khrushchev found acceptable, both domestically and externally, was no longer possible, he was determined to preserve as much unity as he could within the core area of Soviet concerns, Eastern Europe. Within this narrower context Yugoslav revisionism did not seem quite so mortal a sin, especially since some of the practices which the Chinese were condemning under this label - e.g., greater attention to consumer goods, administrative decentralisation, and a more flexible attitude to non-communist nationalists in the Third World - were not so different from Khrushchev's own policy preferences.

Nor had the criticisms which Khrushchev had uttered at the 22nd Party Congress (quoted above) on the dangers of isolationism for Yugoslav socialism fallen entirely on deaf ears in Belgrade. Steps taken in 1960 and 1961 to open the Yugoslav economy to the world capitalist market in order to encourage domestic market forces and increase efficiency had evoked considerable uneasiness in the LCY leadership, particularly among security chief Ranković and his associates. But Ranković's success in sabotaging the economic reforms suggested quite clearly that Tito himself was not entirely enthusiastic over the reforms, especially since initial results had been decidely disappointing.(34)

THE SECOND YUGOSLAV-SOVIET RAPPROCHEMENT

Tito had closely followed the exacerbation of Sino-Soviet relations and sensed the opportunity for renewed efforts at rapprochement some time in 1961. On his initiative Foreign Minister Koča Popović was sent to Moscow in July on a sounding mission and received friendly treatment from Soviet officials. As Yugoslav relations with the West began to turn sour once again - this time, among other things, over Tito's failure to condemn seriously the Soviet resumption of atmospheric nuclear testing just on the eve of the first non-aligned summit conference in Belgrade in September* - Khrushchev, too, began to sense opportunities for a restoration of closer ties.

During 1962 Soviet relations with Yugoslavia improved in direct measure as Tito's relations with the US and other Western countries deteriorated. Yugoslav purchases of Soviet T-54 tanks and other military items were suddenly revealed at the May Day Parade in Belgrade.(35) Following visits by Soviet Foreign Minister Gromyko and the then Chairman of the Presidium of the Supreme Soviet, Brezhnev, commercial relations also began to improve. And in December Tito again visited Moscow, where he was given the signal honour of addressing the Supreme Soviet.

For a brief moment after Tito's return from Moscow Western commentators noted signs of the earlier euphoria over prospects of rapprochement with the USSR and its Bloc clients.(36) Yet a closer reading of Tito's remarks made it clear that no binding commitments had been made or were contemplated, for example, concerning membership in COMECON or

---

* At the conference Tito had said blandly, 'We are not surprised so much by the communiqué on the resumption of atomic and hydrogen weapons tests, because we could understand the reasons adduced by the Government of the USSR. We are surprised more by the fact that this was done on the day of the opening of this Conference of Peace.' (Josip Broz Tito, Selected Speeches and Articles, 1941-1961. Zagreb, Naprijed, 1963, p. 392.

the Warsaw Pact. Subsequent events confirmed the essential truth of Tito's seemingly disingenuous account of his conversations with Khrushchev, delivered in the course of a speech in Železnik after his return from Moscow. Obviously intending his remarks for a wider audience than the workers assembled before him, Tito had said, among other things,

> During our exchange of opinions, which was permeated with understanding, we sought agreement on nothing other than how to avoid anything that disunites us, how to avoid the disputes that took place in the past, so as to exclude gradually various attacks that probably will still be made by us and by them and, finally, to prevent things that neither side will like. We also agreed not to dramatise things that neither we nor they like but to take a realistic approach to their removal.(37)

Among other steps he foreshadowed was a crackdown on anti-Soviet utterances by Yugoslav citizens. Both Milovan Djilas and Mihajlo Mihajlov would soon fall victim to this token of Tito's regard for Soviet sensibilities.

From Tito's point of view, then, he and Khrushchev had basically agreed merely to disagree in future under certain damage-limiting procedural rules - to minimise the consequences of their inevitable disagreements. He considered cordial inter-party ties with the CPSU useful for fostering discipline and ideological orthodoxy in the LCY against the perceived dangers of contamination by Western influences, always a problem because of the ongoing economic and cultural relations on which Yugoslavia depended.

Khrushchev, on his part, viewed renewed rapprochement with Yugoslavia as a valuable counter in the increasingly acrimonious conflict with Peking, as well as a rallying point for the consolidation of his leadership over the loyalist majority of the Bloc. Soviet statements in the polemic with the Chinese suggest that Khrushchev was less enthusiastic than Tito over the acknowledgement of Yugoslavia's right to be different. It was apparent that he now needed Tito more than the latter needed him. Tito certainly supported Khrushchev's struggle against Stalinists at home and the Peking dogmatists abroad and was happy to offer his endorsement of Soviet policies - to the extent that they coincided with his own. Khrushchev should by this time have had no illusions about his capacity to induce Tito to go further than this. But Nikita Sergeevich was nothing if not an eternal optimist, and he continually tried to manoeuvre Tito into a corner by the verbal ascription to Yugoslavia of Bloc status and other <u>faits accomplis</u>. Nevertheless, Tito showed that two could play this game.

A good example of Khrushchev's tactics was the 'correction' of the May Day Theses in Pravda, published first on April 8th and then amended on April 11th, 1963. In the corrected version Yugoslavia was listed along with the Bloc states as a fraternal country 'building socialism'.(38) At a time of increasing American toughness over what was regarded in Washington as Tito's duplicity, this gesture by Khrushchev was bound to be embarrassing. Tito lost no time in writing a personal letter to President J.F. Kennedy to assure him of Yugoslavia's continuing commitment to independence and non-alignment. Mićunović, now Yugoslav Ambassador in Washington, was instructed to convey the same message to Secretary of State Dean Rusk and other US officials.(39)

Khrushchev's standard formula for justifying rapprochement with Yugoslavia to Bloc allies and foes alike during the remainder of his term of office was that Yugoslav internal policies had lately come closer to Marxism-Leninism - i.e., to the standard Soviet model. As evidence he cited allegedly increasing proportions of socialist sector dominance in such areas as agriculture and trade and the tightening of party discipline in the LCY and Yugoslav society (Djilas was back in prison for publishing Conversations with Stalin in the West). The LCY Program, asserted Pravda in an editorial rejoinder to the Chinese, was full of errors, but that did not mean Yugoslavia was not a socialist country. Furthermore,

> The international communist movement has set the goal of aiding Yugoslavia and its leaders to correct the existing errors and to return to the path of unity with the world socialist movement, with the fraternal parties.(40)

In Berlin a few weeks earlier Khrushchev had told the 6th Congress of the SEPD:

> ...It is not suitable for us to imitate the churches and practice 'excommunication' from socialism...

> For example, we have disagreements with Yugoslavia on certain ideological questions, but we must not assert on this basis alone that Yugoslavia is not socialist. We must not do so because the objective indicators of the regime in existence there are socialist. In Yugoslavia the means of production and the power were won by the peoples in heroic struggle, and they belong to the working people. There are no landlords, bankers or capitalists there. The peoples of Yugoslavia are fighting to build socialism and communism. What basis is there, then, for 'excommunicating' Yugoslavia from

socialism and expelling it from the number of socialist states?(41)

But if Khrushchev was untiring in his efforts to portray the convergence of Soviet and Yugoslav views and looked forward to the eventual identity of their positions once Tito 'saw the light', Tito just as insistently emphasised their continuing differences. Thus, in appraising the results of talks with Khrushchev on Brioni in August 1963, he informed an audience in Velenje, in Nikita Sergeevich's presence, that the latter had fully agreed on the permissibility of diverse roads to socialism, as set forth in the 1956 Moscow Declaration, saying, 'I am pleased that complete identity of views exists between us on this question'. Moreover, he went on to assert that Khrushchev had shown deep interest in the operation of the Yugoslav system of workers' self-management, which must have set the latter's teeth on edge, in view of his earlier condemnation of this Yugoslav doctrine as pure revisionism.(42) This game of cat and mouse continued for as long as Khrushchev remained at the Soviet helm, and it was not always clear who would be the cat and who the mouse at any given historical juncture.

As in the past, the 1962-1964 rapprochement entailed costs as well as benefits for both sides. Tito and his aides served with apparent alacrity as emissaries for Khrushchev in the Bloc capitals to buttress the Soviet side in the dispute with the Chinese. One result of the Brioni meetings in 1963 had been Yugoslav acceptance of observer status in COMECON. Accordingly, from 1964 Belgrade began to participate in selected bilateral and multilateral economic ventures with Bloc states. Trips to East Germany and Czechoslovakia by Kardelj resulted in sharp increases in the planned level of trade with those countries.(43) The increased involvement of Yugoslavia in such matters was undoubtedly viewed as positive by all sides concerned. On the other hand, similar dealings with Romania were interpreted, in the West at least, as a Yugoslav attempt to support Romanian resistance to Bloc pressures for economic subordination under the COMECON division of labour.(44) There was undoubtedly a measure of truth in this observation, and the thought must have crossed Khrushchev's mind more than once.

Yugoslav endorsement of the Soviet position against Peking was similarly a two-edged sword. Belgrade consistently warned the Soviet leaders against carrying the anti-Chinese campaign too far and strongly opposed Khrushchev's persistent efforts to summon another international conference of party leaders to read the CCP out of the international movement.(45) Tito realised that Khrushchev's condemnation of 'excommunications' was a selective matter, and it concerned him. Thus, during his return visit to the USSR in June 1964, his last personal meeting with Khrushchev, he rebuffed the latter's attempts to get him to endorse the call for an international conference, although he did grudgingly concede the use of certain formulas which he had earlier rejected, on 'monolithic unity' in their final communique. He was reported to have repented of this concession soon after returning to Belgrade, however.(46)

The remaining months before Khrushchev's ouster in mid-October saw Tito undertaking a whirlwind tour of Bloc capitals, with reciprocal visits by East European leaders to Yugoslavia. Tito evidently relished his new role as mediator and elder statesman in the international movement. He tried to use the opportunity to put across his own favourite ideas on Bloc relations. An editorial in the LCY theoretical journal Komunist in late September sought to raise the practice of bilateral negotiations between Bloc leaders to the level of a basic principle, counterposing it to the 'outmoded' and dangerous practice of international conferences convoked to issue binding declarations. The editorial called these bilateral talks a 'new, positive instrument of international cooperation' and a 'democratic dialogue' among equals.(47)

On October 1st, Yugoslavia officially announced its refusal to attend the pending world conference. Khrushchev had lost another round to Tito. It was to be his last. Two weeks later he was merely an 'honoured pensioner' of the USSR. To the end he had tried to bring Tito back into the fold, playing on Tito's desire for full recognition and vindication in the one arena where he cherished this most, the international socialist community.

That Khrushchev came so close to succeeding was due not only to Tito's ultimate Marxist-Leninist orthodoxy but also to the fact that he sympathised with and sought to encourage the Soviet leader's efforts to change the nature of the Bloc and the internal character of the Soviet regime. In short, Tito believed that Khrushchev offered the best available opportunity to move the socialist community in the directions he, Tito, favoured. In this belief Tito undoubtedly exaggerated the extent to which Khrushchev, or any other conceivable Soviet leader, was willing or able to go to change the Soviet power system.

Both Tito and Khrushchev were gamblers. Khrushchev's ebullient self-confidence, bolstered by a typical Stalinist conviction of the inevitably conclusive logic of the 'big battalions' in settling all arguments, led him to believe that he could eventually bring Tito around to accepting the pre-eminence of the Soviet Union in Bloc affairs. Tito's less demonstrative, but no less vigorous, self-confidence in his ability to control his own party and to charm his way out of diplomatic complications with the West (buttressed by his shrewd understanding of Yugoslavia's strategic value) led him to take dangerous risks in the expectation of influencing Khrushchev to adopt congenial policies.

Each tried to use the other for his own purposes. But there was certainly more to their relationship than that. Both men seemed to enjoy matching wits with each other. The combattiveness noted as a characteristic of Khrushchevism in other essays in this collection was replicated in Titoism as well. The styles of the two men were different, but they spoke essentially the same political language, and their ideological worldviews were basically congruent. They understood each other - as equals - in a way that few other communist leaders have done, before or since.

NOTES

1. See, for example, <u>Khrushchev Remembers</u>. Translated and edited by Strobe Talbott, Boston: Little, Brown and Company, 1970, p. 388, where Khrushchev says he had 'developed great respect and trust for [Tito's] abilities as an imaginative and enterprising leader'.

2. Khrushchev, ibid., pp. 432-433, recounts Tito's intercession for Nasser and recommendation that he was worthy of Soviet support. Tito evidently put the argument of the usefulnes for the Bloc of Yugoslavia's ties with the non-aligned movement in conversations with Khrushchev in December 1962. See Tito's speech in Železnik, Slovenia on his return from Moscow, published in <u>Pravda</u>, 3 January 1963; translated in <u>Current Digest of the Soviet Press (CDSP)</u>, Vol. XV, No. 1, p. 31.

3. Djilas was one of the few Yugoslav leaders who saw the change in a negative light. Milovan Djilas, <u>Tito: The Story from Inside</u>. Translated by Vasilije Kojic and Richard Hayes, London: Weidenfeld and Nicolson, 1981, p. 165.

4. Edvard Kardelj, <u>Problemi naše socijalističke izgradnje</u>, Vol. 3, Belgrade: Kultura, 1954, pp. 338-342.

5. Stephen Clissold, ed., <u>Yugoslavia and the Soviet Union, 1939-1973: A Documentary Survey</u>. London: Oxford University Press, 1975, p. 248.

6. For a survey of the relationship between Yugoslav relations with East and West and the evolution of the domestic political system see Robert F. Miller, *Tito as Political Leader and External Factors in Yugoslav Political Development*. Canberra: Department of Political Science, Research School of Social Sciences, Australian National University, Occasional Paper No. 14, 1977, Part I, esp. pp. 3-25 on the Stalin and Khrushchev periods.

7. *Khrushchev Remembers*, op.cit., pp. 378-379.

8. Clissold, ed., op.cit., p. 250.

9. *Khrushchev Remembers*, op.cit., pp. 379-380. In effect, Khrushchev was offering an exchange of scapegoats for past enmities - Beria for Djilas. Djilas attributes his subsequent prison sentences largely to Tito's desire to placate the Soviet leaders. Djilas, op.cit., pp. 165-166.

10. Clissold, ed., op.cit., pp. 202-207.

11. ibid., pp. 254-257.

12. *Khrushchev Remembers*, op.cit., p. 382.

13. Veljko Mićunović, *Moskovske godine, 1956/1958*, Zagreb: Sveučilišna naklada Liber, 1977, p. 27.

14. See Mićunović's account of Tito's reception in ibid., pp. 79-85.

15. ibid., p. 98.

16. ibid., pp. 89-90.

18. Dennison Rusinow, *The Yugoslav Experiment: 1948-1974*. London: C. Hurst and Company, 1977, p. 90.

19. Excerpted in Clissold, ed., op.cit., p. 263.

20. See Khrushchev's self-serving commentary on the treatment of Nagy in *Khrushchev Remembers*, op.cit., p. 423, esp. n.6; and Mićunović's account of Tito's conversation with Khrushchev and Malenkov on Brioni, Mićunović, op.cit., pp. 156-163.

21. The speech and the Soviet response are presented in Clissold, ed., op.cit., pp. 263-270.

22. See, for example, Tito's interview in   Borba,   commented upon by Elie Abel, 'Tito's Reply Mild in Soviet Dispute', New York Times, 30 December 1956, p. 1.

23. Mićunović, op.cit., p. 212.

24. Mićunović offers some extremely perceptive atmospheric evidence of the changing tone of Sino-Soviet relations in ibid., pp. 230-232,233.

25. ibid., pp. 277-278.

26. ibid., p. 341.

27. Richard Lowenthal, 'Tito's Gamble',   Encounter,   Vol. XI, No. 4, (October 1958), p. 62.

28. Mićunović, op.cit., p. 342.

29. ibid., p. 343.

30. ibid., p. 369.

31. Svetozar   Vukmanović-Tempo,   Revolucija   koja   teče: Memoari. Belgrade: Kommunist, 1971, Vol. 2, p. 322.

32. Lowenthal, op.cit., p. 62.

33. Clissold, ed., op.cit., p. 289.

34. For discussions on the course of these economic reforms see Velimir Vasić, Ekonomska politika Jugoslavije, 5th edition, revised and expanded. Belgrade: Savremena administracija, 1970, pp. 140-141; and Dušan Bilandžić, Ideje i praksa društvenog razvoja Jugoslavije, 1945-1973. Belgrade: Kommunist, 1973, p. 213.

35. 'Yugoslavia Shows New Tanks', NYT, 2 May 1962, p. 4.

36. See, for example, Paul Underwood, 'Tito Closing Rift with Soviet Bloc', NYT, 31 January 1963, p. 2.

37. Pravda, 3 January 1963;   translated in CDSP, Vol. XV, No. 1, p. 31.

38. Pravda, 8 April 1963, p. 1; the corrected version is in Pravda, 11 April 1963, p. 1.

39. 'Tito Assures U.S. of His Neutrality', NYT, 20 April 1963, p. 1.

40. <u>Pravda</u>, 10 February 1963; translated in <u>CDSP</u>, Vol. XV, No. 6, pp. 5-6.

41. <u>Pravda</u>, 17 January 1963; translated in <u>CDSP</u>, Vol. XV, No. 4, p. 19.

42. <u>Pravda</u>, 1 September 1963; translted in <u>CDSP</u>, Vol. XV, No. 35, pp. 3-6.

43. David Binder, 'Tito Strengthens Ties', <u>NYT</u>, 9 May 1964, p. 9; 'East Germans Accuse Peking of Favoring Bonn', ibid.

44. 'Yugoslav Praises Rumania', <u>NYT</u>, 15 February 1964, p. 3.

45. 'Yugoslavs Oppose Meeting', <u>NYT</u>, 10 April 1964, p. 10.

46. David Binder, 'Tito Concession to Khrushchev is Seen in Communique on Talks', <u>NYT</u>, 12 June 1964, p. 6.

47. Cited by David Binder, in 'Yugoslavs Spur Bilateral Talks', <u>NYT</u>, 27 September 1964, p. 10.

48. Djilas, op.cit., pp. 164-165.

49. Mićunović, op.cit., pp. 233-234.

Chapter Eight

KADARISM AS APPLIED KHRUSHCHEVISM

Ferenc Féhér

Is there such a thing as 'Kadarism'? Is Kadar's regime in Hungary different from that of Ulbricht, Honecker, Zhivkov, Gheorghiu Dej, Ceauşescu, Gomulka, Gierek, Novotny, Husak or Hoxha? Or is 'Kadarism' nothing but a journalistic catchword?

My answer is that Kadarism is considerably more than a journalistic catchword (therefore, it is an 'ism'), that Kadarism is a modified version of Khrushchevism (my interpretation of this term is given in the first chapter of in this volume). In this connection it is appropriate to raise the question of Nikita Sergeevich Khrushchev's personal and direct contribution to the emergence of the only political structure created in his political image that outlived him.

The relationship between the two politicians, which gradually developed into a kind of alliance between partners in a complex game, was the result of a long sequence of trials and even more errors on the part of Khrushchev. Indeed, Khrushchev in early 1955 exploited Imre Nagy's heretical acts during his time in office as Prime Minister of Hungary and protégé of Malenkov to engineer Nagy's downfall in order to add to the list of crimes of Malenkov his arch rival in the Presidium. But Khrushchev was far from happy that Matyas Rakosi remained in what he regarded as an unchallenged power position with the then youngest Prime Minister in the world, Andras Hegedus. There were solid reasons indeed for his dissatisfaction. First, Rakosi had already failed once (nearly producing another edition of the Berlin food mutiny in 1953). Secondly, and Khrushchev had made a very disparaging remark about this to Nagy as early as 1 January 1954, Rakosi had doggedly and ingeniously sabotaged the process of rehabilitation of the victims of the Stalinist show trials, an increasingly crucial item in Khrushchev's long-term plans. Finally, Rakosi's dismissal had become a conditio sine qua non for reconciliation with Tito. Despite the fact that the Soviet leadership was not too happy about personnel changes of any kind, in Hungary or elsewhere, and this seems to have been a matter of consensus between the factions after the 20th Congress, they could hardly have had any illusions regarding the political life-expectancy of the Rakosi leadership.

In order to maintain order and the appearance of good relations they made a token gesture by sending, on 4 April 1956, the so-called Day of Liberation, a cable to the Hungarian party and government leadership. This was a symbolic act of support. But by all available testimonies, the Soviet leaders had already in this period made various mental experiments with a possible new prime candidate. Zoltan Szanto was contacted twice. Szanto was, during a short interregnum between Bela Kun's execution in 1938 and Rakosi's release from a Hungarian prison in 1940, the First Man of the Hungarian Communist Party in exile, a heroic old-time Bolshevik with a remarkable amount of common sense, strangely combined with a deep, almost religious, belief in the Soviet Union. Moreover, he was a politician who had remained uninvolved in the Stalinist crimes, having then been the ambassador of Hungary in France.(1) At the time in question, as the ambassador of Hungary in Poland, his official standing was far from high: he was just a member of the Central Committee, a totally mummified body under Rakosi. Nevertheless, he was first sounded out by Ponomarenko, his Soviet opposite number in Warsaw who was temporarily still a member of the Presidium, although in peaceful exile because of Khrushchev's disfavour. Later, when Szanto was returning from the 8th Congress of the Chinese Communist Party in September 1956, where he, along with Kadar, typically represented the Hungarian 'brother party', he was unexpectedly summoned by Mikoyan during the Moscow stopover. In the conversation Mikoyan, then the second man of the Khrushchevite mainstream, made no bones about the fact that the Presidium was not at all happy with their own improvised choice (in June 1956) of Ernö Gerö as successor to Rakosi, despite the grudging approval they had extorted for their decision from Tito. They had had to act hurriedly and with questionable wisdom, Mikoyan admitted, but now they were ready, with appropriate circumspection, to modify their original, mistaken decision. However, they frantically needed options. Szanto unselfishly suggested Kadar, on whose candidacy Mikoyan made no comments; less unselfishly, Szanto suggested himself, which went equally uncommented, and finally, Georg Lukacs, who was immediately rejected by Mikoyan.

In the meantime, there began to emerge very slowly, for the man in the street imperceptibly, but for Soviet 'talent-spotters' not all that inconspicuously, a distinct faction around Kadar. He was not only one of the first in the whole of Eastern Europe to be released from prison in 1954 (where he had been serving time for 'espionage and anti-people activity'), but in fact he was the first rehabilitated leading communist functionary to be restored, albeit gradually and partially, to power. At first Kadar moved very cautiously. As a secretary of the 13th district of Budapest and later in

1955 as one of the secretaries of the Budapest organisation, he directly (and unsuccessfully), at a Central Committee session right after the 20th Congress of the CPSU, charged Rakosi with responsibility for concocting the scenarios of the show trials. (The story of this dramatic, or rather scandalous session, then an object of widely circulating gossip, can be read in detail in F. Vali, Rift and Revolution in Hungary.)

But Rakosi had come to the session well prepared. He brought along the tapes of a conversation between Kadar, then the Minister of the Interior, and Rajk in the latter's cell in 1949 soon after Rajk's arrest. Rajk had obviously resisted accepting the role of a 'volunteer' in his trial; therefore, treacherous and cynical promises of eventual release from custody and of good treatment for his family had to be employed along with physical torture. Kadar, in his official capacity, was the conveyor of these promises. Members of the Central Committee must have thoroughly enjoyed the niceties of this situation, which ended in a 'moral' draw. Rakosi could at least weaken his adversary's position as an umblemished emancipator, but it hardly went unnoticed by CC-menbers that Kadar's first words to his ex-friend and ex-colleague Rajk were, 'I have come in the name of Comrade Rakosi'. Nor was it very likely that Khrushchev, regularly informed by the perceptive and shrewd Soviet ambassador of the day, Iurii Andropov, paid no attention to this clamorous scene. It is highly probable that Kadar's name, so likely a candidate for the list of innocent victims of Stalinism in the Secret Speech, may have cropped up in his mind at that time.

This potential option was enhanced by the methods and principles of recruitment in the Kadar faction, which were so drastically different from the modus operandi of the circle gathering around Imre Nagy. The Nagy group consisted mostly of intellectuals and acted increasingly as a public opposition rather than a party faction. As far as Kadar's partisans were concerned, it was questionable whether this ensemble of people could be called a faction at all. They had certainly tried frantically to create an appearance of mere personal consultations with a man of reputable experience as a Bolshevik militant in a time of trials, and to avoid even a suspicion of factional activity. As Nikita Khrushchev himself had often acted in a similar vein, he could not be displeased with Kadar's tactical skill and sound 'party principles'. Moreover, the Kadarites were all functionaries, prepared to act strictly within the framework of the party constitution. Finally, Kadar recruited only from among those 'reformers' who sought continuity with the past. 'Continuity' meant loyalty to the Soviet Union and it implied the primacy of party prerogatives over all aspects of social life. But as a faction in opposition and comprising several members who were intelligent technicians of power, they had perceived the ferment in Hungarian society and wanted, if not social reform, at least changes in the manner this power was employed.

There is evidence that Khrushchev was familiar with the character of Kadar's activity and, at least to some extent, approved of it. An important event in the chronicle of the Hungarian Revolution is almost always overlooked against the background of the general drama. While Imre Nagy was only foisted upon the Soviet leaders as Prime Minister by the demands of the masses (without him there could be no 'popular' government), it was Suslov and Mikoyan who on 20 October co-opted Kadar and put him into office as the First Secretary of the 'party-in-reorganisation'. They did so in the name of the Soviet Presidium, but certainly with the blessing of Khrushchev. This was a position which then meant very little for the Hungarian population, who anticipated a genuine parliamentary pluralism in which a communist party first secretary would certainly have been a low-key figure. But it was certainly not so intended in Moscow; and Kadar's promotion meant that he, and not Nagy, represented for the Presidium the number one man. They did not go back on their word, even in spite of an exuberant speech by Kadar on October 31, hailing the victorious revolution and the restoration of national independence (a speech which had, in my firm conviction, already been secretly cleared with Andropov). Kadar's name surfaced hardly more than 24 hours later as one of the two top contenders for the position of the First Man during negotiations between Khrushchev and Malenkov, on the one hand, and Tito, Kardelj, Ranković and Mićunović, on the other hand, on the island of Brioni. Even if, as we learn from Mićunović, the Soviet leaders were more favourably inclined toward Münnich, an old-time Muscovite and unquestionably a direct agent of the Soviet security services in many sensitive matters, they accepted Kadar without much ado.

The post-1956 story can best be understood in terms of the ultimate results. Initially the two politicians seemed to be (and perhaps often were) on different wavelengths. At first, Kadar was reluctant to use sufficiently ruthless measures. The Soviet leaders, and in particular Khrushchev himself, who often visited Hungary and whose personal police representative, General Ivan Serov, closely supervised the process of retribution, had to push Kadar hard. On the other hand, at least as popular gossip had it, Kadar firmly resisted being driven close to the limits of pure and simple Stalinism. For example, he is said to have vetoed mass deportations from Hungary to the Soviet Union, a proposal which bore the hallmark of the Khrushchev-Serov modus operandi of 1939 in the

Ukraine, when the duo had millions of Ukrainians and Poles transferred to Siberia.

But ultimately the two men came to understand one another perfectly. They even developed a kind of mutual affection. Kadar was obviously Khrushchev's model pupil; and Hungary under his leadership, the ideal testing ground for proving the adequacy of the recipes proposed in the Secret Speech. What emerged was an ideal combination of a 'firm Leninist stance' against 'counter- revolutionaries' and 'traitors' like Nagy and moderation, once salutory terror had already done its work. This double strategy was crowned by the unexpected general amnesty of 1963, the political and ideological peak of the Khrushchev-Kadar collaboration. The order of Hero of the Soviet Union, then a rare honour outside the Soviet Union, was pinned on the breast of a visibly moved Kadar by Khrushchev himself in front of millions of Hungarian TV-watchers. That was only the most spectacular external symbol of Nikita Sergeevich's deep satisfaction with his excellent disciple. Support of a more substantial kind was constantly given to Kadar against any rivals from the right or the left of his party. On the other hand, in a career as treacherous as that of any successful politician in a totalitarian regime, Khrushchev received in return a striking token of loyalty from his carefully selected follower and disciple. Kadar, returning from Warsaw after negotiations with Gomulka, was caught completely unawares by the communique informing him of Khrushchev's sudden 'retirement'. In a gesture totally unprecedented in communist bloc history under 'normal' conditions, he delivered an improvised and impassioned speech on his arrival at the Budapest Nyugati railway station, offering the only <u>public</u> political assessment of the First Secretary in the Warsaw Pact countries with an openly affectionate tone, and praising Khrushchev as an outstanding Leninist. This was a gesture Brezhnev never forgot. And when Khrushchev died, it was again <u>Nepszabadsag</u>, the Hungarian party daily, which alone carried a warm, if slightly subdued and critical, obituary.

Looking at the relationship from Kadar's angle, there were organic reasons, both in his destiny and political make-up, for his development into the model Khrushchevite. First, with his background as a loyal and unjustly imprisoned ex-Stalinist functionary, he had come to see his political future as inextricably tied to the course inaugurated by the Secret Speech. Had Khrushchev's policy lost out to Stalinism or Neo-Stalinism, the erstwhile Minister of the Interior could not possibly have nurtured illusions about his chances. At best he could have hoped for total anonymity on the margins of society. His political career was thus inseparable from Khrushchev's triumph over his rivals. Secondly, both men had one feature deeply in common: a religiously uncritical faith in certain basic Leninist tenets supporting a ruthless technology of power, without fanaticism, but rather with a sceptical, common sense view of affairs of state. In Kadar this feature held sway without Khrushchev's adventurous escapades from rationality into total irrationality. Thirdly, it was easy for Kadar to accept the Khrushchevite norms of Hungary's relation to the Soviet Union. It was easy, as Kadar was a genuine 'internationalist', a Bolshevik for whom the interests of the Soviet Union counted above all. On the one hand, he was the leader of the 'home party', not a 'Muscovite', a politician who had to take into consideration at least some of the realities around him; on the other hand, although Khrushchev's postulates required an unquestionable dependence, they were not the demands of a lunatic colonisation run by third-rate secret police functionaries in a spirit of radical disregard for elementary realities, as under Stalin. Finally, the idea of controlled, party-directed, and therefore very strictly limited and short-range, social reforms has never been totally alien to Kadar, who in this respect has not become a Brezhnevite, an absolute conservative and an advocate of total social immobility. Some elements of this Khrushchevite political conception have always been preserved in him. It is against this personal background of Khrushchev's direct intervention in Hungarian affairs that the emergence of the model Khrushchevite state should be understood.

Kadarism is thus Khrushchevism, with the difference that Hungary is not a superpower. Indeed, the fact that Hungary is not a 'superpower' is crucial to its viability as the model state of Khrushchevism, and it is Kadarism in that the existence of Kadar's regime is contingent on the physical presence of its leader. This is true of all modern societies in which civil society is subordinate to the state, whether in the form of open dictatorship or of very conservative authoritarianism. What made 'Kadarism' possible? It resulted from a social experiment characterised by its deliberate Khrushchevism and lack of confidence in its viability. No one would have predicted in 1957 that Kadar's would become the third oldest regime in Eastern Europe (after Tito's and Hoxha's) and that it would survive 22 years of crises and upheavals.

Kadar's leadership group emerged from a generation of communist militants for whom sacrosanct orthodox theory was often subordinate to the requirements of emergency situations, and many of its political solutions were discovered by chance. Recruitment for the Kadarist faction in 1955-56 was slow because, unlike Imre Nagy's group, its participants tried to avoid factionalism at all costs. The Kadarists recruited only from those 'reformers' who sought continuity with the past, in spite of the fact that many of them were victims of show-trials during the Rakosi period.

The experiment succeeded because the regime was completely annihilated - if only for 10 or 12 days. In 1956, Russian military intervention only formally restored the original state of affairs. In reality, the Kadarist leadership was for the first time compelled to engage in social engineering and experimentation. Within the ruling bureaucracy many party members remained loyal to Nagy or hesitated in joining the new leadership. Another faction hesitated or even resisted Khrushchev's 'de-Stalinisation' and retained a 'Rakosist' position. As a result, not only the top party leadership, but also the party apparatus so crucial to the regime, was forced to follow Khrushchev. The political survival of the entire regime hinged on the validity of the 20th Congress line and on Khrushchev's authority as First Secretary. Not only was the Kadar regime inextricably bound to Khrushchev, but Khrushchev's own political fate depended largely on the outcome of the Hungarian events. Weak leadership unable to control events or forced to resort to Stalinist terrorist tactics to restore order would have meant the immediate removal of the First Secretary whose authority was already considerably weakened in the eyes of the party apparatus. Thus, by a process of elimination a choice was made, and a solid, principled alliance gradually developed between Khrushchev and Kadar. As a result, during its crucial formative years Khrushchev supported the Kadarist experiment under unexperienced and politically weak leadership.

The development of a 'model Khrushchevism' in Hungary was facilitated by the country's small size; a climate conducive to agricultural production; a small population;(2) a uniform language, and a total lack of raw materials essential to industrial development. All of this contributed to halting forced industrialisation. Khrushchev could support the Hungarian experiment only because it was limited by 'natural' factors.

Furthermore, Hungarian Khrushchevism succeeded because of the country's military weakness and its insignificant role in Russian foreign policy. The fact that there was no Hungarian army presented a reduced risk of rebellion. Because many of those executed after 1956 were rebellious soldiers and army officers, the Russian leadership could not rely on the Hungarian military as an armed ally. When consolidation later proved successful and the military was disciplined, the Hungarian leadership resisted the all-too-energetic development of the military and armament industry threatening revolution. With this reduction of military expenditures the foundations for the Hungarian Khrushchevite experiment were laid. Additional factors contributing to the experiment's success include the absence of national minorities. 'Khrushchevite' Hungary never knew these minority problems (as did Romania, for example, with its Hungarian and German minorities) and could therefore embark on an unprecedented experiment. The <u>national problem</u> as such, however, does generate a social tension evidenced by the subtle, nonvocal resistance of the Hungarian population against Russian domination during national festivals and historical anniversaries.

The most fundamental factor was, however, the following: Kadarism could be Khrushchevism because <u>there was no other Khrushchevite</u> country. This is true in a double sense. The Hungarian party's ambivalence toward Russia, Hungary's greater proximity and stronger ties to the West and its consequent 'chauvinism' toward the 'uncivilised, barbarian' Russians – these facts and others attest to a liberalism connected with Khrushchev's legacy. This explains the Hungarian resentment toward surveillance and active intervention by the Russian Politburo in crucial political affairs. Conversely, however, Hungarian loyalty to Russia is not simulated. It arises from the realisation that 'liberal', Khrushchevite' Hungary owes its existence to other non-liberal countries. It is therefore crucial that the Hungarian population constantly bear in mind the presence of this simultaneously reassuring and threatening environment. Consequently, the need to maintain this awareness essentially defines the role of Hungary's ideological apparatus. The Kadar regime's existence relies heavily on the active and effective usage of propaganda to 'remind' the Hungarian population of its isolated, unique status within the eastern bloc. In Hungary it is primarily, though not exclusively, the intelligentsia which must constantly be warned of the danger lurking outside.

What is the structure of Kadarism? Among other things, the regime is predicated on a genuinely Machiavellian conception. This does not mean that its leaders are ruthless, immoral or unprincipled, but rather that the Kadarist leaders have independently rediscovered and implemented certain fundamental principles of Machiavellian government. They revived the maxim: 'For it must be noted that men must either be caressed or else annihilated; they will revenge themselves for small injuries, but cannot do so for great ones; the injury therefore that we do to a man must be such that we need not fear his vengeance', as well as the following: '[Cruelties] well committed may be called those ... which are perpetuated once for the need of securing one's self, and which afterwards are not persisted in, but are exchanged for measures as useful to the subjects as possible. Cruelties ill

committed are those which, although at first few, increase
rather than diminish with time ... Whence it is to be noted
that in taking a state the conqueror must arrange to commit
all his cruelties at once, so as not to have to resort to them
every day.'(3) It is as if Machiavelli foreshadows the
difference between Stalinist and Kadarist systems. Stalin's
'ill committed cruelties' did escalate to the point where the
system's henchmen were themselves endangered. By contrast,
the Kadarist reprisals(4) could be followed miraculously by
the superficial tranquility of the mid-sixties only because of
the system's truly Machiavellian features. The Kadarist
organs of repression confirmed the first Machiavellian thesis
when, by escalating terror and intimidation in 1957-58, no one
dared resist - not even in the form of a confession of belief
in the defeated revolution. The answer to the question
'resistance or repentance' could mean either life or death
during trials. However, despite opposition by police organs,
the political leadership sought to diminish the number of
'well committed cruelties'. The initial granting of partial
and personal amnesty from 1960 onward was followed by the
unexpected and sensational declaration of general amnesty in
1962, six years after a revolution was suppressed through
unusually cruel measures. By comparison to other European
regimes - for example Spain under Franco, who never granted
general amnesty, or Greece, which proclaimed partial amnesty
only 20 years after the civil war - the Kadar regime is to be
praised for this stroke of Machiavellian brilliance. Its
success can be measured by the level of mass intimidation
experienced and accepted by the people. The Hungarian
population has become aware of the regime's capabilities and
has learned that reasonable arrangements with it presuppose
explicit obedience. The Kadarist system is one based on
effective, i.e., <u>rational</u>, and ongoing repression.

Rational repression as the basis of Kadarism has
superficially changed the character of the Hungarian police
state. Unmistakable efforts by the Hungarian leadership to
reduce overt police repression are indicative of a post-20th
Congress development common to most Eastern European
countries: 'show trials' with victims prepared to testify
against themselves are now relics of the past. 'Socialist
legality' has changed the character of Hungarian police
repression, and police officials may not exercise physical
force against 'political criminals'. Furthermore, the regime
takes almost excessive precaution to ensure its own safety: a
strictly supervised resolution of the Kadarist Central
Committee prohibits interrogation of <u>anyone</u> by police
officials regarding any member of the Central Committee
without prior consent of that body. According to official
reports by the Minister of the Interior, cases of 'anti-state'
agitation constitute only a small percentage of convictions,

and in this regard Hungary is at an advantage vis a vis the rest of Eastern Europe.

This, however, merely documents the rationality characterising repression in Kadar's Machiavellian-Khrushchevite police state. The regime still adheres to the principle that the party's political objectives define legality and not vice versa. There is not even a semblance of independent court jurisdiction: courts are mere executive party organs, and political punishments are decided retroactively by political bodies, as for example in the case of Imre Nagy and his colleagues. Another example of politically motivated legislation occurred in 1982, when Kadar gave in to pressure from the so-called 'workers' opposition' against the liberalism caused by economic reform. Among the main targets of the resumed large-scale police activities were some 'unorthodox' leaders of collective farms who violated certain regulations in order to make the farms profitable. Although many politically important economic advances in agriculture could not have been made without these leaders and their activities (which were not only known by political authorities, but even retroactively legalised), the policy change turned a former virtue into a crime. That the legal system is entirely manipulated by political decisions manifests itself in the various legal prerogatives of the police. These prohibit parallel investigations by defense lawyers and criminalise not just public criticism of police activities but all 'unauthorised discussion of such activities'. So-called 'police supervision' means in practice that the police may indefinitely detain a person on the grounds of certain 'suspicions'. The Kadar regime itself unequivocally states that 'normal' police activity and the party's leading role go hand in hand: police persecution is part of the regime's normal functioning.

Kadar's Machiavellianism was not altogether premeditated. The regime came to power by a coup d'etat against a whole nation and suffered a doubly bad conscience for it. It felt remorse toward the population, the majority of which enthusiastically declared its allegiance to the revolution, and towards Russia for 'vacillating' with regard to principles, such as belonging to the Warsaw Pact, a cornerstone of loyalty. Initially, the Kadarists believed in a possible reconciliation between the popular will and political restoration 'guided' by the Russian Army. It seemed that the Kadarists merely intended to punish organisers of pogroms and certain advocates of a capitalist restoration. There were lengthy negotiations with the Imre Nagy group concerning a possible coalition of that group with the Kadar government. When Russian leadership 'corrected' these ideas,(5) however, the Kadarists realised that reconciliation with both the captive Imre Nagy group and other active organisations was impossible. It was then that the Kadarists embarked on a Machiavellian path which became increasingly appropriate for the Hungarian situation.(6)

Kadar's economics can only be understood in terms of the Russian revolutionary model. The regime derives its strategy from the exigencies of the political superstructure. Thus, post-revolutionary Hungary experienced the termination of so-called <u>extensive</u> economic development and the transition to intensive development.(7)

The economic policy of the Kadarists was not clearly defined from the beginning, but was elaborated <u>en route</u>. Nevertheless, one principle underlies all economic policy, i.e., that economic strategy must enable the political system to operate without major disturbances and obvious dysfunctions. During Stalinism and under the leadership of Matyas Rakosi Hungary was the classic example of forced industrialisation: a small country robbed by two peace treaties (1918 and 1946-47) of almost all its natural resources and compelled to develop heavy industry (e.g., steel production without coal and iron). As a result, a population stripped of its national resources came to despise Sztalivaros, the 'Hungarian Stalingrad', as a symbol of the tragic failure of a misconceived socio-economic strategy and of the system as a whole. The inviolable 'law' of Kadarist economic strategy advocated a gradual and continuous growth of both <u>per capita</u> production and real income, while avoiding social 'complications' at all costs. In this regard, Kadar has even outdone Khrushchev, the born improviser. Of course, Kadar's economic policy runs into problems in the short run, and becomes most vulnerable in long-term planning. The most striking example of problems with long-term planning is the housing policy. Since post-war Hungary required heavy investments whose amortisation was very slow, the Kadarist economic strategy sought to minimise budgetary allowances for 'indirect' amenities'. An alleged plan to increase rents in order to finance housing maintenance, so badly needed in Hungary's industrial centres, was vetoed by Kadar for fear of a possible workers' revolt similar to that of 1956. By thus sparing the monthly budgets of workers from further expenses Kadar displayed a sharp political sense. Yet certain issues cannot be tabled <u>ad infinitum</u>, for indefinite postponement generates considerable tensions and the possibility that problems may no longer be solved at all later.

Two political objectives of post-revolutionary Hungarian economic policy should be emphasised here: to increase the population's net income, and to acknowledge the need for certain fashionable consumer goods, such as cars. The first goal is directed at the gradual abolition of certain 'protectionist' features of the state common to many Eastern European countries.(8) It is politically impossible to carry out such a project, although a limited development in this direction would encourage the development of a new political subject capable of accepting the political primacy of the state while simultaneously waging economic warfare against it by taking advantage of remaining loopholes. If the political leadership acknowledges annual increases in net income as an economic law, then it must tolerate, if not legitimate, 'moonlighting', or what Hegedus and Markus have labelled 'the second economy'. The second economic goal forces the state not only to tolerate consumers, but also to support them. This Kadarist policy cannot be implemented without relapses. Thus, during periods of growing neo-Stalinist 'reaction', the party press and the leader himself must launch into vehement invectives against 'immoderate consumerism'.(9)

Another factor contributing to the success of Kadarism was its agricultural reform policies.(10) When the Hungarian peasantry seemed to have won the revolution immediately after 1956, the Kadar government, in order not to have to forcibly 'pacify' each village separately, nullified a series of Rakosi's decrees. 'Natural taxation', essentially a form of legalised extortion of the total annual agricultural and livestock production, which consequently caused mass starvation in both urban and rural Hungary, was revoked. During 1958 completing socialist collectivisation was of primary concern both internationally and domestically. Two alternatives were discussed in the Hungarian Central Committee: either collectivisation commensurate with the state's economic capacity and credit supply, or collectivisation by force. In a typically Kadarist manner, the question was resolved through compromise. Hence, the agricultural reforms reflected the primacy of political imperatives and were implemented with measured, but effective, doses of physical violence and intimidation. The Kadarist mode of repression was thoroughly rational: in order to 'popularise' the collectivisation program, Kadarists corrupted well-known and expert peasants in order thus indirectly to reach the rural masses. Instead of exploiting the then-collectivised peasantry, Hungary's political leadership understood that a reconciliation with the peasantry and a recognition of its needs and aspirations would be indispensable to the system's preservation. This crucial reconciliation in 1961 made significant concessions to the peasantry, particularly with regard to creating a private sphere of autonomy within the 'household economic unit'. With the 'official' acknowledgement of the domestic domain, the individual becomes exempt from certain 'collective' duties so that he can allocate time and energy to attend to household responsibilities. Hungary has not experienced food supply shortages, as have most other Eastern European countries since the early sixties. This can be directly attributed to the recognition of a private economic sphere within the collective framework. Furthermore, Kadarism encouraged a program of private enrichment among the peasantry. Some prosperous agricultural cooperatives had small industrial enterprises, both as sources of added income and as repositories of otherwise unavailable repair services, while others launched into commercial activities.

As a result of this ingenious policy, the Hungarian peasantry now possesses certain inviolable social privileges. The previously mentioned workers' opposition to economic and ideological liberalisation in 1972-73 exploited the collective envy of the urban population toward the privileged peasantry. The agricultural population responded with a modified strike: production of some goods was halted, thus creating a shortage for the first time in a decade. For fear of a revival of 1956 events, the regime intervened and revoked its new measures, thereby restoring to the peasantry its previous social and economic standing.(11) With this restoration the peasantry was once again pacified.

An entire constellation of typically Hungarian economic factors led to economic reform.(12) An overcautious Kadarist policy in the past had prevented any imminent danger of economic failure. Since a rapprochement with the West was out of the question, Hungary relied heavily and without hesitation on Russian aid. The decision to introduce economic reforms in Hungary was a result of the internal composition of the Kadar regime. These reforms were precipitated by the government's desire to promote 'consumerism' domestically – thus, the call for major structural rationalisation – and popular pressures demanding higher living standards as a compensation for total political servility. Since the Kadarists were experienced in 'resolving' conflicts of interest (for example, in the question of agricultural reform and unequal income distribution between urban and rural sectors of the population), they again followed their deeply pragmatic instincts. The 1966 reforms acknowledged the legitimacy of 'socialist market relations'. Such a position, of course, violated theoretical Marxist orthodoxy (much more so than, for example, Lenin's NEP), but the Hungarian leadership at that time had exclusively practical concerns. In the perhaps most crucial issue of the worker's codetermination and collective ownership of production units, the Kadarists rejected all proposals in favor of liberalising factory management.(13) Thus, from the very outset, Kadarist leadership refused to make concessions to workers' participation in the public productive sphere.

Kadarism as the model state of Khrushchevism must be analysed in terms of its unique political structure within the Leninist framework of a one-party system and the dictatorship over needs. Closely watched and highly praised by Kremlinologists, the Kadar government has succeeded in preventing open social conflict by means of its unofficial tolerance towards existing pressure groups, such as the so-called 'ideological intellegentsia', which has been thoroughly corrupted and co-opted by state power. Also, certain arch-conservative Hungarian church leaders provide some opposition to the existing government, although they have also made substantial concessions to the system's political interests by advocating them in sermons. Leading technocrats, some of them party members, constitute yet another opposition group with independent concerns regarding income and self-realisation in the production process.

A further pressure group is composed of influential peasants and leaders of collective farms. Even certain factions of the political bureaucacy may form an oppositional contingent. The greatest irony, however, lies in the fact that in this alleged 'socialist workers' state', factory workers are the least acknowledged pressure group. Of course, in exceptionally dangerous situations involving industrial workers, painstaking efforts are taken to pacify the discontented as, for example, in 1970, when Kadar made a personal appearance in Gyor to prevent an imminent uprising.

The once-haphazard methods of aborting social conflicts have developed under Kadarism into an intricate and sophisticated system of manipulation and oppression. Negotiations take place through semi-official emissaries and when an agreement has been reached and formal sanctions are necessary. Again, there is a Machiavellian wisdom in this strategy, for it precludes the very possibility of public embarrassment and protest.

The Kadarist political apparatus is predicated on the systematic depoliticisation of everyday life. For the bitterly disillusioned Western New Left this represents a major compromise. For the Hungarian population, however, it is a welcome relief. Historically, the real alternatives during the fifties were not collectivism versus atomistic individualism, but between two types of atomism. Forced atomisation relying on brutal manipulation under Stalinism has been replaced by subtle manipulation under Kadarism. By creating a private sphere for economic and cultural pursuits, Kadarism has depoliticised the Hungarian population. The price of certain consumer goods, Western entertainment, literature and television programs is political anonymity.

To further the goal of depoliticisation Kadarism wages a systematic propaganda campaign on behalf of the family. For career functions divorce is not merely a private issue between spouses, but is subject to official approval. Premarital and extramarital sex are tolerated as inescapable evils, while official propaganda continues to advocate Victorian ethical standards for film, literature and television. However, the Kadarists' Machiavellian instinct for survival prevents them from overstepping the bounds of 'tolerable repression'. Hence, abortion is still available to the unmarried and to the poor despite some regulations, and birth control devices are readily accessible. Despite these concessions, however, the nuclear family as a principle remains unassailable.(14)

With regard to the system's political structure, Hungary under Kadarism has undergone a development different from that of many other Eastern Bloc countries. While it is true that, in the final analysis, the Politburo and/or Secretariat of all Eastern Bloc countries decide, while the Central Committees merely sanction these decisions a posteriori, the post-20th Congress history of Eastern European countries has revealed surprising variations from this norm. In Russia, for example, the Central Committee historically has played and continues to play an exceptionally important role in the political decision-making process, while the Yugoslav Central Committee never contradicted Tito.

In November, 1956, at the beginnings of Khrushchevite Hungary, the Central Committee had to assume a leadership role to compensate for weak political leadership. Kadar did not enter office with a preconceived master plan and therefore had to develop and elaborate policies and strategy in the process. Kadar gained firm control over the Hungarian Central Committee only after the disbandment of the Tancsics Circle, the hotbed of arch-Stalinist opposition. Having established his authority within and outside the party, Kadar proceeded to shift political power to the Politburo. Initially regarded as a sort of Quisling by the population and as a dubious 'revisionist' by most politicians, Kadar was later popularly acclaimed as a shrewd politician. He has been able to maintain the delicate political balance in Hungary only by conscientiously applying the principle of tolerance toward pressure groups. The typical 'lobbies' within communist Central Committees ('army groups', 'Leningrad groups', 'Department I groups', etc., in the case of the Russian CC) are all recognised as legitimate power centres and not divergent political factions. Kadar would not, of course, tolerate organised factions within the Central Committee. In this regard, Kadar follows a Kadarist strategy even within the power centres of his own system.

Of course, ideological pragmatism is no Hungarian invention. However, unlike most other Eastern Bloc countries, Hungary does not stage ideological purges for ideology's sake. Whenever administrative measures are taken on ideological issues, their purpose has been to avenge previous political wrongdoings which have not been handled 'properly'. In some cases, ideological purges become necessary as a concession by 'liberals' to their more adamant conservative counterparts, or they signal a general warning against 'loose talk'. The expulsion of the 'Budapest School' from Hungarian cultural life was motivated by a number of factors. There was pressure to seek revenge for the Korčula protest against the Czech invasion. Kadar felt compelled to make some concession to the then victorious 'workers' opposition', and this symbolic act served as a general warning for an overly self-indulgent Hungarian intellectual class. This policy, however, is indicative of an ideological indifference bordering on cynicism. It is an integral feature of the new Kadarist ethics, which tolerates any and all beliefs not publicly professed. In exchange for the freedom to condemn official ideology in private, the state subject is asked only to act in accordance with party policy. Of course, once one has overstepped the limits of ideological propriety, official retaliation follows quickly and harshly. Kadar's regime, perhaps the most tolerant of all governments in the Eastern Bloc, is also undoubtedly the most cynical.

Now restored to power after its temporary defeat in the years 1972-75,(15) Kadarism faces a serious dilemma and three possible alternatives. The dilemma, of course, is that Kadar, now in his early seventies, is nearing the end of his political career. The regime's first option would be to proceed as usual as long as Kadar still lives. The second possible alternative would be a Stalinist relapse. While the potential for such a development is clearly present, one should not underestimate the potential for violent opposition by the population.(16) Since the Russian leadership reacts sensitively to dangers in Eastern Europe, it is even likely that it would intervene to suppress overzealous advocates of its own cause. The third alternative is just emerging and has assumed different forms. The tradition of intellectual resistance beginning with the Korčula protest and followed by the illegal publication of books abroad has contributed to the development of a Hungarian samizdat, a 'modestly' free press dedicated to the articulation of public opinion. Until recently, this was even tolerated by the authorities. A further indicator of an emerging third alternative is the recent revival of the question of economic reform. In an interview with Svenska Dagbladet, Rezso Nyers, a former secretary and present member of the Central Committee, called the re-emergence of reform a necessary step toward the solution of problems and the realisation of the regime's objectives. According to Nyers, economic goals could not be attained without the introduction of pluralism through social reform. By this Nyers does not mean a multi-party system, but rather things such as the granting of autonomy to trade unions. This suggests a kind of 'Tito-isation' of Kadarism insofar as certain social sectors would be acknowledged as being legally and de facto independent, i.e., not subject constitutionally to party arbitration or intervention. (Nyers, of course, is a spokesman for the technical intelligentsia, party functionaries, selected working class strata, etc.) What stands in the way of a Hungarian 'Titoism', however, is one crucial constitutive element, i.e. national independence.

NOTES

1. These facts were imparted to me by Szanto with whom I had friendly relations in the last years of his life, in the late 60s - early 70s, and whom I came to know as a man of integrity and also a realistic watcher of party affairs, to be sure within the very narrow-minded confines of dogmatic Bolshevik doctrine.

2. With its 10 million people, Hungary is the second smallest of the COMECON countries in Eastern Europe, after Bulgaria.

3. Nicolo Machiavelli, The Prince, New York, 1950, p. 9 and p. 34.

4. The three-year reprisals led to at least 2,000 to 3,000 executions, the imprisonment of tens of thousands and the internment of ten times as many as the above combined. In numerical terms, the reprisals were second only to events in the wake of Greek Civil War in post-war Europe. The data cited in the White Book on counterrevolution published by the Hungarian government obviously falsifies the number of victims executed by classifying them in other categories. In calculating orders of magnitude, I rely on personal testimonies and recollections.

5. A few days before the abolition of the Budapest Workers' Council (the centre of resistance against the 'workers' state'), Malenkov secretly visited Budapest. One does not need mystical powers to surmise the topic of discussion betwen him and the all too hesitant Hungarian leadership.

6. Kadarist Machiavellianism is efficient compared to Gustav Husak's cynical and amateurish administration, which alternates between intimidation and reconciliation. Husak, intellectually a far better prepared candidate for First Secretary and a man of exceptional courage (he was one of the very few who survived the torture cells of Czech Stalinism without a false confession), failed entirely in his Kadarist assignment. The very fact that he could not make this separate peace with the most vulnerable and corruptible stratum, i.e., the oppositional intelligentsia, documents his failure, despite the employment of certain crude 'Kadarist' techniques.

7. By 'extensive industrial development' I follow the well known Hungarian economist, F. Janossy. It is roughly the period which Preobrazhenskii described as 'primitive socialist accumulation' characterised by heavy investment in industry (primarily that sector producing the means of production) and the forced relocation of the peasant population into centres of industrialisation. There are natural limits to that expansion, as Rosa Luxemburg suggested, with regard to the limits to capital accumulation (lack of available peasant manpower, the danger of a total collapse of agriculture). The intensive phase begins when industrial growth is realisable only through rationalisation and the introduction of new technology.

8. For a discussion of the protectionist character of Eastern European states, see my 'The Dictatorship over Needs', op.cit. The 'comfort of unfreedom' within these societies discourages people from acting independently and forces individuals into total dependence on the omnipotent totalitarian state.

9. The liberal Kadarist policy of consumerism has often been criticised by the European and American Left as a 'return to capitalism'. Such criticism is not only highly ironic (considering the long-term scarcity experienced by the Hungarian economy) and inherently romantic for its insistence on an untenable, orthodox Marxist vision of eliminating markets, but most importantly it misses one significant point. The options for wage-workers in Eastern European countries are not either domination over production or consumerism. Rather the consumerist permissiveness serves as a compensation for the total exclusion of the population from public political participation, their poverty and subjugation.

10. The following is based on the account presented by Ferenc Donath's <u>Reform es forradolom</u>, Budapest: 1977, pp. 160-170. Once a prime defendant in a show trial during the fifties, Donath survived to become Secretary of State under Imre Nagy's second government, only to be indicted and to survive again. A leading communist party expert in agricultural questions and an oppositional politician, Donath is the best possible source in this area.

11. Although Donath's contention that a 'truly socialist' transformation took place in Hungarian agriculture may not be true, substantial changes did occur. One of these is their higher living standard, and another is their participation in questions regarding production. By contrast, industrial 'production strategy' is still decided entirely by central political authorities. Still, the question of property remains relevant to the peasantry, for it does not exercise the right of disposal over property.

12. Questions of economic reform can only be answered with respect to particular instances. Thus, the German Democratic Republic, prosperous even by Western standards, has avoided economic reform as a result of numerous interacting circumstances - the economic priority it enjoys in the COMECON since the 1953 uprisings, its highly trained and technologically most advanced industrial manpower in the whole Socialist Bloc and the advantages of inter-German trade agreements with its Western counterpart. Other countries, on the other hand, desperately need to rationalise in order to save their poorly functioning economies, and yet they resist reform out of nationalistically motivated hostility toward <u>any</u> reform. Some resort to economic reforms out of sheer necessity, i.e., in order to prevent total political collapse. Novotny's Czechoslovakia in the mid-sixties resisted the liberal innovations introduced by the 20th Congress and, as a result, simply collapsed economically. A second type is exemplified by Yugoslavia. With its policy of close affiliations with the Common Market, certain principles of economic reform became inevitable and irrevocable. Finally, Hungary represents a third type.

13. Andreas Hegedus, for instance, suggested the introduction of a shareholders' system in factories in order to at least symbolically acknowledge workers as collective owners.

14. When Agnes Heller and Mihaly Vajda published their
     article on 'Family Structure and Communism' –
     subsequently translated in English in Telos 7, Spring,
     1971, pp. 99-111 - dealing with new alternative forms of
     family life, the then Prime Minister threatened 'to take
     the pen out of their hands'.

15. Kadar's reinstatement can be explained by various
     factors. When Russian leaders ratified the Helsinki
     agreement, they needed a liberal like Kadar.
     Furthermore, the second Polish uprising persuaded them to
     act cautiously in order not to provoke further rebellion.
     Finally, there were unconfirmed rumours that the
     Eurocommunists (in particular the Italians) demanded that
     Kadar be present at the European Communist Conference
     before they would attend themselves.

16. One could even find a precedent for this. In October,
     1964, when Khrushchev was overthrown by the
     Brezhnev-Suslov-Kosygin coup, Kadar was informed of the
     event during negotiations with Gomulka. Obviously still
     in shock, Kadar delivered an impromptu speech upon his
     return to Hungary which was actually a eulogy for the
     overthrown leader. Allegedly, tens of thousands of
     letters addressed to the Hungarian Broadcasting Company
     threatened that if Kadar were dismissed from office for
     that speech, a general strike would break out.

Chapter Nine

KHRUSHCHEV'S POLICIES AS A FORERUNNER OF THE 'PRAGUE SPRING'

Zdeněk Mlynář

The attempt to reform a Soviet-type socio-political system, which was carried out in 1968 by reform-oriented forces within the Communist Party of Czechoslovakia (CPC), has been up to now the most significant attempt to change the system 'from above' in any of the Soviet-Bloc countries; that is, the governing communist party was itself the initiator. This is, after all, generally recognised even today; and comparing 1968 in Czechoslovakia with developments in Poland in 1980-81, it is usually emphasised that in contrast to the 'Prague Spring' Polish developments clearly began with the pressure of the masses against the system 'from below' and certainly not with the initiative of the governing party itself.

This fact must have had its unique causes directly in developments 'above', in the framework of the official political structure and within the communist party itself. This factor is usually underrated, however: the period of Antonin Novotny's leadership of the CPC (1953-1967) is often described, without differentiation, as a time of classical Stalinist government, against which the revolt of the 'Prague Spring' suddenly flared up.

The key to understanding the real development in the CPC and in Czechoslovakia generally are, in my opinion, the very specific and often contradictory characteristics of Khrushchev's policies. In the framework of this chapter it is not possible to give a profound historical analysis which would meet the requirements of an academic study. Therefore, I shall attempt only a brief formulation of the main problems which need to be examined objectively and in detail in the interest of a better understanding of the particular and unique features of the period before the 'Prague Spring' in 1968.

In contrast to the other Central-European and East-European countries of the Soviet Bloc, in Czechoslovakia before World War II the communist party had a tradition of legal operations within the parliamentary system. It grew originally out of the strong social-democratic movement which already had historic roots in the second half of the 19th Century. The decisive phases of its development, at a time when Stalinist domination had succeeded (the so-called 'bolshevisation' of the CPC began in the year 1929), were also always characterised by a certain resistance by non-Stalinist tendencies within the CPC. On the whole, one can say that the domination of Stalinism always prevailed here with a time-lag, despite a degree of resistance by the party and also a certain hesitancy by the leadership of the party itself.

At the same time the interests of Moscow always ultimately and entirely prevailed, and the more tardily and hesitantly this came about, the more ostentatious were the forms of Moscow's victory. This phenomenon is also valid for the last Stalinist phase: the main political trial of the CPC General Secretary, Rudolf Slansky, was the last to occur in the whole of the Soviet Bloc - in November 1952, four months before Stalin's death. At this trial eleven high functionaries of the CPC received death sentences - a number several times higher than the number of victims of similar trials in other countries of the Soviet Bloc.

The leadership of the CPC, headed by A. Novotny, which after Stalin's death became a partner of the CPSU under Khrushchev, was therefore composed of people who had come to power directly as a consequence of the greatest sham political trial, and all its members were clearly responsible for that trial. Even a year after Stalin's death further political trials took place in Czechoslovakia (in one of these the death sentence was still applied). Only in 1955 was the forced collectivisation of agriculture completed and the last remains of the small trade sector liquidated - all under the official Stalinist slogan of 'sharpening the class struggle' for the success of socialism. After the 20th Congress of the CPSU in 1956 the CPC and its leaders were considered, and quite justifiably so, as the strongest Stalinist bastion against Khrushchev's policies. After the Hungarian uprising the germs of anti-Stalinist criticism were also completely suppressed in Czechoslovakia. These had begun to grow within the CPC from spring to autumn in 1956 (even if mainly only in the course of ideological disputes among the party intelligentsia). In the autumn of 1956 Czechoslovakia had come to represent a wedge inserted between Poland and Hungary and greatly contributed to the notion that the resistance to the system in both countries could be suppressed as isolated uprisings.

Because of this role, which contributed to the stabilisation of the Soviet Bloc at a time of great danger for Khrushchev's policies, Novotny's leadership of the CPC gained the support of Khrushchev - notwithstanding that the internal political forces were not inclined towards Khrushchev's course of 'de-Stalinisation'. In a different form a similar role was repeated in 1958, during the conflict between Khrushchev and Yugoslavia at the time of the Eighth Congress of the League of Communists of Yugoslavia (LCY) in connection with the Program of the LCY: Czechoslovakia was here in the front line of the fighters against 'revisionism' and eased Khrushchev's difficult position by trying to set the boundaries of the concept of 'de-Stalinisation' and reform, as against Yugoslavia's unacceptable revisionism, which had plainly overstepped the bounds of systemic change.

The leadership of the CPC, with Novotny at its head, successfully won Khrushchev's positive support during the following years. They did so without going, in their domestic policies, as far as Khrushchev went in the USSR in one important problem area - the reconsideration of the political trials. In this respect, the leadership of the CPC really showed itself, several years after the 20th Congress, to be an obvious relic of classical Stalinism. In reality, of course, this aspect far from exhausts the significance of changes for the development of the CPC which occurred in the USSR under Khrushchev.

Khrushchev's 'de-Stalinisation' policy had a continuous effect on the CPC which, although at first not obvious from the outside, was in actuality very strong. This policy gradually awakened hopes in the broader strata of CPC members and among party functionaries that this time a new and previously non-existent possibility was opening up: to build on the most democratic principles of the historical tradition of the CPC and yet at the same time not come into conflict, but on the contrary remain in harmony, with the political line of Moscow.

The old principle that within the CPC Moscow's influence is accepted cautiously and dilatorily now appeared under new circumstances. The Novotny-led CPC waited to see whether Khrushchev's orientation would prove to be long-term and durable. This waiting meant, on the one hand, that the leadership did not support any initiative within the CPC which could result in Khrushchev's 'de-Stalinisation' policy being actively taken up and applied in Czechoslovakia. On the other hand, it also meant that within the CPC there arose no marked conflict between reforming and anti-reforming forces. If one does not count individual attacks on certain party intellectuals for spreading 'revisionist' views, it is possible to say that both conflicting developmental tendencies were tolerated within the CPC during those years.

A landmark in the process was probably the end of 1961: at the 22nd Congress of the CPSU Khrushchev consolidated his position; entered upon a new cycle of de-Stalinisation politics; and adopted a new Program of the CPSU, which planned a policy of gradual changes and reforms for the coming twenty years. I shall mention the significance of this CPSU

Program in more detail because it contained several concrete ideological formulations which were also used concretely in preparation of the ideological conception of the 'Prague Spring'.

It was generally agreed that the 22nd Congress of the CPSU signified a victory of political atmosphere in that the evolving changes and reforms of the existing economic and socio-political system were officially declared not only possible but necessary and inevitable. The necessity for reform and change was thus not a heretical demand but an official requirement of the ideology of the communist party. Of course, what reforms and when they should be realised was not at all clear: thus, a field for ideological and political power conflicts was opened up. It is possible to consider the ideological and political content of Khrushchev's CPSU Program debatable (and from the standpoint of Marxist theory even primitive), but where disputes and conflicts on the direction of further development were concerned - there, clear criteria were pointed out in politically obligatory fashion: the perspectives of communist society in the spirit of the theoretical hypotheses of Marx and Lenin.

Antonin Novotny, a man who came to lead the CPC in the last phases of Stalinism and a strong exponent of Stalinist methods, probably came by himself to the definite conclusion, following the 22nd Congress of the CPSU, that the victory of Khrushchev's orientation was a lasting and long-term factor and therefore linked his future fate to this orientation. At that time in Czechoslovakia there were emerging signs of a crisis in the centralised method of planning: the five-year plan that had been adopted was so unrealistic that in 1963 it was necessary to admit its collapse publicly. The economic crisis obviously threatened to grow into a political crisis as well. Novotny suddenly reacted to this situation in a completely different manner: instead of returning to the old orientation he decided to open the door to prospects for a reform solution. From the leadership of the party he dismissed all his colleagues who had come to office in the wake of the political trials of the fifties. The trial of Slansky was reviewed and, although with certain limitations, even those people who had been sentenced in political trials were rehabilitated. Pragmatically oriented functionaries inclined to limited reforms entered the party leadership. Studies for the preparation of conceptual reforms of the whole system of economic management were made legal. In the sphere of ideology and culture the pressure of censorship was eased, and gradually a liberal atmosphere evolved. Novotny expressly announced that the 'Program of the CPSU is also the Program of the CPC'. He opened wide the possibility of taking over all the ideological concepts and reforming trends inspired from the Soviet Union; he adopted the motto of the communist future and announced that 'our generation will yet live under commmunism'.

The last five years of the Novotny regime in Czechoslovakia (1963-1967) can thus in no way be called simply 'years of Stalinism'. The leadership of the CPC during this period was not, to be sure, a leadership which could be called reform-communist. It tried to keep all attempts at reform development under its own control, with the intent of keeping its own power position dominant over all other interests and necessities. However, this leadership was at the same time conscious that significant reforms in the economic sphere and in the socio-political system could not be avoided in the future. It actually made possible the preparation of conceptions for alternative development within the party itself (although not in public political life). Under the condition that the process of formulation preserved its internal character and was under the control of the party leadership, even such reform concepts could emerge whose contents meant far greater systemic changes than those officially programmed by Khrushchev in the USSR.

During the years 1963-1967 the influence of reform-oriented currents within the party (and also within other official structures, including the press and mass communications media) thus gradually grew ever stronger, and the conservative-oriented forces became increasingly defensive. At last, in the summer of 1967 Novotny again began to try to limit the influence of the reform-oriented forces by administrative suppression; however, by then it was too late, and in the internal party conflicts among various groups Novotny's group was finally defeated.

As far as the content of this process is concerned, the ideological concepts embodied in Khrushchev's CPSU Program played a role in the preparation of the 'Prague Spring', particularly in two basic directions. The thesis of the Program that communism cannot be built except on the basis of the effective development of productive forces and therefore that 'science must become the main productive force' in society served to demonstrate a fundamental criticism of the existing mode of economic and political management. This criticism had, of course, arisen earlier, but now it had an official ideological shield. The thesis on the irreplaceable role of science and technology made possible the adherence to the current of reforming forces of practically all groups of intellectuals as social strata: these social strata had felt in the past extremely restricted in their social interests and needs under the slogan of the 'dictatorship of the proletariat', and the new ideological concept gave them the possibility of aggressively defending their interests and needs. The role of technology and the demand for rational and effective economic management - both presented as necessary conditions for building communism - won a particularly influential group of technocrats over to the side of the reforming current.

The CPSU Program won for the humanistically oriented communist intelligentsia an official ideological protection in its attempt at a completely opposite interpretation of Marxism to the one offered for years by Stalinism. From the official Soviet thesis that science would become the principal productive force there was created in Czechoslovakia an integrated ideological conception which perceived in the process of the so-called scientific and technological revolution a decisive social process, whose social and political consequences were to be interpreted in the spirit of Marx's theoretical hypotheses. Among the communist aims included in this conception were not only the quantity of material products but even more the emancipation of man from the fetters of the classical division of labour. Automation under socialist conditions should lead to a greater measure of freedom and autonomy for all social subjects and every individual, and to a decline in the role of political and ideological means for directing social life. The existing social reality in Soviet-type systems was conceived as only a very early phase of development, which in essence conforms to the old concept of progress and human needs as formed during the first industrial revolution and the development of capitalism linked to it. The communist future was not limited by anything that had already been achieved: on the contrary it should mean a radical change in all economic, social, political and cultural conditions existing in Soviet-type societies.

Although such ideological concepts were certainly illusory and time-bound (besides also being influenced by favourable conjunctural developments in the advanced capitalist countries), they nevertheless made it possible, within the framework of the official party ideology, to consider a program that was not limited to an effort apologetically to defend the existing situation. The party ideology had become during this time capable in principle of abolishing all existing ideological taboos and putting questions which could not previously be asked in this form.

The second most significant thesis of the CPSU Program, which influenced the ideological preparation for the 'Prague Spring' within the communist ideology itself, was the thesis of the so-called all-people's state and the development of an all-people's democracy and social self-government. While in the USSR itself these concepts had always remained mostly abstract slogans, in the framework of the reform-communist ideology in Czechoslovakia there emerged an effort to work out on their basis a relatively complete idea of how the complex of institutional and legal relations would look in a political system of so-called all-people's democracy. The official requirement of the then existing Soviet ideology, whereby the state and political authority expressed the 'interests of all the people', was formulated more concretely: in order for 'the interests of the whole of society' to be able to be expressed correctly it is necessary that the interests of all social groups and individuals be freely expressed, and thus by democratic means a genuine total-social interest must be constituted out of the conflict of interests of the parts.

Such an ideological construction, of course, already made practically possible a fundamental critique of the previous linkages between political power and society: the totalitarian model of those relations contained in Stalinist ideology could have been completely rejected in the framework of the official party ideology and replaced by an essentially pluralist model.

It is clear that the contents of the resulting reformist concepts, as elaborated by the Czechoslovakian communists, far over-stepped the framework of the ideological concepts of Khrushchev's CPSU Program. The contents of the Czechoslovakian reform concepts were influenced both by the different history of Czechoslovakia and also by critical Marxist concepts which had arisen earlier in other countries, namely, Yugoslavia and, after 1956, Poland. The fact remains that the ideological ideas inspired by Khrushchev created one of the indispensable conditions for reform concepts to develop within the CPC in the framework of the official ideology of the communist party in the years from 1963 to 1967.

The ideological and political developments in Czechoslovakia from 1963 were almost from the beginning discordant with tendencies which at that time were gaining predominance in the whole of the Soviet Bloc. In reality the CPSU Program had already been more of a swan song for Khrushchev than a real political victory. A year later, as ideological concepts aimed at much more vigorous systemic changes began to take shape under his aegis in Czechoslovakia, Khrushchev was toppled by forces in the Soviet political bureaucracy who, in contrast, demanded 'an end to experiments' and a stabilisation of the Soviet-type system. At this time Gomulka, in Poland, was manifesting the same tendency of the political bureaucracy towards stabilisation, and the original Polish experiment with a 'new model of socialism' (in the name of which Gomulka had come to power in 1956) was terminated by an anti-reform offensive of conservative forces. In Hungary the period of strictest repression had indeed ended after the defeat of the uprising in 1956; but there was no trace of the atmosphere of reformist optimism which pervaded Czechoslovakia, rather there prevailed an atmosphere of heavy consciousness of the insurmountability of limits within the framework of the given system.

For a long time before 1968 the reform-communist development in Czechoslovakia was thus, in fact, an isolated phenomenon. It was a delayed product of a former phase of the development of the Soviet Bloc; the Czechoslovakian reform communists did not take proper notice of this isolation - not even in the year 1968. They succumbed to the illusion that within the Soviet Bloc context they were playing the part of an avant-garde, and as far as they felt their isolation, they understood it as the isolation of an avant-garde.

However, it was perhaps just this illusion that enabled the CPC to formulate the ideological-political conception which over-reached in its contents the framework of Soviet conceptions and necessarily led to direct conflict with developments in the USSR. Thus, the historical fact emerged that the CPC was in reality still a political organism that was closer to certain West European communist parties (namely, for example, the French CP and in a certain sense the Italian CP, also) than it was to the communist party in the USSR. The ideological-political conceptions of Czechoslovakian reform communism therefore really represent, in the context of the entire communist movement, rather the initial phase of the future so-called Eurocommunism than the culminating phase of Krushchevism. Indeed, the CPC would hardly have been capable of taking such an ideological and political step if it had been conscious in time of its real character (conflict with the USSR). It could have done so, however, in the illusory belief that it was only developing something that had already begun and that would develop even further in the Soviet Union. This, of course, does not apply to the individual creators and bearers of the reform concepts in Czechoslovakia: among them were people who in various degrees were conscious of the contentiousness of the situation with respect to the USSR. It does, however, apply to the CPC as a whole, particularly to its political leadership both before and during the year 1968.

It can also justifiably be said that among the factors which make it impossible simply to repeat in the future in Czechoslovakia the developments of the sixties (that is, a new attempt at systemic reform 'from above') is the fact that any developmental phase which is coupled in the USSR with the name of N.S. Khrushchev is not likely to be repeated.

Contributors

Bill Brugger is Professor of Politics at the Flinders University of South Australia. He is the author of Democracy and Organisation in the Chinese Industrial Enterprise: 1948-53 (Cambridge University Press, 1976); China: Liberation and Transformation: 1942-62 (Croom Helm, 1981); China: Radicalism to Revisionism: 1962-79 (Croom Helm, 1981); co-author of Modernisation and Revolution (Croom Helm, 1983); and editor of China: The Impact of the Cultural Revolution (Croom Helm, 1978) and China Since the Gang of Four (Croom Helm, 1980).

Ferenc Fehér left Hungary in 1977 after a long record of dissidence as a member of the Budapest School of G. Lukacs. He is the author of works on Dostoevsky, Sartre and Lukacs published in Hungarian, German, Italian, Serbo-Croatian and essays on the theory of the novel in German, French, and Portuguese. He is co-author (with A. Heller and G. Markus) of Dictatorship Over Needs (Blackwell, 1983); co-author (with A. Heller) of Hungary, 1956 Revisited (George Allen and Unwin, 1983); and co-editor (with T.H. Rigby) of Political Legitimation in Communist States (Macmillan, 1982).

Robert F. Miller is Senior Fellow in Political Science, Research School of Social Sciences, Australian National University. He is the author of One Hundred Thousand Tractors: The MTS and the Development of Controls in Soviet Agriculture (Harvard University Press, 1970); Tito as Political Leader and External Factors in Yugoslav Political Development (Department of Political Science, RSSS, ANU, 1977); and monographs and articles on politics and administration in the USSR and Eastern Europe.

Zdeněk Mlynář is a former ideological and political official of the Communist Party of Czechoslovakia who served as a Secretary of the Central Committee under Alexander Dubcek during and after the 'Prague Spring'. For continuing to advocate reform communism he lost his party position in May 1969. He was subsequently expelled from a research post in the Academy of Sciences for participation in the Charter 77 Movement, leaving Czechoslovakia in 1977 for Vienna, where he has since resided and worked as a free-lance political writer and consultant. His most important publication is Nightfrost in Prague: The End of Humane Socialism (C. Hurst & Co., 1980).

Aleksandr M. Nekrich, formerly Senior Research Fellow of the Institute of History, USSR Academy of Sciences, has been a Fellow and Associate of the Russian Research Center, Harvard University since 1976. He is the author of numerous books on Soviet domestic and international politics and recent history. Among them are 22nd June 1941 (Moscow: Nauka, 1965); The Punished Peoples (W.W. Norton, 1978); and (with M. Heller), L'Utopie au Pouvoir (Calmann-Levy, 1981).

T.H. Rigby is Professorial Fellow in Political Science, Research School of Social Sciences, Australian National University. He has written extensively on various aspects of the Soviet political system and its development. Among his best known works are Communist Party Membership in the USSR, 1917-1967 (Princeton University Press, 1968); Lenin's Government: Sovnarkom 1917-1922 (Cambridge University Press, 1979). He is co-editor (with F. Feher) of Political Legitimation in Communist States (Macmillan, 1982).

Dennis Woodward is Lecturer in Politics at the Chisholm Institute of Technology in Melbourne. He was formerly a Research Fellow in the Contemporary China Centre, Research School of Pacific Studies, Australian National University. He has published articles on Chinese agriculture and the People's Liberation Army, as well as works on Australian politics.

Graham Young is a Research Fellow in the Contemporary China Centre, Research School of Pacific Studies, Australian National University. His publications include articles on the politics of the Chinese Communist Party and on Chinese revolutionary theory.

240